T0369157

FIVE VOICES ON A SUNDAY MORNING

Candid Musings on the Rich Pageantry of Everyday Life

ED GROELLE

iUniverse, Inc.
New York   Bloomington

Five Voices on a Sunday Morning
Candid Musings on the Rich Pageantry of Everyday Life

iUniverse books may be ordered through booksellers or by contacting:

iUniverse
1663 Liberty Drive
Bloomington, IN 47403
www.iuniverse.com
1-800-Authors (1-800-288-4677)

ISBN: 978-1-4401-2056-5 (pbk)
ISBN: 978-1-4401-2055-8 (cloth)
ISBN: 978-1-4401-2057-2 (ebk)

Printed in the United States of America

iUniverse rev. date: 02/24/2009

Like everyone else, I am going to die. But the words – the words live on for as long as there are readers to see them, audiences to hear them. It is immortality by proxy. It is not really a bad deal, all things considered.

J. Michael Straczynski

Acknowledgments

The Kenosha News is in no way involved with the publishing of this book. I am grateful to the newspaper for seeing the possibilities of the book and in giving me permission to use the articles after they have been printed in their newspaper.

I discovered, when putting together this book, that sometimes writing a book is easier than producing it. Of course, I can say that because several neighbors of mine, whom I have never personally met, wrote the majority of this book's content. I am very grateful to them for allowing me to use and assemble their literary blood, along with mine, into this book. Thank you, Kenda, Tom, Jim, and Laurie.

For whatever reason, a book always seems to be more enjoyable when a photograph and a short biography of the author are included. With that in mind, the same is presented here.

+++

Ed Groelle harbored several burning ambitions as a child while growing up on a Wisconsin dairy farm. The first and most important was to get the hell off of the dairy farm as soon as possible. This ambition, coupled with an instinctive inability to tolerate boredom, led to a variety of jobs over the next fifty years, every one preferable to dairy farming; Factory worker, TV antenna installer, Hospital orderly, TV Repairman, Soldier, Lead Radican and Station Chief at a Dewline (Distant Early Warning) station in the Canadian Arctic, thirty years as an IBM field engineer, ten years as a Microsystems Analyst and network technician, and after retiring, eight years ago, briefly as a security guard. He is a graduate of DeVry Technical Institute, Chicago.

Ed puttered at poetry writing most of his life and did not begin serious writing until after retiring. He wrote as a columnist for the local daily newspaper writing forty columns, all contained within this book. He was eventually requested not to submit any more columns since he was becoming more popular than the national syndicated columnists. Of course, the newspaper vehemently denies that this was the reason, citing instead his 'unreasonable' salary requests. He is currently co-authoring a second book, *In A Moment*, a biography of a blind friend, which should shake up the literary world when it hits the shelves in a few months.

Today, he spends his time playing Sheepshead, bicycling, writing, and volunteering, mainly with the blind and visually impaired. He has been married 45 years to Charlene and has two beautiful daughters, Laura and Melissa.

 **Tom Noer**'s research has resulted in writing three books and 22 articles on the history of U.S. foreign policy. His first book, *Briton, Boer, and Yankee: The United States and South Africa, 1870-1920* was selected one of the ten *Academic Books of the Year* by Choice magazine. His second book, *Cold War and Black Liberation: The United States and White Rule in Africa, 1948-1968* received the Stuart Bernath prize from the *Society for Historians of American Foreign Relations* as the outstanding book of the year.

His most recent work, *Soapy: A Biography of G. Mennen Williams* was selected the book of the year by the *Michigan Historical Society* and named a *Notable Book of the Year* by the

Michigan Library Association. He has received research grants from the *American Philosophical Society, the Harry Truman Library Association, the John F. Kennedy Library, the Lyndon Johnson Library, the National Endowment for the Humanities, the Spencer Foundation, the Gerald Ford Library, the Bentley Library,* and *Phi Alpha Theta.* He was a participant in the *U.S. State Department Scholar-Diplomat* program in Washington, D. C. and was a research fellow at the Charles Warren Center at Harvard.

In 1980 he was selected *Teacher of the Year* by Carthage College and in 1995 was named *Valor Distinguished Professor of the Humanities.* He is currently working on the politics of the architect, Frank Lloyd Wright.

Laurie McKeon is the youngest child in a biggish Catholic family.  She has an undergraduate and law degree from the University of Notre Dame. (Go, Irish!) After a stint as a trial attorney, she stopped "practicing" law and started to enforce it as the mother of six children. Getting the very most out of her expensive education, she spends the bulk of her day doing laundry, filling out school paperwork, trying to remember which teenager is currently grounded, and driving an endless loop around the greater Kenosha County area.

She has been married for 21 years to the endlessly patient Dave McKeon (it's gone by like five minutes … underwater), and is the mother of Annie, Chris, Jack, Nate, Pete, and Posey.

Kenda Buxton was born and raised in the Dairy State. Although she has never milked a cow, she does own a farm.

As a child, this small-town girl planned to be the first woman in the Major Leagues and dreamed of playing right field for the Chicago Cubs. (Seemed like a pretty safe position – no chance of being mowed down by a base runner or beaned with a foul ball, yet you still get to suit up every day and put on those nifty shoes with cleats.) Unfortunately, a chauvinistic band teacher killed that dream when he scoffed, "Girls can't play in the Majors." For that remark, Kenda got her revenge ... she didn't grow up to play a sissy piccolo for the Boston Philharmonic either.

When the Cubs didn't come calling after high school graduation, Kenda turned to banking for a career. Although not nearly as much fun as playing baseball for a living, it does provide a few important things like a paycheck and health insurance. And hey, if you think the only place you'll ever see an in-field brawl is on a baseball diamond, then you should work in a bank for twenty-eight years.

Although Kenda would love nothing more than to serve as a human ATM machine twenty-four hours a day, when her boss finally shoves her out the door at night (ignoring her protests of, "Please, I'd love to stay even longer!") she enjoys pursuing the three "R's"; reading, running, and 'riting.' Aside from the columns she's penned for the Kenosha News, Kenda has written fan fiction for many years and self-publishes her stories on her website. She also runs several miles each morning before work, and like Amy Carter, never shows up at a boring dinner party without a book in her hand.

Kenda is married to a Democrat hog farmer who doesn't hunt, (betraying the popular supposition that all farmers are Republicans who *do* hunt) and together they lavish all of their free time and spare money on their three spoiled dogs.

James Wynne is a manufacturing quality engineer who lives in Kenosha with Joyce, his wife of 29 years. He has two grown children (a son and daughter) and two grandchildren.

FIVE VOICES ON A SUNDAY MORNING

Candid Musings on the Rich Pageantry of Everyday Life

Prologue - A must read

by Ed Groelle

In view of the fact that this book is a collection of articles, one would assume that this is where the first article would normally be located. However, it has occurred to me that, if this book's distribution area extends outside of this locale, and the reader is not fortunate enough to live in this area of the country, it would be very helpful if some of the places and people mentioned in the articles were to be explained before diving in.

To that end, I have listed a few names and places mentioned in the articles with a brief description and explanation.

Enjoy, and refer back to this page, if necessary.

Kenosha, Wisconsin - A Midwest town (85,000) located in the extreme Southeast corner of the state midway between Milwaukee and Chicago. It is bordered on the east by Lake Michigan and on the south by Illinois. The city directly south is Waukegan, Ill. and to the north, Racine, Wis. In the past, Kenosha was an important industrial, manufacturing town: Automobiles (Rambler, Chrysler), Tools (Snap-On), Fire engines (Pirsch), Music Instruments (Le Blanc), Electrical devices (Dynamatic), Clothing (Jockey), Stainless steel fittings (Ladish Tri-Clover), and a host of other smaller concerns. An impressive list, but unfortunately, many of these no longer exist.

Communities surrounding Kenosha - Peasant Prairie, Paddock Lake, Somers, Bristol, Carol Beach, White Caps, Lake Geneva

Kenosha News - Kenosha's only daily newspaper. Some consider it to be one of the best small town newspapers in the country.

Howard Brown - The big honcho at the Kenosha News. A rather likeable guy with an acceptable sense of humor.

Steve Lund - The Editorial Editor at the Kenosha News who volunteered for the enviable job of managing the "Sunday Morning With ..." column, and as a result, is required to contend with people who have convinced themselves that they possess exceptional writing talent.

Darts and Laurels - An editorial feature of the News, which either commends or criticizes local activities.

Sound Off - A popular feature of the Kenosha News in which anyone, who wants their moment of fame, can anonymously phone in a fifteen-second opinion on any subject.

Barden's store - Once a very popular downtown, family-run, clothing department store, which fell victim to the big chains. The store building has never been occupied since closing its doors several years ago.

Yooper - The Wisconsin nickname for anyone who lives in the Upper Peninsula of Michigan, especially applied when they venture south into Wisconsin.

Smelt - A delicious, small, silvery, Lake Michigan fish that spawns every spring a few feet from the shoreline. They are netted, usually in the middle of the night, by people who actually get a kick out of being cold and wet while bathing in kerosene lantern light.

Perch - Probably one of the best-tasting fresh water fish in the world. At one time they were abundant but their population decreased significantly due to being killed off by the alewives coming in through the St. Lawrence Seaway.

Cohorama - A three-day festivity that sort of celebrates the planting of Coho salmon in Lake Michigan in an effort to kill off the alewives that were destroying the perch fishing. A prize is awarded to whoever catches the largest Coho salmon during these three days. Beer and brats are always available for purchase and consumption.

Highway 50 bookstores - Adult book stores located along the last stretch of Highway I-94 just before it enters Illinois. They were a target of long, legal battles in an attempt to shut them down. They eventually were bought up and razed when the State needed room to expand I-94.

Brats - Spicy pork sausages that are legally required to be prepared over charcoal and washed down with a Wisconsin beer. Very popular at tailgate parties and any other excuse for gourmet outdoor dining.

Wisconsin Dells - A popular tourist destination in central Wisconsin, especially for the kids. There is a water park or miniature golf course within walking distance from any point in the area. Sometimes described as a tourist trap or tacky but it has, undeniably, a certain self-deprecating appeal, which can be satisfying, especially for those who enjoy feeling guilty about taking a vacation.

Kenosha Trolley - An eye-catching downtown tourist attraction or a total waste of money? Your choice! These old, restored street trolleys go around and around in a two-mile loop, sort of like a model train under the Christmas tree. You can ride it all day for a quarter.

Sheridan road - This is a road that runs from Chicago to Milwaukee hugging the shore of Lake Michigan. It really was built to tie together the downtowns of Waukegan, Kenosha, and Racine. When the malls arrived and the downtowns were abandoned, the maintenance of Sheridan Road fell to the bottom of the to-do list for most communities. It is a two-lane, three-lane, or four-lane road with extremely varying degrees of upkeep determined mainly by the income of residents along its route.

Christmas Lane - This is a two-block stretch of homes that display innovative, and sometimes, audacious Christmas decorations in an effort to raise money for charities. There are rumors around that some of the residents actually have mortgaged their homes in an effort to outdo the neighbors. It's a must-see, drive-by, Christmas season activity for anyone living within a fifty-mile radius.

Alternative street parking - This is a local ordinance that requires everyone to park on alternative sides of the street whenever the snowfall exceeds one inch. Which side of the street is determined by odd and even dates. This ordinance is essential for effective snow plowing but a real pain in the keester to comply with.

Kenosha Unified School Administration - An entity that operates a massive school system with a budget larger than the GNP of some countries.

The Spot - A very popular, car-hopped, drive-in that stays open in all weather conditions. It has been in operation longer than anyone can remember.

Casino Referendum - There is a proposal to build a casino in Kenosha, an ideal location halfway between Chicago and Milwaukee, just off I-94. The voters passed the referendum approving its construction but the tenacious, vigorous, opposition from other existing casinos has effectively postponed it's construction.

Boat Storage Facility - A ginormous rectangular building built right on the shoreline of Lake Michigan used to store and repair boats. It sits on what, unquestionably, must be the most expensive and desirable real estate in town. It blocks a portion of the lake view for condominium owners who were upset that they were not told of its construction before purchasing their condos. City officials deny this, citing a mention at a meeting held several years prior. All things considered, it is a tax source much needed to sustain the Kenosha School District.

American Brass - A manufacturing plant that specialized in brass products. When it could no longer compete with foreign industry, it was demolished and replaced with a couple of stores and another school.

Green Stamps - Anyone over fifty will probably remember these. Every retailer gave little green stamps with every purchase, which you would then be required to lick and paste into a booklet. When filled, these books could be redeemed for items from a catalog. It worked until around 1980 when people started feeling kind of foolish licking all those stamps (which also served as a very efficient method of spreading germs), only to get a lousy toaster or iron.

Dayton Hotel - An old hotel in the downtown area used mainly to house indigent and down-and-out men.

KAFASI - Kenosha Area Family and Aging Services offers programs for senior citizens. It manages hundreds of volunteers whose services enhance the lives of the elderly, ill, poor, etc.

Antiques, a source for memories of what once was

by Ed Groelle

The world of antiques has never been of interest to me, but as I unrelentingly become more of an antique myself, my interest is sometimes aroused. When visiting any antique store, I am usually astonished by what is considered to be an antique. A large number of items classified as antique these days were at one time items that my family had used in our day-to-day existence ... which is what small time dairy farming really was. I was raised on a typical dairy farm of the day near Manitowoc, i.e. 80 acres, 25 cows, 40 pigs, 2000 chickens, four horses, and one good working cow dog. There were lots of hand tools for very select purposes and an assortment of machinery that you now see from time to time in someone's yard serving as a decorative conversation piece. You can probably imagine all the antiques the farm contained as defined by the antique standards of today. I once was in a restaurant where there were antique tools hanging on the wall. I was particularly intrigued with one item, a handmade pliers similar to one we once used to crimp copper rings in the snouts of pigs to discourage routing. I didn't order pork.

My maternal grandfather was a blacksmith/farmer, and as was common in those days, he fabricated most of his tools. I visited his shop once as a child and remember a vast array of odd-shaped tools and an odor like hot brimstone and horse sweat. He operated the blacksmith shop on a small corner of his dairy farm. His three daughters worked the farm while he pontificated in his blacksmith shop. His farm was poor and not exactly state-of-the-art. He was not much of a farmer anyway, as the shop was obviously his first love.

When he retired he gave our family all of his blacksmithing tools; forge, anvils, hammers ... the works. This would be an absolute treasure trove to any antique hunter today. The tools were brought to our farm and we used them for many years. I particularly remember using them to carve toys from scrap lumber. That is probably where I developed my love for woodworking.

A fire completely destroyed the barn while I was away in Europe for a couple of years, and when I returned, there wasn't much remaining. A few years later my father convinced a road construction crew operating nearby to dig a trench with their bulldozers and bury anything remaining from the fire. He considered it all to be worthless junk.

The farmland is still there, of course, but today it is one 80-acre field worked by a large conglomerate. The antiques are still buried there and I know where they are. Some day, in the distant future, an ambitious archaeological student will discover them, and in an attempt to gain fame, will dig them up. He may even make a couplabucks selling the antiques. He will also discover the outlines of the barn foundation and will, in all probability, spend years attempting to ascribe astronomical or religious significance to their alignment with the stars. He may even try to prove that the circular concrete slabs, which served as foundations for the two silos, were altars for some sort of virgin sacrifice. I hope he succeeds. At least, it would explain the scarcity of virgins in the neighborhood.

If an antique hunter is ever offered an opportunity to go back in time to scour the landscape for antiques, I would recommend that he first visit the farms and then the local taverns. The most popular tavern in our neighborhood was a farmer's haven named Jake's Circle Inn. Upon entering this tavern you were immediately hit with an odor I remember rather vividly yet today; stale beer, urine, and Plow Boy tobacco. The taverns at that time were ergonomically designed for drinking with a heavy hardwood bar and a mandatory brass rail running along its base. For furnishings there were the ubiquitous spittoons strategically placed to be within firing range from any stool at the bar and dozens of advertising signs on the walls furnished free by roving salesmen. Along the sidewall were slot machines, which my grandfather lifted me up to play. I'm not sure they were legal or not at that time, but I know they were legal in Wisconsin at some point. I'd like to own one of those mechanical marvels.

Jake's was buried long ago by the construction of the intersection of Hwy 43 and County H. What became of all those antique spittoons, slot machines, signs, exotic bottles, etc.? Whenever I drive through there I wonder what is buried under that intersection. Maybe Jake is somewhere down there, still tending bar.

Antique hunters and collectors render a valuable service to us all. They provide a measure of living reality to our memories.

Haircuts — the defining personal touch

by Laurie McKeon

My grandpa used to say that the only difference between a good haircut and a bad one was about a week. Maybe this is true for guys, because unless they're trading in a mullet or a mohawk, all guys' haircuts look about the same after a week. This was especially true for my grandpa since he was bald. But, for a woman, a bad haircut is a BIG deal that can take weeks or maybe months to get over. The mental trauma inflicted by a bad hairstyle can last for years. I should know.

When I was a child, the youngest of five kids, four girls, all a year apart, my totally efficient mother had little time and absolutely no patience for anything hair related. No ponytails, pigtails, braids, or barrettes for the Giunti girls. Oh, no! My mom swore by the pixie cut, that really short little haircut that in the fashion history of the world only looked good on Mia Farrow for about a day. Needless to say, I spent a fair portion of my childhood being mistaken for an incredibly well-dressed, little boy, which probably explains a lot. Never one for hypocrisy or trendy hair fads, my mom had her own hair styled after your basic Army Ranger with a little fringe of bangs. And, God love her, she still is sporting the modified crew cut to this day. I am embarrassed to admit how many people think she is undergoing chemotherapy because of her abnormally short hair. Teachers in school used to whisper to me, "So, how is your mom?" and I'd have to explain, "She's just fine. That's her hair do. She pays money for that cut."

When I was in fourth grade my mom let us grow out our hair. We did ... for about five years. Every one of us had waist length hair all through high school and for most of college. None of us could ever imagine having our hair any shorter than shoulder length. I still flinch and clench a little when I hear the buzz of the hair clippers. Posttraumatic haircut syndrome ... it's real!

Ask any woman about her worst haircut and she can tell you with a quiver in her lip and a tear in her eye the exact date, salon, and stylist. Women will go to enormous lengths to correct or avoid a bad haircut. My college roommate spent her whole first semester junior year wearing a visor to cover up a perm gone bad. I know women who happily drive hours and spend a week's grocery money for a great haircut. Money well spent. A good friend of mine recently needed a quick trim before she went out of town. Her regular stylist could not fit her in so she went to someone new. Now, many women will just sit in the chair watching with horror as their haircut goes south, too afraid to hurt the stylist's feelings or make a scene ... but not my friend, Jane. The minute she saw those scissors take a wrong turn she jumped up from the chair, hair soaking wet, whipped off the cape, threw down two twenties (so she wouldn't be accused of stealing the crappy cut), and speed dialed her regular stylist begging for an emergency appointment. She got in ... hair crisis averted.

For most guys, a haircut is just a way to get the fuzz off the back of their necks. For women, except my mother obviously, every haircut is full of potential. We all think that THIS haircut is going to be the one ... the one that makes us look younger, hipper, smarter, and thinner. Each salon appointment holds the possibility of transforming us into our very best hair selves and at the very least, all women, even my mom, expect to walk out of the salon looking just a little bit better than when they went in. That's a lot of pressure to put on a haircut.

My husband cuts his own hair with some cheap barber clippers (cringe), while hanging over the garbage can. Sure, he looks like an escaped convict for a week but, after that, he looks like every other middle-aged dude with short hair.

I just got my hair cut. I'm not sure what I think. Check back with me at the end of the week.

A quote often contains much wisdom

by Kenda Buxton

With just three days left in the year, it's time once again to reflect upon where we've been. If you're like me, it's also time to wonder why you're still sitting in the same spot doing your reflecting that you were sitting in last year, while pondering if this shows lack of ambition, lack of good fortune, or lack of being born filthy rich.

Go west, young man, go west - In 1851, newspaperman, John Soule, encouraged pioneers to explore the land beyond the Rocky Mountains. If Mr. Soule were living today, he'd urge, "Go north, old man, go north." Then he'd rent a bus to the senior citizens who need to buy their medications in Canada so they have enough money left each month for luxuries like food and electricity.

Silence is golden - Is there anyone other than telemarketers who doesn't think the national Do-Not-Call list is the best invention since the telephone? If Alexander Graham Bell had known we'd eventually hang up on three-quarters of the people who call us, he'd have invented the microwave oven instead.

I'm hiding, I'm hiding, and no one knows where, for all they can see is my toes and my hair - When U.S. Forces pulled Saddam Hussein from a hole in the ground, he possessed two assault rifles, a pistol, a taxicab, and 750 thousand U.S. dollars. Apparently, a guy can make pretty good money driving a taxi in Iraq. Which leaves me wondering how many times he heard from his passengers, "Say, has anyone ever told you that you look just like Saddam Hussein?"

This town ain't big enough for the both of us - In October, our state senate voted to overturn Wisconsin's ban on carrying concealed weapons. I knew all those years of watching Bonanza would come in handy some day. As soon as I find my plastic six-shooters, broomstick horse, and cowboy hat, I'm challenging anyone who ticks me off to a duel outside the Silver Dollar Saloon.

I am beginning to learn that it is the sweet, simple things of life, which are the real ones after all (Laura Ingalls Wilder)

6

- Little Laura Ingalls was thrilled the year Santa Claus brought her a penny, a tin drinking cup, and some hard candy. Patricia Van Lester was probably wishing she'd settled for a penny, a tin cup, and some hard candy when she was trampled by hoards of Wal-Mart shoppers while racing to grab a $29 DVD player, but then again, maybe not. Ms. VanLester has a long history of filing lawsuits. Given that, she'd have probably sued Santa for bringing her the meager haul that Laura was once grateful to receive

If I'd have known you were coming I'd have baked a cake - President Bush made a surprise visit to U.S. troops in Baghdad on Thanksgiving Day. Our military men and women applauded their Commander in Chief, while Democrats were quick to say this was a ploy on Bush's part to drive up his popularity before next year's election. On the other hand, Republicans were quick to point out what a brave and noble deed the president had done, while on yet another hand, Iraqi citizens were quick to complain that the president's stay was too brief, and that he should have toured war-ravaged towns (perhaps in Saddam's taxi). By the time the president returned to the states, he fully understood the meaning of the phrase, 'You can't please all of the people all of the time.'

All you need is trust and a little bit of pixie dust (Peter Pan) - Michael Jackson will need a lot more than pixie dust to clear his name when it comes to the latest allegations of child molestation made against him. Mr. Jackson may be as innocent of wrong-doing as he claims, but it's past time he learns that forty-five-year old men shouldn't host sleepovers for young boys, and unlike the fictional Peter Pan, we all have to grow up eventually.

Here's hoping the new year brings our troops home from Iraq, no more reality TV shows, and a Democratic presidential candidate we actually want to vote for. As 2003 makes way for 2004, another quote from Laura Ingalls Wilder sums it up best, "We may not know where we're going, but we're on our way."

Take this test; impress your friends at Trivial Pursuit

by Thomas J. Noer

When not slaving for endless hours over my Kenosha News column, I teach history. When I'm asked why students should study history I have a number of wise responses; it teaches you how to evaluate various forms of evidence, it forces you to use critical thinking, it helps you appreciate various cultures, etc. etc. But, I know that the REAL reason students study history is so they can kick butt in *Trivial Pursuit* and *Jeopardy* and understand all the references on *The Simpsons.*

History is an endless source of trivia and my brain is saturated with obscure names and facts. Did you know that the word 'trivia' comes from the Latin for 'three roads'? Where the major routes to Rome met, travelers posted messages and notes on posts and trees that became known as 'trivia.' With stuff like this in my head you can see why I can never remember my computer password or which side of the street to park on in winter.

To test your historical/trivia knowledge, below is a pop quiz asking you to determine what each group of three individuals has in common. Be warned! This is difficult and if you get half right I will be very impressed. Answers and scoring are at the end, but don't peek.

1. Architect Frank Lloyd Wright, magician Harry Houdini, artist Georgia O'Keefe.
2. Author Mark Twain, singer Judy Garland, President Bill Clinton.
3. British queen Elizabeth I, poet Emily Dickinson, President James Buchanan.
4. British king Henry VIII, actor Mickey Rooney, actress Elizabeth Taylor.
5. Artist Michelangelo, poet Walt Whitman, composer Cole Porter.

6. Football coach Knute Rockne, actress Carol Lombard, magazine publisher John F. Kennedy Jr.

7. Movie stars Charlie Chaplin, Cary Grant, and Bob Hope.

8. Singer Elvis Presley, N Sync member (I can't say 'singer') Justin Timberlake, basketball player Horace Grant.

9. President Calvin Coolidge, columnist Ann Landers, playwright Neil Simon.

10. Presidents John Adams, Thomas Jefferson, and James Monroe. (besides all being U.S. Presidents)

11. Physicist Sir Isaac Newton, dictator Adolph Hitler, movie star Drew Barrymore.

12. TV newsman Walter Cronkite, former senator Bill Bradley, director Stephen Spielberg.

13. TV star Lucille Ball, singer Cher, TV newsman Peter Jennings.

14. President Theodore Roosevelt, humanitarian Mother Theresa, Palestinian leader Yasir Arafat.

15. Explorer Christopher Columbus, writer Henry David Thoreau, South African leader Nelson Mandela.

16. British monarch Mary Queen of Scots, artist Andy Warhol, sportscaster Marv Albert.

17. Novelist George Eliot, novelist George Sand, novelist Acton Bell.

18. Girl Scout founder Juliette Gordon Low, the Incredible Hulk Lou Ferrigno, 1995 Miss America Heather Whitestone.

19. Scottish terrier Fala, golden retriever Liberty, English springer spaniel Millie.

20. Darts and Laurels, Cathy, Tom Noer's columns.

Answers:

1. Each was born in Wisconsin.

2. All left-handed.

3. None ever married.

4. All married six times.

5. They were gay.

6. Died in plane crashes.

7. Each was born in England.

8. They were twins.

9. Born on the Fourth of July.

10. Died on the Fourth of July.

11. Vegetarians.

12. Famous Eagle scouts.

13. High school dropouts.

14. Winners of the Nobel Peace Prize.

15. Served time in jail.

16. All bald and wore wigs.

17. All were women (Mary Ann Evans, Aurore Dudevant, Anne Bronte)

18. They are deaf.

19. Dogs owned by U.S. Presidents (Franklin Roosevelt, Gerald Ford, and George H. Bush)

20. All often serve as wasted space in the Kenosha News that could be better devoted to publishing complete transcripts of School Board meetings or more stories about Brett Favre and the Packers.

If you got ten or more correct, you are either a history professor, were a history major in school, or spend way too much time reading the tabloids.

If you got five or more correct, you are reasonably sane, but still have a lot of brain cells stuffed with really insignificant material.

If you got fewer than five correct, you are pretty normal, but a bad partner in Trivial Pursuit. Tune in next time for a special 'Back to School' column with ten easy steps to save American education!

I love France — no apology offered

by Ed Groelle

OK, I'll admit it. I love France. Someone once said, "France would be a very pleasant country if it weren't inhabited by French people." I disagree. That person should find a good proctologist and request a personality transplant because the problem is with him. I have lived in France for two years, visited France many times, and have seldom encountered the negativity some tourists will insist upon recalling. Learn a few French words, use them profusely, respect the French penchant for privacy, and you will be astounded at how much their demeanor will improve.

When I first visited France fifty years ago there was no English presence at all, either written or spoken. Today, public displays in English are still conspicuously absent, but English is now a required subject starting in the fourth grade. Most young people have a working knowledge of English and are always eager to test their skills. Ol' Charlie de Gaulle would be turning over in his grave if he knew this.

If you are intending to set off exploring France for the first time I'd like to point out to you a few of the many interesting cultural differences you are about to encounter. Upon landing at De Gaulle airport, you will immediately notice that everything is at least twenty percent smaller; cars, trucks, waistlines, even toilet seats, which may be a problem for some broad-minded people. Space is an expensive luxury in France, so unless money is no object, it's best to roll with that. The only items that will not be twenty percent smaller are the prices; $10 for a pint of Kronenberg beer, $6 a gallon for gas … sky-high prices everywhere. Accept and treat this sobering reality as part of France's charm.

Now to the French driving. French rules of the road are basically the same as in the U.S, but the laws and courtesies are much more obvious. There is no passing on the right (ever), no riding the left lane (passing only), wearing seatbelts is mandatory (the built-in auto alarms to remind you become increasingly louder and irritating until you comply or lose your mind), no cell phone use while driving, and trucks cannot drive over fifty-five mph or use the left lane. You will rarely see any of these laws violated. They are religiously observed and ruthlessly enforced, not only by the police but also by private citizens who take a particular delight in rather aggressively pointing out bad driving habits using internationally understood hand and finger signals.

There are few elderly drivers and teenagers must be eighteen to apply for a license. A professional driving school must be attended with three to four months of extensive testing, training, and studying before a temporary license is issued. This is an expensive procedure that typically costs more than $500. After receiving the license, a new driver is on probation for a year. Any infractions during that time will result in effectively starting from scratch. Driving is just too privileged and expensive to be taken lightly by irresponsible driving, at least, not until that license is permanent. Then, if you desire, you can become an innovative driver, like many French nuts. Just be sure to stay somewhere within or near the definition of the rules.

Considering the adherence to rules of the road, you'd expect driving in France to be an enjoyable adventure, and it is ... at least in the countryside. City driving is another story and can be compared to a carnival bumper car ride. The rules are still there and basically observed, but very compressed in time and space. The problem is that there is no room and no one ever seems to slow down. Motorcycles use the center area between lanes of traffic with impunity. One must always be looking in the mirror to avoid them.

Street signs are another problem. Those that exist are in places where they are impossible to see until it is too late and since street names seem to change every few yards it is futile to navigate by them. You can forget about consulting a map since there is no room to pull over and consult it anyway. In case you are wondering, France honors a valid U.S. driving license for one year, so there is no problem renting your very own bumper car ... after that, Good Luck!

I find it amusing when someone says, "I don't like driving in Chicago. Too much traffic!" Chicago does not have a traffic problem. Compared to cities like Paris or Cairo, driving in Chicago is a pleasant romp in the park. If you feel Chicago driving is hectic, please be kind to yourself and book a bus tour to see France, then, sit back and relax.

France is a fantastic tourist destination but not a Garden of Eden … far from it. They have high unemployment, inflation, uncontrolled immigration, stifling bureaucracy, decreasing birth rates, and a host of other problems peculiar to a modern society. But, like I said, I love it, if only for the bread so delicious it can bring tears to one's eyes.

I can't wait to return.

Money-saving ideas for the decorating challenged

by Jim Wynne

I've been watching a lot of home improvement shows lately, mostly on the cable channel HGTV. I do this because my wife watches these shows a lot. HGTV is primarily aimed at females because females believe that if the house today bears any resemblance whatsoever to what it looked like yesterday it needs to be remodeled. Actually, the most popular of these shows, *Trading Spaces*, is on TLC. I'm sure it galls the people at HGTV to have dedicated 24/7 programming to home improvement and then have the most popular show on a network dedicated mainly to graphic depictions of grisly surgery, childbirth, and pet euthanasia. The premise of *Trading Spaces* is that neighboring homeowners, abetted by diabolical professional decorators, desecrate rooms in one another's houses. They festoon walls with cheap fabric, paint linoleum floors, and drag garbage in from the curb to use as accessories.

After watching these shows for a while it is possible to develop a short list of popular, money-saving ideas that may be used to desecrate one's own residence. One of the most popular today is the use of what the decorators call 'faux' finishes. 'Faux' is an Armenian word that means 'unsightly,' and the process involves desperate and invariably unsuccessful attempts to make the refuse that has been dragged in from the curb more presentable. Another use of faux finishing involves painting a wall or expensive piece of upholstered furniture a light color such as ecru, and then dabbing on a darker color, usually taupe, with a sponge. This has the amazing and apparently unexpected effect of making the wall or sofa appear as though someone dabbed paint on it with a sponge.

Faux finishes are also suggested by decorators for surfaces that should be replaced, but can't be because of a tight budget. For example, if you can't afford a new kitchen counter top, you can make a design statement by giving it a faux finish. In this case, the statement is, "Try not to notice that I painted my counter top because it looked like hell and I couldn't afford a new one."

An entire decorating style has developed around the use of garbage to accessorize a living space. These days, one does not put things in the living room ... one *accessorizes* the living space. The technique of bringing trash into the house and proudly displaying it in the living space is called 'shabby chic.' A living space effectively decorated in this style immediately brings to mind the idea that there was a good reason that the salvaged items were thrown out in the first place.

There are also a lot of gardening and landscaping shows on HGTV. My own experience with decorative gardening boils down to a simple concept; when you plant something, it will probably die. Nothing that I do will affect the outcome, which is somehow predetermined. You can follow the planting and feeding directions to the letter and then the thing will still just die if it feels like it. Sometimes you're better off if the plant does die. If the nursery tag on it says that it is a 'modest grower' and will be two feet high at maturity it means that it will be bigger than your house by the end of the summer and its roots will go through your sewer line like a hot knife through butter.

According to the HGTV shows I have seen, there are two things that every landscape design must have; a water feature and a touch of whimsy. Water features are similar to fountains, except that water features cost about $2000 more and are made from rusty 55-gallon drums that originally contained radioactive waste. As for whimsy, it is important to have some focal point in the garden that is mildly amusing. Not hilarious, mind you, because an effective garden plan should create an outdoor living space that makes it possible to be introspective and contemplative while communing with expensive dead shrubbery.

Now that I think about it, it seems that most of what passes for interior (and exterior) decoration these days consists of what used to be considered garbage-picking and acts of vandalism. The upside of it all is that if your living space is shabby, you can dab an ugly shade of paint all over everything, including the broken table your clueless neighbor threw out last week, and suddenly be very stylish.

For myself, I must admit that I have partially succumbed to the do-it-yourself craze, having chosen a project that involves taking an old coffee table and making a cable spool out of it, and I mean a cable spool with a whimsical faux finish that makes a statement and will be just the ticket for casual entertaining.

Or maybe I just need to watch more ESPN.

Vote early - Vote often

by Kenda Buxton

The last time I paid attention to a presidential election, Snoopy was a candidate. It was 1972 when Charlie Brown's beagle launched a campaign with a straightforward declaration, 'Snoopy for President.' That slogan, along with Snoopy, appeared on T-shirts, buttons, and lunchboxes. I was ten years old and found Snoopy a lot more appealing than the major contenders for president, Richard Nixon and George McGovern. Considering that the Watergate scandal erupted shortly after the election, we probably would have been better off under a cartoon dog's leadership, which is exactly why the only candidates I'm endorsing this year are those from the cartoons of my youth.

Quick Draw McGraw – Like President Bush, Quick Draw McGraw hails from a western state where he's the only horse in town wearing a sheriff's badge. Quick Draw's sidekick is a burro named Baba Looey, who dispenses words of wisdom to the dimwitted Quick Draw. Since many politicians seem to rely on jackasses for advice, Quick Draw has a good chance of winning this year's election.

Augie Doggie and Doggie Daddy – In the tradition of John Adams, John Quincy Adams, George H. W. Bush, and George W. Bush, Augie Doggie and his father, Doggie Daddy, could be another set of father/son presidents. How can you not be drawn to a respectful young pup who always refers to his father as, "Dear Old Dad"?

Fred Flintstone – Since he was never elected Grand Poobah of the Water Buffalo Lodge, Fred lacks political experience, but he's one of the few cartoon characters who can provide us with a First Lady. Like Barbara Bush, Wilma Flintstone was never seen without a string of pearls around her neck ... or maybe they were dinosaur bones. Oh well, either way, ever since Jackie Kennedy, Americans have loved a First Lady with style.

Underdog – You have to love a president whose motto is, "When trouble calls, I am not slow. It's hip, hip, hip, and away I go." We haven't had a president with a girlfriend since Bill Clinton. Whoops! I meant since Woodrow Wilson. After the death of his first wife, Wilson courted and married his second wife while in office. Underdog's girlfriend, Sweet Polly Purebred, sang, "Oh where, oh where, has my Underdog gone?" each time she was in trouble, resulting in our hero swooping down to save her. It'll be difficult *not* to vote for a candidate who won't spend his time off at Camp David, but instead, will spend it rescuing damsels in distress.

Davey and Goliath – It's important to keep the conservative voters happy, which is why Davey Hansen and his dog Goliath are throwing their hats into the ring. The Evangelical Lutheran Church in America owns the characters of Davey and Goliath. This means Davey doesn't support abortion or same sex marriage, but then, he is only eight years old and more concerned with issues befitting a boy his age, like demanding better tasting bubble gum in packets of baseball cards and getting to stay up past his bedtime. Obviously, time stopped for both Davey and me in 1970.

Beetle Bailey – Beetle had a short life in animation. He was never able to obtain the popularity on television that he still has today in newspaper comic strips. However, I think Americans will forgive Private Bailey for his low TV ratings. After all, we're left with no doubts that Beetle *did* report for duty.

Bugs Bunny – An election wouldn't be complete without that "Wascally Wabbit" as Elmer Fudd would say. Bugs will work for nothing but carrots and a few laughs. The former making him stand out amongst his wealthy political peers, the latter meaning he'll feel right at home in Washington.

Mr. Magoo – Granted, the lovably stupid Quincy Magoo isn't the most outstanding choice for president. He's not sure where he's going, mangles his sentences, and is easily confused. On the other hand, that means he's not much different from our current commander in chief. So, hey! *Mr. Magoo for President!*

With campaign slogans that will range from, "There's no need to fear, Underdog is here." to, "Eh, what's up, Doc?" to, "Yabba dabba doo," the next presidential election could be the most animated one yet. Unfortunately for us, even cartoon characters are too smart to get involved in politics.

Broadway, move over for Kenosha, the musical

by Thomas J. Noer

It's great to be back among the *Kenosha News* family, but it's different as I am now writing for Sunday rather than Friday. On Friday, you can be frivolous since the weekend is approaching and people are ready for mirth. But, Sunday readers want serious columns on major issues! Unfortunately, you are not going to get serious in this space because for me, Sunday means musicals. There is nothing better than sipping a cup of coffee, laughing at the *Kenosha News* editorials, and listening to *Sunday Brunch on Broadway* on the radio. Who cares about the stock market when you can sing along to *The Music Man*?

The hottest two musicals on Broadway are *Mamma Mia*, a pasted together collection of the hits of the Euro-trash group *ABBA*, and *Urinetown*. (The title pretty much says it.) If these can be hits, why not *Kenosha*? Below is the libretto (a fancy term for 'the words') of the soon-to-open musical, *Kenosha*!

It is set in one of the local taverns on a late afternoon. A stunned-looking young man in a Brooks Brothers' suit enters, checks the market results on his pager, and then sings the opening number, *Investorday*, to the tune of the Beatle's *Yesterday*.

> Investorday, all my money was in my 401 K
> thought it was there to stay.
> Oh, I believed in investorday!
> Stupidly, I put it all in old *Enron*.
> Now my kid's tuition is nearly gone.
> Oh, I believed in investorday!
> Suddenly, my losses were really mounting.
> So I called in *Andersen Accounting*.
> Oh yes, I believed in investorday!

As the depressed Yuppie sips a Cosmopolitan, Ed Block and Debbie Ruffalo enter from opposite doors clutching Kenosha Symphony programs and join in the rousing duet, *This Band is MY Band,* sung to the tune of Woody Guthrie's, *This Land is Your Land!*

> This band is MY band! This band's not YOUR band!
> I'll decide who's on the bandstand.
> We can't agree which tune to play
> So our Board just flew away.
> The way we fight over every cello
> We make the School Board seem almost mellow.
> This band belongs to only ME!

While they argue over what song to play on the jukebox, a senior citizen wanders in clutching a white envelope. She orders a cheap beer and breaks into the moving, *Its Unfair!,* sung to the tune of George M. Cohan's, *Over There!*

> It's unfair! It's unfair!
> Every year, there's the fear, when its there!
> The assessment letter! The assessment letter!
> I appealed but they don't care!
> I just hate that damned mill rate!
> Watch the date. Don't be late. You can' t escape!
> The assessment letter! The assessment letter!
> Who said owning a home was so darn great?

As the she nurses her beer, there is a loud commotion in the parking lot as the entire Kenosha School Board arrives and fights its way into the room. After trying to fire the bartender, they sing their poignant version of Stephen Sondheim's, *Send in the Clowns.*

> Aren't we a joke? Don't we appear
> Bigger idiots year after year?
> Our egos are vast. Our voices are great.
> We've made Kenosha the joke of the state!

Where are the clowns? There ought to be clowns. Send in the clowns.

Don't bother. WE'RE here!

They order a round, but the bartender recalls their drinks and a disheveled traveling salesman enters singing the showstopper, *Sheridan Road*, to the tune of Lerner and Loewe's, *The Street Where you Live*, from *My Fair Lady*.

I often drove down that street before.
And the turns were always so very neat before.
Now going South I can see downtown.
But to get there I've got to turn around.
I often drove down that street before.
But the old road never had me so beat before.
Now to take an order, I go to the Illinois border!
When I drive on the street they've destroyed!

The bartender gives the dazed salesman a free boilermaker when a dashing, distinguished, incredibly handsome historian from a local college wanders in. He plugs in his word processor, orders a gin and tonic, and sings the show's finale, *To Write*, to the tune of Leonard Bernstein's, *Tonight*, from *West Side Story*.

To write, to write. I need a column tonight.
Or else there will be no words to print!
Be light, be bright. 700 words is very tight.
It's Wednesday and I don't have a clue!
Its late. But wait! It doesn't have to be too great.
Just something to make the reader smile.
A song! Not long! Cause music's never wrong.
Just make sure that the lyrics scan!
Its true. I'm through. I wrote it just for you!
And it's always great fun … to write!

Curtain! Applause! Look out, Broadway! Kenosha, the musical, is on the way!

Would you like a cappuccino with that hymn?

by Kenda Buxton

When I first heard the phrase, *Video Café Services*, I thought Starbucks and Blockbuster had merged, and that you could now rent a movie while waiting for your Caramel Espresso Latte Broccoli Mocha Frappuccino. Life was a lot simpler when coffee was advertised by Mrs. Olson and came in just one flavor we called ... well, coffee. But recently I've found out *Video Café Services* aren't about renting movies or buying coffee I can't pronounce. *Video Café Services* are somewhat like going to church, but without the uncomfortable seating arrangements, the uncomfortable clothes, and your stomach growling as you think of Mom's pot roast cooking at home. Evidently, someone's stolen the idea I had forty years ago, "Boy, if we could just eat and watch TV while we sit here, coming to church wouldn't be so bad." Well, because of *Video Café Services*, now we can. If I'd only known how popular these services would be, I'd have ignored my mother when she said, "You watch plenty of TV at home", and marketed my "food and TV" concept to ministers across America.

Since the call to worship now means television, doughnuts, blue jeans, and tennis shoes, you can count me in. To begin with, any time I can sit in front of a TV and eat, I'm all for it. And since this is done at a church service, and if I pray hard enough for a miracle, I'm sure God will banish the calories from the chocolate chip muffin I'm stuffing into my mouth, while the minister preaches against the sins of the flesh. This beats the days when attending church meant a dress with lace that made me itch, black patent leather shoes that pinched my toes, and a pastor determined to get me into Heaven the old-fashioned way ... by thumping his Bible and working up a sweat over the thought of my soul being lost if he couldn't convince me a little pain was worth the price of eternal life.

Thanks to *Video Café Services*, eternal life no longer means scratchy dresses, ill-fitting shoes, or even a pastor in many cases. Some churches rely on a video library filled with sermons preached by famous ministers. But hey, who needs a pastor anyway, when your church can have what's referred to as a "directional leader"? I'm not sure exactly what a directional leader does, other than put a videotape in the VCR each Sunday morning, but it sounds like a pretty cushy job to me. You show up early enough to make the coffee, set out the doughnuts, pour some orange juice, and pick the "sermon of the day" from your video library. How hard can that be? No more agonizing over your weekly sermon and no more worries about offending half the congregation, while putting the other half to sleep. If anyone has questions about how to get to Heaven, you just find the video marked, *How to Get to Heaven* and play it. Better yet, let the person rent it for two bucks and allow the church a little tax-free income, which can then be used for more doughnuts.

Doughnuts, coffee, and TV aside, this is where you're thinking, "But where's the music, Kenda?" I'm glad you asked, because no *Video Café Service* would be complete without traditional hymns like, *What a Friend We Have in Jesus*, or contemporary Christian rock music, or even heavy Christian rock. The choices are overwhelming for a Baptist woman who attended a church where, as teenagers, we were warned not to sing, *When the Roll is Called Up Yonder* with too much gusto, for fear we'd start dancing in the aisles like the kids on American Bandstand, a show none of us was supposed to be watching. I didn't say we *weren't* watching it. I just said we weren't supposed to be.

So now that Christian rock music makes dancing seem less sinful, and several local churches hold *Video Café Services*, I just might have to bake some chocolate chip muffins, put on my best blue jeans, and join them. I have one question though, "If I don't like what the pastor is saying, can I change the channel?"

Old TV characters don't die, they plan parties

byThomas J.Noer

Have you ever wondered what happens to TV commercial characters when their ads are canceled? Of course not! You have far better things to do. That sort of dumb stuff is why I am here. So click on your remote as I take you to, *Ancient Ad Village: A TV Commercial Character Retirement Community* for a meeting of the Planning Committee for the annual dinner/dance.

The *Frito Bandito,* Chair of the group, *The Marlboro Man,* and *Madge* the Palmolive beautician are sitting in rocking chairs nibbling snacks served by *Mr. Peanut.*

"Hey, cigarette man, you got a date for the dance?"

"Well, it's hard to find someone what with me connected to this oxygen tank. How about you?"

"Si, amigo. I'm hooked up with *Chiquita Banana.* Love her hats!"

"Guys, lets get on with it. I have to do *Betty Crocker*'s hair this afternoon."

"OK Madge. You were put in charge of refreshments. What do you have?"

"Well, I guess it is the usual. The *Hamm's Bear* and *Spuds McKenzie* are bringing the beer, *Tony the Tiger* and *Captain Crunch* are in charge of cereal, and *Charlie the Tuna* is doing a seafood salad. For dessert, the *Keebler Elves* are making cookies, the *Tootsie Roll Owl* is bringing treats, and the *Nestle's Dog* has some special hot chocolate. I asked Mrs. Anderson and Juan Valdez to brew coffee."

"Same stuff every year," gasped *The Marlboro Man*! "You know that old lady in Room 48 is going to yell, "Where's the Beef?" and that crazy kid down the hall will want his Maypo."

"Can't we get The *Taco Bell Chihuahua* to bring some burritos?"

"He and *Morris the Cat* are out of town visiting that obnoxious *AFLAC Duck*. I can't believe he and that ugly *Geico Gecko* are still working and we are all collecting unemployment. They must have a great agent. Well, I guess I can get *Elsie the Cow* to whip up some sandwiches."

"Alright, but make sure she uses real butter. We don't want to fool with *Mother Nature*."

"Madge what about the punch?"

"It's done. I got some bottled water from The *Culligan Man* and *Punchie* gave me some Hawaiian Punch. In fact, you're soaking in it! Just kidding. Trust me, the food will be fine. We had Mikey try it."

"Come on Madge, you know that Mikey will eat anything!"

"Settle down! You always cough when you get upset, my filtered friend. Let's move on, nicotine addict."

"Have *Mr., Goodwrench* and *Buddy Lee* finished building the dance floor?"

"Well, they did, but The *Pillsbury Doughboy* and The *Michelin Man* jumped on to do their aerobics and it broke. We've got to get those two on a diet."

"What about entertainment?"

"We have the *Doublemint Twins* twirling their batons. *Snap, Crackle and Pop* have worked up a comedy routine, *Dino the Sinclair Dinosaur* is singing a duet with *The Texaco Man*, and there will be a race between *The Energizer Bu*nny and *Speedy AlkaSeltzer*."

"Who is handling clean-up?"

"Well, Bandito, *Mr. Clean* is in charge along with the *Ajax White Knight* and the *White Tornado*. The *Brawny Man* will provide paper towels and *Mr. Whipple* will bring the Charmin."

"Hey Marlboro, do you think *Mr. Clean* is gay? I mean, what's with that earring and the shaved head?"

"Nope, I saw him on a date with *Mrs. Butterworth*. Man, is she sweet! I wish I had asked her to the dance. I guess I will have to break down and call the *Ring Around the Collar Lady*. She did a nice job on my shirts last week and will be more fun than that Clap On/Clap Off woman I asked last year. Anyway, I hear she's fallen and can't get up."

"What about music for the dance, Madge?"

"We have a problem there. *Reddy Kilowatt* did a great job on the lights, but the *Maytag Repair Man* was supposed to fix the sound system and nobody ever called him. We will have to go live and use those *Coca Cola Singers* and their stupid, *'I'd like to make the world sing in perfect harmony'* song."

"We can't dance to that. Can't you find anyone else?"

"Well, the three *Budweiser Frogs* want to sing, but they only know one tune and the *Raisinettes* want too much money. I guess we can get the *Ricola Cough Drop* Boys to play their Alpine horns, but its tough doing a polka to that."

"This has the makings of a real disaster! Whose stupid idea was it to have this affair anyway?"

"Oh, some idiot columnist in Kenosha, Wisconsin desperate to fill some space thought it up."

"Well, tell him, when he finishes this, he had better call the *Tidy Bowl Man!*"

Abused, amused, or enthused by it, you gotta love it

by Ed Groelle

Well, as Arnold Schwarzeger said in *Terminator 3*, "I'm back!" The Kenosha News has recognized its pressing need for some alternative writing on the Local Page and has reinstated me for the next two years. My fans who picketed the newspaper's downtown office probably were instrumental in that decision. They want a total of twenty-six articles from me but I'm not worried. I figure long before that commitment is satisfied the job will be outsourced to India anyway.

Today's subject is English, the language, not the people. I arrived at that subject by the usual method of waking up in the middle of the night in the fetal position with an idea, immediately mixing a large glass of gin and diet 7-UP, firing up my PC, and then just starting typing. It's easy and gets even easier with a second gin.

There are only three aspects of English that give some users trouble ... pronunciation, grammar, and spelling. In the area of spelling, I personally don't have a problem because I have a little man that lives in my brain who comes out with a little hammer and starts tapping me on the rear of my eyeballs whenever he sees a misspelled word ... sort of like a live-in spelling *au pair*.

There are certain spellings that always give people trouble. There is the persistent "i before e" dilemma, of course, but this is easily detected and corrected because the little man immediately calls my attention to the mistake. One word you see consistently misspelled is the word *$%&#* which is commonly seen in comic strips as a surrogate for an off-color or cuss word. The correct spelling is *$%&#*. Just remember that the "%" comes before the "&" and you should be OK. The English tend be a bit snobbish, so they will sometimes add an 'e' at the end and pronounce it with a

28

silent $. But then, what can you expect from a nation that drives on the wrong side of the road? Their spelling should be graciously accepted, but it is not strictly proper in American English. Also, while I'm on the subject, the plural is "$%&#ies" not "$%&#'s." Don't make this common mistake.

I am a devoted stickler for proper English usage but it seems that no matter how carefully I check and double-check my submissions there is always at least one error when it is published. I have a nagging suspicion that someone at the Kenosha News inserts at least one error on purpose so as to not make themselves look bad by comparison.

Have you ever noticed that titles are rather enigmatic in English? The French have M. and Mme. for *Monsieur* and *Madam*, the Spanish have Sra. and Sr. for *Señora* and *Señor*, but in English, what do the titles stand for? Mr., of course, is for Mister, and Mrs. for Mistress (now perhaps a defunct, politically incorrect title) but what about Miss? I personally think it stands for "missing a ring." And Ms is a complete mystery but it may just stand for that … a mizz-tery.

Using apostrophes in possessives should not be the stumbling block people make of them. It's really quite simple. The rule is that if the possession is singular the possessor has an apostrophe before the 's.' For example, it's St. Catherine's hospital. If Cathy had more than one hospital it would still be St. Catherine's Hospitals but … if there were more than one Cathy with more than one hospital it would be St. Catherines' Hospitals. No mystery there. Hyphenated possessives really can get some peoples' panties in a twist. It's mothers-in-law (plural), mother-in-law's (possessive), or if you are not crazy about her and use the street vernacular, muthas-in-law, the same rule applies.

English is loaded with ambiguities such as those words that have one spelling but two pronunciations like 'lead' and 'dove.' Some languages get around this problem by calling the reader's attention to an atypical pronunciation by adding a silly mark above the vowel. We could do the same with 'lêad' or 'dõve', but I really don't think it is such a good idea. My little man has more than he can handle now.

BTW, do you know which word in the English dictionary has the longest definition? It's 'set.' No kidding!

English often makes no sense at all but if it is your mother tongue, hang in there. It really is worth mastering.

Are you 'Old School'? A complete and handy guide

by Thomas J. Noer

In my never-ending quest to keep up with American culture and language I have noticed a wonderful new term, *Old School*. It is used as a compliment for people, ideas, and objects that are time-tested and show traditional values. A football player who plays tough all game is *Old School*. A business leader who succeeds through hard work is *Old School*. Below are some examples of things *Old School* and those that clearly do not qualify.

Flannel is *Old School*. Spandex is not! Flannel shirts are warm, loving, and sooth your tired body. They invoke memories of camping trips, raking leaves, and Saturday mornings. Spandex is artificial, tight-fitting Yuppie wear for bottled-water-drinking exhibitionists. Have you ever tried ice fishing in spandex long underwear?

Barbers are *Old School*. Hair stylists are not! Barbers are old, Italian guys who wear comfortable shoes, can talk about sports and politics, and have lots of ancient magazines scattered around. Stylists are thin, young, wear designer black shirts, and charge way too much money. What do you talk about with a stylist? How to make a Cosmopolitan?

Barbie is *Old School*. *American Girl* is not! Barbie is an enduring image of unrealistic expectations for young girls. Mothers and even grandmothers can share Barbie stories and costumes. *American Girl* dolls are way too hip and designed only to drive parents to bankruptcy buying the latest fashions. Ken would never go out with an American Girl.

Pick-up trucks are *Old School*. SUV's are not! County music could not survive without pickup trucks. Can you imagine throwing your wet dog in the back of a Lexus LX470? Let's see you haul a couple of dozen bags of cement in your Nissan Pathfinder? Flannel shirts are perfect for pick-up trucks and unacceptable for SUV's.

The World Series is *Old School*. The X-Games are not! Baseball is played by tobacco-chewing millionaires and watched by beer-swilling adults. Sometime in their youth everybody tried to hit a ball with a stick and we all know, *Take Me Out to the Ballgame*. The X-Games are tattooed, anorexic teens in baggy shorts trying to kill themselves on skateboards. Ever see someone at the X-Games eating a hotdog? No, they are all Mountain Dew-addicted vegetarians.

Cruises are *Old School*. Adventure vacations are not! Cruises permit (no, require) you to eat six to eight gigantic meals a day and to listen to incredibly bad singers and comics. They are a floating Las Vegas. Adventure vacations take you to exotic and dangerous locations where you can crash down rapids, climb killer mountains, or hike across barren deserts. They make you pay for this.

Pot roast is *Old School*. Sushi is not! Sunday afternoon at grandmas ... sit around in your flannel shirt, drink a few shots of brandy, talk about the World Series, look at your niece's collection of Barbie's, and then its time for the family dinner of SUSHI? Yes! Grandma has prepared her famous raw tuna with wasabi sauce. Yummm! Hope there are some leftovers for lunch tomorrow. Maybe granny has been sipping Cosmopolitans.

Western movies are *Old School*. Special effects movies are not! The whole family can enjoy good guys shooting bad guys, cowboys singing to their horses, and dusty ranchers standing at the bar drinking red-eye. Two hours of things blowing up, car chases, and aliens are not the same. Do you want to see John Wayne beat up the evil cattle baron or listen to 45 minutes of lame philosophy in *The Matrix*?

Progressive dinners are *Old School*. Flash mobs are not! For those of you under thirty, progressive dinners are moving feasts with cocktails at one home, appetizers at a second, main course at the next, and dessert at a fourth. Everybody tries to outdo each other in cuisine (and in cleaning up their house). For those of you over thirty, flash mobs result when someone circulates an address and time on the Internet and hundreds of computer geeks show up and mill around. Give me a nice progressive dinner with pot roast anytime.

Newspaper columns are *Old School.* Chat rooms are not! Newspaper columns provide wit, wisdom, and profound thoughts. Chat rooms just run up your phone bill. More importantly, have you ever tried to bring your computer into the bathroom? Newspaper columns are perfect toilet accessories as many of you may be proving right now.

A cure for Packeritis?

by Jim Wynne

This is the year of the World Cup. The quadrennial world championship of soccer is a huge event all over the world except for the United States. Aficionados of the game, when asked to explain why it isn't more popular in this country, usually answer that Americans have not taken the time to learn its "nuances." In answer to this contention, and in the interest of educating the public, I have taken considerable time to familiarize myself with the game. In fact, I recently watched nearly ten minutes of a game on the Spanish-language cable channel.

While watching the game was an edifying experience in itself, I was delighted to hear one of the announcers use what sounded like the Spanish word, *albondigas*, which means 'meatballs.' It is the only word I remember from my high school Spanish class other than the word for 'washroom,' which I remember only because the teacher wouldn't let you go there unless you asked in Spanish. One of the slower students had the misfortune of experiencing sudden-onset intestinal distress during Spanish class one day and caused a memorable commotion when he desperately and unsuccessfully tried to remember the word for 'washroom' and wound up in tears asking in Spanish if he could go immediately to his uncle's blue car.

I can't imagine what the context might have been in which the announcer referred to meatballs during a soccer game. I suppose it's possible that what the announcer said was something that just sounded like *albondigas*, but I don't think so. At any rate, for the benefit of readers who lack the type of comprehensive knowledge of the game that I now have, I will explain a few of the nuances.

As far as American professional soccer teams go, there are three positions: Midfielder, Fiery Spaniard, and Determined Croatian. The other seventy players on the field at any given time are not really players at all. They are hyperactive people who run helter-skelter up and down and back and forth across the field in order to create the illusion of purposeful action. The intended verisimilitude is not achieved, however, as it is soon apparent that these 'players' are running around aimlessly. And the term 'professional' is a little misleading. Due to the lack of popularity of the sport in this country, few tickets are sold. If you call the ticket office of an American professional team and ask what time the game starts, they ask you what time you can be there. So players, instead of being paid actual salaries, are compensated with *Chuck E. Cheese* tokens.

Goaltenders wear unique uniforms because they are not members of either team. Their job is to protect the basic integrity of the game by making sure that there is never any scoring beyond the one-goal limit. By rule, the final score of all soccer games is either 1-0 or a scoreless tie. Goaltenders are armed with pistols and after a goal has been scored they are empowered to shoot anyone who looks like he might be trying to score another. This explains why players are often seen frantically impelling the ball *away* from the goal with their heads.

In soccer, the game clock runs backwards. That is, it shows the elapsed time rather than the time remaining, which means that it is necessary for spectators, players, and officials to do a small mental calculation in order to determine how much time is left in the game. Because soccer fans are generally incapable of such mental activity, no one really knows when the game is supposed to end, so they sometimes go on for several days.

Other than players running willy-nilly up and down the field, there is no meaningful action whatsoever in soccer games, unless one team's Fiery Spaniard trips the opposing team's Determined Croatian, or vice-versa. When this happens, one of the officials on the field will pull a colored card out of his shirt pocket and show it to the crowd. In most of the world, this is a signal for spectators to begin throwing things on the field, randomly beating the snot out of one another, and dismantling the stadium. It doesn't happen in this country because the spectators generally lapse into a coma-like stupor shortly after the game begins and don't wake up until halftime, which is usually two or three days later.

If given a bit more space I could explain a few more of the fine points, but I think the average reader, who didn't understand soccer before reading this column, will now be able to watch at least five or six minutes of a game before losing consciousness. And, you can be sure that upon waking up the next morning, you can start watching the game again without having missed anything.

Graduation, your future, and more Mondays than you wanna think about

by Kenda Buxton

It's a tradition that dates back to the first Neanderthal boy earning a bachelor's degree in "Grotto Artistry", and to the blue collar Neanderthal parents paying for that boy's education with pterodactyl eggs. Graduation ceremonies answer the question, "Tell me again, Wife, why are we forking over pterodactyl eggs for that boy to learn how to draw on cave walls?"

Graduation ceremonies are once again taking place across the country. Due to their outstanding contributions to society, politicians and celebrities are speakers at many of these ceremonies. I know this because every time a famous person appears at a graduation ceremony, it states on the program that, "Celebrity So and So is speaking, due to his outstanding contributions to society."

From a college administrator's standpoint, famous people are assets to a graduation ceremony. Not only does their appearance guarantee every graduate will show up just to get an autograph (or, depending upon political affiliation, heckle and yell, "War monger!" or "Baby killer!"), but they're great at urging young people to go forth and "Conquer the world!" or "Bring peace and harmony where there's been none!" or "Find the promise of tomorrow in today!" ... whatever that means. Actually, I do know what it means. It means the speaker couldn't bear to see the enthusiasm melt from those eager young faces if he laid the truth on them by saying, "Hate to break the news to ya', kids, but it's all downhill from here. Mom and Dad won't be paying your bills any more and sleeping until noon is a thing of the past because your idiot employer will expect you to show up at some ungodly hour shortly after daybreak.

You'll spend the next fifty years being aggravated by your health insurance company, your cell phone company, and your mother-in-law, while groveling for a boss you hate just so you can keep a job that makes you wonder why you got a college degree to pursue that job in the first place. And, just when you think there's a light at the end of the tunnel because the mirror says, "Man, have *you* gotten old!", the government will raise the retirement age to 94 and three quarters, and the kids you've just put through college will move back in with you."

The above example is the reason college administrators don't ask regular shmoos like me to speak at graduation ceremonies. Without giving it a try, I know conquering the world is not only impossible, but dangerous too, considering the number of people you tick off when you kick open their doors while declaring, "I'm here to conquer you!" Instead, I'd tell the graduates, "Forget any lofty ambitions you have about conquering the world. Conquering the challenge of getting up and making it to work on time during the 2,496 Monday mornings you'll face from now until retirement is the only thing most of you'll be up for. If you do it with a migraine headache or after being up all night with a sick kid, it's equal to the effort of overrunning a small country anyway."

On the subject of bringing peace and harmony where there is none, I'd say, "Once you get married, graduates, you'll have all you can do to keep peace and harmony in your own house. Your desire to spread it around will dwindle greatly after multiple arguments with your spouse over issues of great significance, like who didn't refill the sugar bowl, and whether your car is parked too close to his tool bench, or his tool bench sets too close to your car."

So now, as students don caps and gowns and as famous people step up to podiums to impart words of wisdom on this new generation of adults, I'll impart my final words of wisdom:

"It's all downhill from here, graduates, but hey, look at the bright side. You've only got 2,496 Mondays until retirement."

Back to school with reservations

by Laurie McKeon

There is pallor over our house that is palpable. We're all in mourning over a summer that was way too short and is gasping its last breath. Although some of us are in denial (my sons), there is no avoiding those three little words that every kid (except my youngest daughter) hates to hear, 'Back to School.'

I know that most moms can't wait to get their kids out of the house and back into the system and I can appreciate that, but I'd do much better living in an endless summer. The school year means early bedtimes, really early wake-up calls, regulated meals, homework, practice, games, and the never-ending car loop, not to mention test anxiety, gym uniforms, school supplies, and the constant press to stay on schedule. During the school year there is no room for error and the slightest glitch has a ripple effect that can last for days. For me, the school year is nine long months of innumerable opportunities to miss the mark. But, in the summer, our schedule has some flex to it. No one has ever gotten a detention for being late to the swimming pool. And it's not only the kids going to school that I dread, it's also all the leg work required to get them there that makes my palms sweat.

Last Sunday I bit the bullet and went out to buy school supplies before all of the pink pearl erasers were gone. Hey, we learned our lesson last year. When it comes to getting the good school supplies … you snooze, you loose. As I trolled the store, multiple supply lists in hand, I joined a throng of other parents, eyes glazed over, searching for the four-ounce container of Elmer's School Glue. Each child needs very specific supplies, and I must admit, it makes me nervous even thinking about deviating from the list. Will my second grader be sent home because she has forty-eight crayons instead of the required twenty-four? I can't find blue erasable pens. Will black suffice? Somewhere in the universe there is a heap of five-inch Fiskars with "McKeon" stamped on them, because we never seem to keep a pair for more than one year. The big kids want mechanical pencils (nerds) that the little kids aren't allowed. Everyone needs boxes of Kleenex and someone needs a graphing calculator with scientific notation, whatever that is.

Buying, sorting, and labeling the supplies are bad enough, but the real torture comes with outfitting the troops. One would think that with four boys born within five years, we'd have hit the hand-me-down mother lode. But, due to some freakish genetic combination, our four sons have absolutely no physical similarities. We have a slim, a husky, a regular, and a really short. You can fake it with shirts but, when it comes to pants, we're reinventing the wheel every single school year. After years of trying to belt a slim son into an older brother's husky pants, or worse, stuffing a husky into a used slim, I've finally realized that there will never be any economies of scale for us. The good news is that our kids go to a Catholic school and wear uniforms. The bad news is that our kids go to a Catholic school and wear uniforms. They actually must have "school" pants. Throwing on some jeans and calling it a day is not an option. We are on a never-ending hunt for khaki and navy blue pants that meet the dress code but don't look like they belong on a fifty-year-old actuary. It's harder than it sounds, especially for the huskies.

Finally, the most painful piece of this back to school dance is all the paper work involved. Every single child has a packet the size of the New York City phone book full of forms that must be completed before they can cross the threshold of knowledge. Emergency forms, physical forms, vaccination forms, volunteer forms, authorization to use the internet, authorization to get a cough drop forms, permission to be in the school directory forms, permission to play sports forms, acknowledgement that we read the handbook forms (Yeah, right! Cover to cover), proof that they have had the chicken pox forms, hot lunch forms, milk count forms, order forms for spirit wear, order forms for picture day and every single form ... six times over. I'm getting carpal tunnel just looking at them. I know for a fact that if my mom had to complete one tenth of this paperwork to send me and my four siblings to school, she would have just let us stay home and watch Phil Donahue all day ... every day. Don't think I'm not tempted.

While we try to enjoy those last minute summer flings, the specter of school casts a large shadow over our days. And all I keep thinking is, "If I fill out ten forms a day for the next ten days, will I get all this paper work done on time?"

Maybe I need that graphing calculator to figure it out.

Cell phones — another investment opportunity missed

by Ed Groelle

Someone once said that advanced technology is indistinguishable from magic. Of course, no technology is really magic, but can be similar to many other mysteries that abound like, why does Massachusetts keep reelecting Ted Kennedy or why do people drive around a health club's parking lot looking for a space near the entrance so they won't need to walk very far to exercise.

Cell phones fall into the category of mysteries until they are explained and then they fall into the category of mind boggling. I recently decided to unravel the 'mystery' of how cell phones work by wading for several hours through the gobblygook and technical jargon on the Internet. I'll try to condense my findings with an example.

Let's pretend you are standing in a six-sided compartment or 'cell' similar in shape to a bee's honeycomb but differing in that it is approximately ten square miles in area and has a 150-foot antenna somewhere in that area. You've all seen these antennas. They have six or more vertical cylinders on out-stretched arms located on towers, churches, water towers, and anywhere there is enough height to facilitate their function of communicating with cell phones. Cities, churches, farmers, etc. all vie for these antennas to be erected on their property because the cell company pays them $500 plus each month for that privilege. Each station has a base station attached and can service 168 users at one time. No two adjacent cells use the same frequencies. This ensures there are no transmission collisions. There are more than 176,000 of these cells with antennas across the US and probably ten times that amount all around the world.

OK, you are standing in one of these cells and get the sudden urge to phone your wife to tell her she is cuter than a basket of kittens. Turning on your phone immediately activates some complex technical activities. First, your phone will contact the nearest antenna and its base station through a special control frequency. Using your phone's ID number, it will know who you are, where you are, and if you have paid your last cell phone bill and therefore be allowed to use the network. If not, you will get a *No Service* display. Let's be honest here ... cell phones don't only work on battery power, they run on money. It's a huge and lucrative business.

As you dial your wife's number the base station receives it and determines if her phone number is in its cell. If it isn't, it will hand it off to a central station that monitors many cells. This central station will determine if the number you have dialed is a cell phone or a landline number. If it is a landline number, it can hand it to the telephone company. If it is a cell phone number, it will kick it up to a master station for processing. The master station will find the cell phone and also determine if it is outside your paid area. If it is, you will get the dreaded "Roaming" message. "Roaming" is the top-secret cell company code word for, "Let's really soak this guy."

If you are in a car and you move toward the edge of your cell, your cell's base station sees your signal strength diminishing and the station in the cell you are moving toward sees your phone's signal strength increasing. At some point your phone gets a signal to change frequencies and switches itself to the new cell.

Simple, isn't it? Cell phones are the most complex devices you use on a daily basis. They can process millions of calculations per second, all transparent to the user. What is amazing is that all of that functionality that once would fill a room now fits into a package not much larger than pack of cigarettes.

If someone had predicted the existence of cell phones thirty years ago I would have laughed derisively and said, "It can't be done." The probable next evolutionary step with cell phones will be direct communication with satellites making cell phone antenna towers obsolete. I've said it before and I'll say it again, "It can't be done." ... but, this time I'm not laughing.

Crazed Kenosha columnist shares desperate diary

by Thomas J. Noer

Editor's Note: It is a little known fact that the Kenosha News requires its columnists to keep a daily diary to make sure they are working hard. Mr. Noer has chosen to reveal his in the piece below. This is a serous breach of his contract, but our lawyers have determined that we cannot block publication. Mr. Noer has not answered our phone calls and there are reports he has left town for the week. In the meantime, Mr. Noer has been placed on *Double-Secret Columnist Probation!*

Noer diary entries

Sunday, September 14.
5:30 AM - Lurk by front door waiting for delivery of Kenosha News.

7:00 AM - Stop looking out window and brew coffee. Make note to cut back on tip to carrier.

7:15 AM - Hear thump of newspaper. Open and see the same *America's Most Wanted* photo of myself. Read column on New Holidays and laugh hysterically! Stand by phone waiting for congratulatory calls from grateful readers.

12:00 PM - Phone has not rung. Watch six hours of football.

Monday, September 15.
7:00 AM - E-mail Kenosha News demanding payment for last column and suggesting large raise.

3:30 PM - Sharpen pencils for next column.

3:31 PM - Realize I don't use pencils. Turn on computer and stare at screen.

5:30 PM – Type, 'October Column'

6:43 PM - Turn off computer and go home.

Tuesday, September 16.

7:15 AM - Ask spouse for possible column topics.

7:20 AM - Remind spouse I AM STILL waiting for answer.

7:25 AM - Spouse leaves for work.

8:00 AM - Ask colleagues at work for column ideas. They suggest Iraq, the deficit, and rebuilding urban infrastructure.

8:03 AM - Realize none of my colleagues read my column. Consider column about those who don't read my column. Consider column about academic's total lack of humor.

Wednesday, September 16 thru Saturday, September 20.

Forget about column.

Sunday, September 21.

4:00 PM - Attend Kenosha Library function honoring local authors and talk to 'real writers.' Drink lots of wine and determine to find idea for October column tonight! Watch end of Packer's loss in Arizona. Too happy to write.

Monday, September 22.

4:45 PM - Check from Kenosha News arrives. Spend entire check on order of fries at McDonalds. Consider getting job at Kenosha County golf course.

Tuesday, September 23.

3:00 PM - Come up with three ideas for column:

1. Underrated/Overrated. Denim is overrated, Corduroy underrated. Bratwurst overrated, Philly Steak sandwiches underrated.

4:45 PM - Abandon underrated/overrated column.

2. Advice column. Clever responses to letters like Ann Landers and Dear Abby! Type, 'I am a 16-year-old girl who recently began chatting with a convict on the Internet.'

5:58 PM - Abandon advice column.

3. Kenosha Poem Column. A heroic epic about our city,

The Odyssey with trolleys!

All hear my saga of those who dwell in a land.

With cheese on their head and beer in their hand!

7:08 PM - Abandon poem column.

Thursday, September 25.

7:05 AM - Scan front page of Kenosha News for current hot issues to write about. Decide column on three-person basketball tournaments will not work.

7:18 AM - Read 'Darts and Laurels.' Suddenly nauseous.

Monday, September 29.

4:40 PM - Write column about Reality TV shows set in Kenosha. Survivor in Barden's store! Joe Millionaire in a Packer sweatshirt! Its funny, but only 134 words. Decide to let it rest for a few days.

Wednesday, October 1.

5:23 PM - Re-read Reality TV piece. Hit delete key. Call spouse and ask if she would write a note to Steve Lund asking that I be excused from column, "Tom has a sore throat and a slight fever and can't write this month." Spouse hangs up.

Thursday, October 2.

3:33 PM - Outline column on joys of fall; beautiful leaves, crisp air, no more mosquitoes. Remember that I will need to clean all those dam leaves out of my gutter while fighting swarms of annoying bees. Also remember I had to turn on my furnace during freezing October weather. Tear up lovely fall column.

Friday, October 3.

1:34 PM - Ponder how people like Dave Barry and George Will can write something good every week! Decide I am an untalented idiot.

Sunday, October 5.

5:43 AM - Awake drenched in sweat. Assume it is column phobia but soon realize I turned furnace way too high. Panic! Got to get something done TODAY! Spot secret Kenosha News Columnist Diary next to bed.

Monday, October 6.

4:48 PM - Put on disguise and drive to Kenosha News to drop off hastily written Diary column. Spend fifteen minutes trying to find new entrance. Four salespersons try to sell me full-page ads and autographed photos of Howard Brown. Slip computer disk to receptionist and sprint to car before anyone asks me what I am doing there. Make plans to be far out of town on the Sunday when this one appears.

Unlike tuition, advice is free and worth every penny

by Laurie McKeon

As colleges across the nation hold their graduation ceremonies many notables will be giving inspirational commencement addresses. Although I have yet to be formally (or informally for that matter) asked to speak to this year's newly-minted graduates, I too, have some solid words of wisdom.

To the Class of 2008: Hurray for you! You've made it! You've climbed the mountain, written the thesis, gotten the sheepskin, and repaired all of the nail holes in your student apartment with toothpaste in the futile hopes of getting your security deposit back. Way to go! But now, as you enter the cold, cruel, world of adulthood with its myriad responsibilities of car payments, student loans, insurance premiums, and utility bills, I'd like to give you a few words of advice.

You will never be any smarter than you are today. Trust me! Never again in your natural life will you be so sure that you have all the answers and be so willing to share them with others. Right now, today, you know it all. And that's great, because this is your special graduation day but, starting tomorrow ...

~ Buy a belt. Low slung pants may be all the rage on your college campus, but in the real world, the world that has absolutely no interest in your prowess at beer pong, no one wants to see your butt cleavage, plumber's crack, paisley boxers, back tattoo, muffin top, or thong. Pull up your pants and put on a belt. While you're at it, pick up some decent shoes. Unless you are embarking on a lucrative career as a lifeguard, flip-flops are unacceptable in the work place. (Or the White House)

~ Along those same lines, lose the ball cap, skullcap, stocking cap, doo rag, or any other funky head attire. Believe it or not, back in my day, it was considered very poor form for a gentleman to wear a hat indoors. While that bastion of decorum has long gone by the wayside, totally due to major league sports merchandising, it is still inappropriate to wear that Cub's cap to the office. A possible exception is if you just signed a major league contract. Although, if it's with the Cubs, you'll be way too embarrassed to wear the hat.

~ Get a job. I may be stating the obvious, but jobs pay money and money buys food. The days of some campus employee in a hair net placing food on your cafeteria tray are over. All that Easy Mac is on your tab now. And, if you ever want to be able to buy the wine that comes in a bottle, rather than a box, you're going to need a job.

~ Show up every day. Contrary to popular belief there is no "three cut" policy in the work force. Your employer expects you there every day, so unless you have a written note from the Center for Disease Control or your father owns the company, go to work. Also, FYI, there is no spring break, summer vacation, Christmas break, or senior skip day. And, sorry, it's too late to switch your major to education.

~ Be on time. Now that you are a full-fledged adult, your mom, roommate, boyfriend, or parole officer is not responsible for getting you out of bed. Buy an alarm clock, program your phone, get a dog, or work the night shift. Nothing is more impressive to an employer than showing up every day, on time.

~ Put in a full day's work no matter how boring, tedious, repetitive, or hard. This is why they call it 'work.' If it were big, super fun every day they wouldn't have to pay you. And, sad to say, when you put in your full day's work no one is going to throw you a party, hand you a medal, or give you a trophy. You get a paycheck. Be grateful!

~ Listen way more than you talk. I understand that you are now a college grad and just aced your integral logistics final, not to mention that B+ in statistics, but you should probably wait until the ink on your company ID dries before telling the woman, who's been running the shipping department for the last eighteen years, that she's doing it all wrong.

~ Oh, by the way, that money that is missing from your paycheck is for taxes, and yes, you have to pay them. You are now footing the bill for roads, schools, safety, and national defense, not to mention a lot of pork barrel and boondoggle. Stings a little, don't it? Welcome to the club.

~ Finally, say thank you. Many, many people have sacrificed a lot to get you to this day. Your parents, siblings, teachers, and friends all have earned a stake in your future. You're one of the lucky ones. You've made it through. Now get out there and make us proud.

Graduation, your future, and facing 2,496 Mondays between now and retirement – Part 2

by Kenda Buxton

Part 1 of *"Graduation, Your Future, and More Mondays Than You Wanna Think About Until You Can Finally Stop Showing Up at Work"* appeared in this newspaper on June 13th. Right about now you're probably thinking that twelve months seems like a long time to wait for a sequel, so what's the point, right? Well, it took seven years for *The Brady Girls Get Married* to air after the Brady Bunch wasn't a bunch any more. If the American public could wait patiently while Sherwood Schwartz spent nearly a decade writing a Brady Bunch sequel, then the three people who read this column can wait patiently while I put in hundreds of hours of hard work, dedication, tooth gnashing, which, by the way, is not recommended by the American Dental Association, and multiple breaks for anything chocolate that comes in a wrapper labeled Hershey's, which the American Dental Association doesn't recommend either, but you know what? I don't care.

One year ago, I took away the hopes of millions of graduates, okay, maybe four or five, by telling them what no new graduate wants to hear; that adult life really isn't full of new beginnings, glorious achievements, and endless happiness, but instead, is filled with the drudgery of showing up at a job for the next 2,496 Mondays. Make that 3,496 Mondays, if you miscalculate how much money you need to sock away in your privatized retirement account.

Believe me, whoever said it's a cruel world out there was right. Because I don't want to keep any new graduates from enjoying this cruelty every Monday morning for the next fifty years, and because I've been known to mumble in my sleep, "Tell me, what makes you the right candidate for the job?" I'm passing along some tips that guarantee you, too, can gain employment for all those Mondays just waiting to be conquered.

~ **Dressing for the Interview:** Don't be like the young woman who asked me, "Do I have to dress up for the interview?" This left me wondering if she planned to show up in her pajamas, Big Bird slippers, and before she'd brushed her teeth.

~ **References:** If I've fired your best friend, don't use her name as a personal reference. Call me prejudiced, but I'm now old enough to know that birds of a feather really *do* flock together.

~ **Salary:** Spend time investigating the average salary of someone working in the position you're applying for. We'd all like to start at the top, but when your salary requirements exceed what your potential boss is making, then you're asking for too much. But if you get it, let me know, because that means I'm long overdue for a raise.

~ **Children:** How many you have is up to you. Just don't bring them to the interview and then assure me that you have reliable day care.

~ **Piercings and Tattoos:** Unless you're a bull, I don't want to see a ring in your nose. Unless you're a sailor, I don't want to see your tattoos either.

~ **Be on Time:** If I have to call to find out why you haven't shown up for your interview, only to discover you're still in bed at noon, I'm smart enough to figure out that getting to work on time will be a problem for you.

~ **Personality:** Yes, I know the thought of working for the rest of your life is worse than the thought of being sentenced to death by hanging, but bring a little enthusiasm to the interview. I'm the only one in this interview who gets to act like I hate showing up for work. After all, I've been doing it for twenty-five years. I've earned that right.

Graduates, while I can't promise life will be filled with endless happiness and glorious achievements, I can promise you'll have a better shot at being employed if you're on time for the interview and wear anything but your pajamas and Big Bird slippers. Oh, and remember to act enthusiastic about the prospect of working. You might as well get used to it. It's a performance you'll have to pull off every Monday for the next fifty years.

Buy your cards now for Noer's nifty new holidays

by Thomas J. Noer

When I was young (before fire was discovered) there were only a few commonly shared holidays. There were the big four; Christmas, New Year's, Easter, and Thanksgiving as well as Memorial Day, July Fourth, Labor Day, Halloween, and Father's and Mother's Day. There was also May Day and Arbor Day, but I never really understood those. In the past few decades there has been an uncontrollable growth of holidays. Greedy greeting card companies, gift shops, and florists have combined to shame us into buying cards and presents for Sweetest Day, Secretary's (now Administrative Assistant) Day, Bosses' Day, Grandparent's Day, and dozens of others.

This is only the tip of the holiday iceberg as I have discovered there are over 2,000 officially recognized holidays that celebrate people, games, foods, ethnic groups, and strange behavior. Did you know, for example, that there is a national Hop Scotch Day? A Stay Home with Your Kids Day? An International Tool Day? Brazilian Independence Day? There is even a Sour Herring Day (don't ask what you do on this one), and don't forget, September 10th is Bret Favre's Birthday (but you all probably knew that).

Ever alert to changing cultural trends, I have some new holidays for Kenosha News readers to celebrate. Feel free to send me other examples of new and silly holidays designed to make you buy cards and look stupid:

National Telemarketers Day - Given the new restrictions on the industry, many telemarketers are lonely and depressed and could use some cheering up. Phone them (preferably during dinner or late at night) and offer them a chance to change their phone service, get a new credit card, or buy aluminum siding. Make sure you mispronounce their name so they will feel special. If they hang up, feel free to hit the callback button.

National Senior Reminder Day - Send a card to a forgetful senior friend reminding them, "Your car keys are in your purse!" or, "Your glasses are on the table next to your bed!" or, "Did you look in the bathroom drawer for your prescription?" or "Where do you think you left your coat?" Be sure to mark this new holiday date on your calendar so you don't forget. Today is Sunday, so remember, there is no mail.

Eat Like Elvis Day - My son recently found a restaurant in Chicago that serves Elvis Toast, which is thick slices of white bread fried with peanut butter and bananas. I can only welcome this trend and propose a day when each of us invites an anorexic fashion model to dine on biscuits and gravy, Twinkies, and mashed potatoes smeared with syrup. Maybe they will put on a few pounds and cover their bare midriffs with checkered bibs.

Teen for a Day - People of all ages get to be a teenager for 24 hours! After you wake up at noon and breakfast on Pop Tarts, salsa, and Mountain Dew, you spend the next thirteen hours playing video games and talking on your cell phone about how your parents are 'like so totally uncool!' Be sure to utter long sighs and roll your eyes when any adult enters your room. Remember, it is crucial to know if Jim really likes Susie.

Gay Day - Given the success of *Queer Eye for the Straight Guy*, it is time for an official day of male sexual reversal. Straight guys have to go to a spa, visit a fabric shop, and observe three hours of *Designer Challenge*. Gay guys must wear cut-off sweatshirts and baseball caps while drinking boilermakers and watching *Monday Night Football*. Everyone sends a card to Michael Jackson.

Alternative Parking, Bluebag, Smoking Night. Celebrate the annual evening of mass confusion when Kenosha's finest roam the city to ticket cars whose owners forget the beginning of auto roulette season. Set your alarm for midnight, fill your car with grass clippings and brown bags (or bluebags and hazardous waste. I can never remember which), and then drive to Racine for the night. If your vehicle has a designated smoking area, you can have a cigarette, but only if it is an even-numbered day in an odd-numbered month and you live in Pleasant Prairie.

International Swedish Gourmet Day - It is a little known fact that the Vikings left Sweden to try to find something decent to eat. After years of lefse and lingonberries, even the food in England sounded good. On December 21st, the shortest day of the year, everyone must eat lutefisk, tuna casserole, and rutabaga pie followed by two large glasses of Aquavit. Remember there already is a National Sour Herring Day! (No kringle! That's Danish!)

As you can see, the possibilities for new and useless holidays are endless. You should know, however, that June 24th is National Columnist Day and I expect cards, flowers, and lutefisk!

This poem concerns a Minnesota farm girl who lived with our family for a year while attending a college in Kenosha.
She graduated, moved back to Minnesota, and eventually married.
About a year later, she dropped out of sight.
We never heard from her again. That was over forty years ago.

Keke

by Ed Groelle

Two years ago
Give or take a few months
This woman-child breezed in
Unpacked her trunks

Klunky shoes
Torn jeans
High school baton
Effervescent dreams

Like Pandora's box
Let loose to attack
My world of Mozart
and aching back

She took part of our life
Attached it to her own
And started cutting old strings
To watch reflections alone

Requests for advice
Were extremely rare
I had little to give
The freedom wasn't there

It lay behind rusted doors
The key of years didn't fit
No need to disturb it
For a young girls benefit

I wanted to sense her life
To observe without condition
But the sadness now realized
Somehow I missed her invitation

Girls are like that you know
Their charm haunts and lingers
Then like the memory of dreams
Helplessly slips through your fingers

It seems she didn't stay long enough
But all the promises have been kept
She turned alone to a new horizon
And took a giant step

She isn't here anymore
This sunny bittersweet day
The bubble is missing
Keke has gone away

Strictly for the birds

by Kenda Buxton

I'm losing a lot of sleep over the possibility that we're all going to die of the bird flu this winter. Well, maybe not quite all of us, only as many as 150 million of us world-wide, according to one expert who refused to give his name because Bill Hall, a spokesman for the U.S. Department of Health and Human Services, said the U.S. government doesn't make predictions on flu pandemic death rates.

I might find that comforting (as though the government has the possibility of a flu pandemic under control) if I wasn't having nightmares about being stuck on my roof in a fevered state while begging for fresh water and a helicopter ride. Oh, wait, that's my nightmare about a hurricane blowing through Kenosha County. My nightmare about a pandemic revolves around begging for fresh water and Tamiflu. Why do I strongly suspect that wealthy politicians and guys like Donald Trump have already stocked their medicine chests with truckloads of Tamiflu, while the rest of us are told there won't be enough of this wonder drug to go around if we should all start coughing, sneezing, and reaching for the NyQuil at the same time?

Because I excel at spending 23 out of every 24 hours worrying about what illness might kill me, and because I'm pretty good at preparing and organizing, when I'm not worrying, that is, I've come up with a plan I call B.I.R.D.F.L.U. Yes, it's simplistically clever, isn't it? You know how our government loves programs that can be referred to by acronyms. Nevertheless, at a time when we're on the brink of a world health crisis, I vow to do my part to keep things easily understandable for our president. That's the beauty of my B.I.R.D.F.L.U. plan, any birdbrain can implement it.

Here's how the B.I.R.D.F.L.U. project will work. Under my plan, you'll be asked to:

Be Alert for Suspicious-Acting Birds: If there's a lot of coughing and sneezing going on around your backyard birdfeeder, this is cause to be alarmed. Do not, under any circumstances, hand these birds a Kleenex! Birds that cough and sneeze (bet you didn't even know birds *could* cough or sneeze) may have the bird flu. Maintain your distance and call my B.I.R.D. F.L.U. hotline for assistance. Eight or nine days after your call, someone from FEMA will arrive to remove the birds for testing.

Isolate Everyone Between 20 and 40: The bird flu seems to strike people between the ages of 20 and 40 the hardest. Since the future of the Baby Boomer's Social Security depends on the Generation Xer's showing up at work every day for the next several decades, it's important that we keep them healthy.

Replenish Over-the-Counter Flu Remedies: These may not ward off the bird flu, but then again, they might. As one government official said, "If we were sure what was going to work against this virus, we would still be unsure. But we can't be sure of anything in unsure times like these." It's assurances like this that have me losing all that sleep and building an addition onto my house for the six tons of TheraFlu I just ordered.

Dead Poultry – Avoid Contact At All Costs: Unless it comes in a bucket with the letters KFC on the outside, it's probably in your best interest not to spend your free time with dead chickens during the midst of a bird flu outbreak.

Forgo Travel Outside of the U.S.A.: It's past time we enjoy all this country has to offer, anyway. After all, where else can you go but to a good old American Wal-Mart to buy all those over-the-counter flu remedies that might or might not save your life in unsure times like these? Oh, and on your way out, don't cough on the twenty-year-old cashier. Remember, if you're not one of the 150 million who perish during the pandemic, you're going to need your Social Security check.

You might think my plan is strictly for the birds, but in unsure times like these, when we can't be sure of anything, you can rest assured that I'm spending many sleepless nights making certain the Generation Xer's survive the pandemic and that the only dead poultry we encounter is coated with the Colonel's secret recipe.

Tom's terrific travel tours and vacation packages

by Thomas J. Noer

It's August and many of you are deep into vacation planning. Sure, you could spend another boring week 'up North' fishing and swatting mosquitoes or make the usual trek to Branson, Missouri or Orlando, Florida. But, for more adventurous travelers, I offer my own special vacation packages to liven up your summer. Colorful brochures are available upon request.

Affordable, Adorable, Afghanistan - With all of our focus on Iraq, many have forgotten this mountainous beauty. Catch a colorful camel caravan in Karachi (say that fast three times) and in no time you will be dining at the Taliban Table in downtown Kabul. Rooms are cheap and some still have walls. Women should bring a burka and all should wear boots, as there is a lot of unexploded ordinance in the area.

Senior Citizen Special Tijuana Trek - Tired of paying outrageous prices for your prescription drugs? Just hop on our generic bus and 39 hours later you can fill your needs for just a few pesos. The trip back is something special as we all share our Lipitor, Prozac, and Viagra. Border crossings into San Diego can cause some delays depending on the number of drug agents working that day.

The Scam Tour - Martha Stewart leads this trip to the most memorable companies that ripped off shareholders and employees. Have your picture taken in front of the Enron statue in Houston and talk on the phone to WorldCom executives hiding from creditors. Conclude with a lunch at a Pennsylvania prison where members of the Riga family will entertain you with rollicking accounts of looting the Adelphia Company. (Optional side trip to Arthur Anderson Accounting). It's "a good thing."

The Super, Yooper - Long for some snow and slush? Need to break-in your ice scraper? Well, it's always winter in Michigan's neglected Upper Peninsula. Sleep at the bottom of an abandoned copper mine or in an ice fishing shack and use your food stamps to dine on cold pasties and smelt. There is nothing like Saturday night in exotic Escanaba to make you appreciate home. Yah, hey der!

The Highway 194 Literary Excursion - A close, convenient, and colorful cruise of the many interesting bookstores stretching from Highway 50 to the Illinois border. The tour bus parks in the back so don't worry about being seen by neighbors. Remember they are open 24 hours, so take your time. When we are done you might want to buy some helicopter parts at the massive military museum nearby. You must be eighteen years old to purchase anything.

Where's Jimmy Tour - Join other crime sleuths to find the body of Teamster leader, Jimmy Hoffa. We depart by truck (what else?) to check out the long-rumored site in Giant's stadium in New Jersey and then on to investigate more recent reports of spots near Detroit. The tour includes stops at diners where Elvis has recently been seen.

Yummy Yucca - Did you ever wonder what we have done with fifty years of nuclear waste? Find out as we travel in a specially sealed boxcar from the abandoned Zion, Illinois power plant to Yucca Mountain, Nevada and explore our only nuclear storage center. You will be aglow after climbing a mile down and playing with the Plutonium. Radiation suits required.

The Lewis and Clark Trail - Retrace the steps of this famous duo as we follow the path of Jerry Lewis and Dick Clark. Start at Times Square to see where Dick appears like a vampire on New Year's Eve and then on to the set of the annual Jerry Lewis telethon to throw ink on photos of Dean Martin. Everyone gets free samples of Brylcreem and Botox.

New York Taxi Time - The excitement begins when you try to flag down one of these fascinating yellow vehicles and count how many times they ignore you. Then hear Joan Rivers voice scream at you to, "BUCKLE UP!" The excitement continues when you give directions to drivers who speak no English and experience the thrill of mass road rage in the nation's biggest traffic jam. Finally, learn interesting new words when you fail to leave a tip.

Famous Fairs, Festivals, and Feasts - Got a hankering for corn, brats, and raffle tickets? Come with us as we explore the wonderful world of church fund-raisers in Kenosha. Watch your kids exhaust themselves jumping and down in an inflatable torture chamber, break balloons with darts to win valuable key chains, and buy pies with no filling at the bake sales. Open to all denominations as long as you buy a few chances on that donated stereo system.

All of these exciting adventures are available from the Noer Travel Agency. Space is limited so be sure to book now as I'm taking off soon for a week's vacation in the Dells. Love to ride those ducks!

Trash, like beauty, is in the eye of the beholder

by Laurie McKeon

All over the country property taxes have gone sky high. It's a great big bummer and I often wonder, "What exactly we are getting for our tax dollars?" Here, where I live, there aren't a lot of village amenities ... no water, no sewer, and no sidewalks ... just a few streetlights and fire hydrants. But, do you know what? Our garbage service ROCKS! It's the best. Trust me. I know garbage and we are living in trash collection heaven.

I hate to admit this, but I have a long history of garbage issues. Sure, in theory, garbage collection sounds pretty simple. You put the trash in the bag, sort out the recyclables, tie the bag up when it's full, take it to the garage, and then drag it all out to the curb on trash day. Repeat this process daily for a week. This works for most people, but for me ... not so much. Regardless of the system, and we've had pretty much all of them; private garbage collection, city service, mandatory recycling, designated bags, color coded bags, and whatever. I'm always struggling with garbage.

My trash removal nadir came when we were living in Ohio, where I was actually fired by our private garbage service. This is a rather long embarrassing story involving many corrugated boxes and a rather terse (okay, bitchy) phone call by me, inquiring why said boxes had not been removed, culminating in a handwritten note on the back of a *Don Haynes Trash Removal* receipt addressed to me saying, "Git (sic) somebody else."

When we moved to Wisconsin a few years ago, we rented a house in Kenosha while we were building our home in Pleasant Prairie. Although we lived there for a year, we never really got a handle on the garbage system. During our first few months in Kenosha, I swear, our garbage never got picked up. Every week, we would put our garbage at the curb, fervently praying that it would be gone when I came back from dropping the kids at school. Every week, as I turned the corner on to our street, there it was ... our forlorn garbage, still at the curb, deemed undesirable by those in the know (or at least those in the truck). Attached would be a little red tag, our garbage report card, telling us what we had done that week to preclude our trash from being removed. Not only was the offending bag left at the curb, but usually the rest of our trash was left as well. Guilt by association, I guess.

Some weeks we used the wrong colored bags, some weeks our recycling wasn't spaced the proper distance from the regular garbage, and once, we had the audacity to place some recycling in a box instead of the requisite blue bag. To be perfectly honest, all of our neighbors seemed to figure out the system. Frankly, the problem was us.

So, last year when we began a new trash removal service, I was more than a little leery. Great! Here's another garbage system to learn, another truck to chase down the street, and another series of garbage rejections. But, week after week for over a year now, our trash has been removed promptly, regularly, and with no givebacks. Go figure.

Last week I tested the limits of the system. I kicked off the summer by cleaning our nasty, cluttered basement, filling reams of Hefty bags with broken hockey sticks, two wheeled trikes, leaky rubber rafts, dented lamp shades, and all other sorts of unidentifiable junk.

Ultimately, I left a dozen bulky bags at edge of the driveway for pick up along with some empty paint cans, in a box, no less. I'll admit, I was a little nervous. As I was driving home after dropping the boys at football camp, I saw the garbage truck parked in front of the house. I actually waited at the end of the block, steeling myself for the inevitable, but, when the truck pulled away, all the trash was gone ... everything, even the paint cans. It was a garbage miracle.

Who needs fire hydrants, sidewalks, and streetlights? My house can burn to the ground and my kids can ride their bikes in the street in the dark. Keep picking up my trash and I'll pay the tax ransom. Just make sure our trash collection professionals are getting their cut.

How about one last look at St. Catherine's Hospital?

by Ed Groelle

Written after the shut down of a 90-year-old hospital

I just retired. That's no big deal. After four careers and almost fifty years of work, it seemed like the accepted thing to do. What makes my last ten-year career so special to me is that it was at St. Catherine's Hospital. I wanted to share some of my thoughts with the community.

My job and my curiosity had taken me to almost every nook and cranny in the buildings. I know where there are stairs that lead nowhere and doors that open into brick walls. A few days before my last day, armed  with a flashlight, I made a tour through the entire hospital from the labyrinthine underground tunnels to the spooky fourth floor attic. It was a lonely and emotional trek.

The hallways and rooms are now silent and dark. Without people, the interior has begun to take on a sagging and resigned atmosphere. There are a lot of abandoned personal mementos everywhere; last work schedules, patient care instructions, stuffed animals, etc. If you stand quietly in one of the empty rooms you can easily remember the faces and hear the voices of the past occupants.

There are benevolent spirits in there. All the patient rooms echo with the aura of hopes and prayers of past patients. There are ghosts of nuns and nurses standing by the bedsides dispensing compassion and medicine. I am not clinically trained, but the surgery and treatment areas look as though they could be used in a minute. The shiny instruments and sterile, cryptic, packages are there, just waiting for a skilled hand to pick them up.

My family and I have been patients. There are probably very few Kenoshans who haven't had a personal involvement with St. Catherine's Hospital. I'm sure they, like me, never pass by today without feeling an ache in their hearts. St. Catherine's Hospital had to stop operating some day. Her loving heart is worn out and keeping her on life support would only be compassionate cruelty.

I only wish the powers that be would open her halls to the public for just one day so everyone could pay their last respects. It would be a moving experience and a healing gesture for the community.

If Mars is the answer, what was the question?

by Kenda Buxton

At first, I was skeptical about President Bush's 'Mission to Mars.' Like many people, my initial thoughts were, "Let's fix the problems we have here on Earth. Let's feed and shelter the homeless. Let's make world peace our goal. Let's put every American to work. Let's get a Super Wal-Mart in Kenosha, and while we're at it, a Red Lobster too."

Although Kenosha may not get a Super Wal-Mart, it can only be a matter of time before one shows up in outer space, because on January 14th, President Bush spoke at NASA, saying in part, "We will build new ships to carry man forward into the universe, to gain a new foothold on the moon, and to prepare for new journeys to worlds beyond our own. With the experience and knowledge gained on the moon, we will then be ready to take the next steps of space exploration: human missions to Mars and to worlds beyond."

As the president encourages us to boldly go where no man has gone before, as he raises his fist and declares, "To infinity and beyond!" as he urges us to once again take one small step for man, one giant leap for mankind, here are my top ten reasons to send Americans to Mars. Yes, the Top Ten idea was borrowed from David Letterman with no shame whatsoever. The rest of the stuff was borrowed from Star Trek, Toy Story, and Neil Armstrong. After all, the sincerest form of flattery is imitation, and what the heck, it also saves on original thinking.

Number Ten: We can thumb our noses at *Dr. Phil's Ultimate Weight Loss Solution, the South Beach Diet, the Atkin's Diet, Weight Watchers, Jenny Craig,* and every other person making millions off of Americans' bad eating habits. On Mars, we'll *all* look chubby in our space suits, so why worry about dieting? Given this, Dr. Phil is already at work on his new book, *"The Ultimate Guide to Getting Along With Your Family During Extended Space Travel ...*

The Seven Keys to Overcoming the Temptation of Unplugging the Oxygen to Your Husband's Space Suit When He Refuses to Stop and Ask for Directions to Mars."

Number Nine: We've been looking hither and yon for Osama Bin Laden since September of 2001. We might as well hither on up to Mars and look for him there, too.

Number Eight: A Martian winter can reach 207 degrees below zero. When we get our heating bills for *that*, a Wisconsin winter won't look so bad.

Number Seven: No need to worry that Janet Jackson's top will be ripped open due to a "wardrobe malfunction" during the Martian Super Bowl half-time show. A spacesuit is made to withstand even the poor judgment of so-called entertainers.

Number Six: Speaking of Janet Jackson, although many of us have long thought her brother Michael was from another planet, the good news is that it doesn't appear to be Mars.

Number Five: The Martian year is equal to 687 Earth days. That means we'll have 322 additional days before turning another year older.

Number Four: As of yet, no political candidates have plans to visit Mars.

Number Three: Since Mars is currently uninhabited, it will take us a while to start a war by looking for fictional weapons of mass destruction.

Number Two: Those nifty little remote control robotic rovers, Spirit and Opportunity, will keep all the men on Mars busy for hours.

And the **Number One** reason to put Americans on Mars: What better way to get us to quit worrying about the high cost of health care and prescription drugs, skyrocketing property taxes, and the lack of decent paying jobs, than to spend trillions of dollars sending us someplace with no doctors, no pharmacies, no housing, and no industry.

And so, as we mount a wagon train to the stars and make space our final frontier (both phrases shamelessly borrowed from Gene Roddenberry) there will certainly be, at times, danger ... Will Robinson danger. But as Ralph Kramden was fond of saying, "One of these days, Alice, bang! zoom! To the moon, Alice! To the moon!"

Even the irrepressible Ralph couldn't have imagined we'd someday reach the moon and then be headed for infinity and beyond.

Columnist reveals his most intimate writing secrets

by Thomas J. Noer

Three years ago I offered my first column titled, *Ten Ways to Improve Kenosha*. Since then I have written pieces ranging from *Kenosha the Musical* to *Updated Children's Classics* to *Practical Advice to the Class of 2003*. My monthly efforts have provoked a number of questions from curious readers asking about the glamorous life of writing for the local newspaper. Today, for the first time, I respond to their inquires and reveal the sordid details of life as a Kenosha News columnist!

1. Where do you get all those brilliant ideas for your column? Writing is a lonely business and you cannot be distracted by other people. To assure complete solitude, as soon as I have a possible column topic, I hop on the Kenosha Trolley for a couple of trips and then go window-shopping in downtown Kenosha. I then sit in the middle of the American Brass demolition site and write my column in magic marker on old bratwurst wrappers.

2. Just how much do you get paid for this drivel? It is a little known fact that none of the local columnists actually receive any money for their efforts. Instead, we get Kenosha News coffee mugs, preferred parking passes for Cohorama, and the use of Howard Brown's old tennis racquets.

3. Why don't you ever write a SERIOUS column about REAL issues? Well, I've tried. I penned a wonderful piece on the consequences of significant tariff reform, another on how to use nuclear weapons to solve the bigheaded carp problem, and one suggesting Martha Stewart was having Michael Jackson's baby. Somehow, they just did not have the right feel for sunny Sunday mornings.

4. Why do your columns have such lame headlines? Most readers are unaware of the Kenosha New's editorial process. I always submit a witty column with a catchy headline. The piece is then fed into the massive Kenosha News computer that inserts numerous typos and grammatical errors, deletes my clever bold script, and rewrites the headline to discourage readers from reading any further. This piece will probably be titled, 'Significant Tariff Reform.'

5. The News now has color in the comic section. How come your column does not have color or any other attention-grabbing visuals? The only visuals in my space is a photo that makes me look like a cross between Benito Mussolini and Daddy Warbucks. Some parents actually use the picture to scare their children into going to bed on time.

6. Why are you so addicted to columns with lists and quizzes?

Select one of the following:

a) It is an easy way to organize stuff

b) Readers can skim it quickly and get on to *The Family Circus*

c) Academics love lists and quizzes as it makes us feel smart

d) All of the above

The correct answer is d). If you gave any other response immediately call *Sound Off!* and yell about George Bush or Hillary Clinton.

7. How come your column is always paired with David Barry's and why does he get his photo and quote on the front page? Dave Barry is a NATIONAL columnist, is very funny, and gets paid an obscene amount of money. My column provides a dramatic contrast in all three areas. I SHOULD be paired with James J. Kilpatrick as he writes boring junk about court decisions. My stuff is far funnier.

8. How many people actually read your column? The marketing experts at the Kenosha News have done extensive surveys to determine who reads each section of the paper and have found that 97% of subscribers will read any story about the Green Bay Packers, 54% read the garage sale listings, 12% read Miss Manners, and .0004% peruse my column. This may seem small, but beats the .000001% who read *Darts and Laurels*.

9. Do you get much response to your columns? I used to get lots of irate letters accusing me of Kenosha-bashing that included vague physical threats and copies of Illinois real estate listings. Lately, however, I generally get comments like, 'are you still writing that column?' and 'Boy, that last piece was really stupid!' I think this shows the growing maturity of my readers and the fact that many think I am really a drag version of Molly Ivins.

10. It seems like you have a few pet topics that you write about in nearly every column; the Packers, Sheridan road, abandoned buildings, alternate street parking, etc. Why don't you get some NEW material? OK. Did you hear about the bus load of Packer fans who couldn't turn off Sheridan Road, got ticketed for parking on the wrong side of the street, tried to take the trolley to Lambeau Field, but wound-up living in the vacant Barden's store where they were busted for smoking? Wait! That's next month's column!

You two can write real good

by Jim Wynne

Recently, after having read one of my columns, a coworker asked me how I learned to write so good. While I'm not sure that how to write good is something that can be teached, I thought it might be a good idea to offer a few pointers for any one who has a desire to improve his writing skills.

The first thing that you should do is to always use the male personal pronoun. In other words, instead of saying, "This is advice for anyone who wants to improve his or her writing skills," just write, "his writing skills." Aside from avoiding the clumsy 'his or her' construction, there are some women (mainly ones with hyphenated last names) who will be irritated by it, and that alone makes it worthwhile. Also, don't worry about subject-verb number agreement. It's perfectly okay to write, "anyone who wants to improve *their* writing skills" because such usage is evidence that the writer was not really thinking about what he was writing, and too much thinking while writing is never a good thing, as anyone who reads the letters to the editor in this paper must realize.

Many people seem to have trouble with punctuation. The most misused punctuation mark, by far, is the apostrophe. My advice is to use the apostrophe indiscriminately, just as everyone else seems to do. If a word ends in 's' and you're not sure whether to use an apostrophe or not, go ahead and throw one in. This is especially true of the word 'its.' In this newspaper's sister publication, the *Bulletin*, no one knows when to use an apostrophe in 'its.' And if professional writers don't care, why should you?

The aspiring writer should never allow himself to be intimidated by big words. While at one time it was considered good form to use a dictionary and look up the meaning of a big word before using it, these days meaning is less important than the sheer mass of verbiage that you use. Thus you can refer to an ordinary abbreviation such as 'YMCA' as an acronym, even though it is not an acronym and has never been an acronym. You would have no way of knowing that though, unless you looked it up, and who has time for that? In this newspaper a few years ago, on the occasion of the opening of a Pleasant Prairie candy factory, a story was published about the grand opening festivities, which, according to the piece, included a "train that circumvents the warehouse." While it may be that the train actually did avoid or elude the warehouse by way of a loophole, I doubt it, but what does it matter? The writer knew what he meant.

Contractions like 'it's' are another bit of sand in the ointment of good writing. Take my word for it ... no one cares whether you say "your" or "you're." The sentence, "Your not using you're head" makes perfect sense to ninety percent of the population, so why bother trying to figure out which is correct? Likewise, don't worry about homophones. In the past few weeks in different publications I've seen instances of reporters writing about being in dire 'straights' and having one's curiosity 'peaked.' Take a tip from the professionals ... do your best to spell the word phonetically and get on with your life.

One of the main reasons that no one cares about how to write good anymore is that we now communicate a great deal via written messages on the Internet, and since many people who use the Internet can neither type nor spell, written communication has reverted to a language of abbreviations, hieroglyphics, and the modern-day equivalent of cave painting. They use sideways pictures called emoticons such as {;>) which is supposed to look like a person winking. They don't say that something is funny, they say 'LOL' or 'ROTFLMAO' (laugh out loud; rolling on the floor laughing my ...). They also often refuse to use upper case letters and punctuation of any kind and call each other by weird names; "hey blamo ufabno (woo gitty) down by mr stankys lol—pigmeats gonna be their to ..." The result is that you need to read a message about twelve times, at least, to partially figure out what the sender was trying to say. It's no wonder that people who spend hours every day communicating like this have trouble with formal English, IMHO.

So don't let the fact that you know nothing about grammar, spelling, and punctuation make you think that you can't write good. The only rule to observe is that you should start at the beginning and make your way to the end by way of the middle, and if you apply yourself, the first thing you know yule be writing more better than myself. LOL.

Marriage — hang in there. It's worth it.

by Laurie McKeon

We've been invited to seven weddings this summer ... SEVEN! (Four Catholic, one Methodist, one nondenominational and one Catholic-Hindu hybrid). That's a lot of fondue pots. I love weddings. I really do. I love the ceremony, the music, the dresses, the flowers, the reception, the dancing, the bouquet toss, and the whole shebang. My eyes start tearing up the minute I hear the first strains of Pachabel's Canon. By the time the couples say, "I do" ... forget about it ... I'm a blubbering idiot.

In this day of instant divorce, long-term cohabitation, and chronic "hooking up" (whatever that means), I am so impressed by these young people who are consciously choosing marriage. Generation X (or is it Y? Z?) gets a pretty bad rap for being lazy, whiny, and coffee swilling slackers who are only interested in video games and cell phone ring tones. But, I've got to tell you, the betrotheds we know are seriously stand-up people with major careers and good intentioned life plans, complete with low interest mortgages and IRAs. So far this summer, we've been invited to the upcoming nuptials of an investment banker, a sales intern, a dental student, a medical student, a lawyer, an IT specialist, two youth ministers, and an accountant. Not a loser in the bunch.

To be willing to make a public statement asserting love and commitment takes some guts, and obviously, from the weddings I've seen so far, a whole lot of tulle. I am honestly so touched by the earnestness of these newlyweds, touched by the love they have for one another, the dreams they have for the future, and their untarnished belief in the institution of marriage. You can see the hope in their eyes and the anticipation in their shaky voices as they make their vows before God, family, and friends. Were we ever that young, that unguarded, and that innocent? I recently saw one of our wedding photos and we did have that same dewy look that the newly married have. My husband had some really dorky glasses, too. While I wouldn't trade places (the first five years of marriage are a lot of work), I do envy them that newness of a journey and the enormous possibilities that their lives together will hold.

As I enter my twentieth year of wedded bliss (some years more blissful than others) I like to tell my husband, "It's gone by like five minutes ... under water." There are so many things I want to say to these newlyweds. Things like, "Go ahead and go to bed angry, otherwise you might not be getting much sleep." "A little champagne and roses goes a long way." "Think mean things about your in-laws, but do not say them out loud." But, would that spoil the surprises and take away some of the lessons that come from living in a marriage? I hate to say too much for fear of "scaring single" those yet to march down the aisle.

Mostly, I want to tell these fine young couples to love each other. It's harder than it sounds. As your married life grows to incorporate in-laws, careers, children, and all the joy and stress that they bring, your partner will be the first one you turn to for help and also the first one you turn to in anger. Things will not go as planned, ever, so stop trying so hard. Someone will get sick, someone will lose a job, the babies will come at the most inopportune time, or they won't come at all. Money will be tight and tempers will run short. Some days you'll look at each other and barely remember what brought you together. Remember, you're on the same side. Err on the side of kindness and cut each other some slack. If you want this union to last for the long haul, be willing to apologize, even when you know beyond a shadow of a doubt that you are so right, and be even more willing to forgive. Because, in a marriage, there are moments, days, weeks, and even years of such sublime joy and unexpected wonder that you really need to share it with the one you love the most.

Learn eavesdropping in your spare time

by Kenda Buxton

You've gotta feel a little sorry for a guy who's spent the last few months on his hands and knees in the Oval Office running additional telephone lines for wire tapes, only to be accused of illegal activity when his top secret domestic spying program was leaked. Which just goes to show you that, even when it comes to super-secret-highly-classified government stuff, some blabbermouth always spills the beans.

As our president said, "The fact that somebody leaked this program (perhaps the White House maid who has to vacuum around all those phone lines?) causes great harm to the United States. There's an enemy out there."

This was followed by, "I am not a crook," and "If I were to make public these tapes, containing blunt and candid remarks on many different subjects, the confidentiality of the office of the president would always be suspect."

Whoops! My mistake. I was domestically spying on the wrong president when it came to those last two remarks.

Well, anyway, there's an enemy out there, and as President Bush also said, "If somebody from al-Qaida is calling you, we wanna know about it."

That seems like a valid concern, though I can assure the president that no one from al-Qaida is calling *me*. First of all, I'm a charter member of the Do-Not-Call List. As well, if any pesky telemarketers or sneaky terrorists happen to reach me by phone, I will deny being Kenda Buxton, while claiming she's unavailable because she's busy doing selfless good deeds around the globe. All right, so what I'm actually doing is a load of laundry, cooking supper, and defrosting the freezer, but half the art of beating the terrorists at their own game is not revealing what *really* keeps America running.

Because the president is a busy man, when he's not spending time clearing his Crawford ranch of the brush that apparently keeps regrowing there, I think we, as citizens of this great nation, should take the burden of wiretapping from the man. Since 90% of Americans spend 95% of each day talking on cell phones, we'll easily conquer this eavesdropping challenge. Considering most of us overhear cell phone conversations on a frequent basis, all we need to do is carry a notebook and a pen and record what's been said. Just last week, I followed a woman around the grocery store who consulted her husband about every purchase. She was on the phone with him throughout her shopping excursion, and because of my eavesdropping diligence, I can tell our president exactly what brand of toilet paper the man told his wife to buy. Who knows? I may have just saved some unsuspecting Charmin delivery guy from an al-Qaida hijacking attempt.

Aside from eavesdropping on cell phone conversations, I suggest our communication system revert to the old party line where, like on the *Andy Griffith Show*, we pick up the phone and ask Sarah to connect us to whomever it is we'd like to speak with. This ensures that not only Sarah eavesdrops on everything we say, but so does Aunt Bea, Barney, Opie, and Floyd down at the barbershop. What better way of knowing if your neighbors are giving an apple pie recipe to al-Qaida?

If further treachery is needed to thwart al-Qaida, we can take a lesson from *Green Acres* and mount our telephones atop the nearest telephone pole. Then, like Oliver Douglas, whenever we need to report what we've overheard to the president, we'll scurry up the pole and place our call, while pretending to be telephone linemen.

Or, like Maxwell Smart from *Get Smart*, we can wear a shoe phone, complete with a rotary dial embedded in the sole. Even if we get caught by an enemy operative, unless that person is older than forty, we'll be safe because no one under forty knows what a rotary dial phone is, let alone how to use it.

Remember, folks, as our president said there's an enemy out there, and if he's calling your neighbors, it's your job to find out why. Whether you accomplish the eavesdropping by cell phone, party line, or shoe phone, you can take pride in doing your American duty for which President Bush will surely thank you, when he's finished listening in on what you're saying.

A line on the ice — Standing watch on the top of the world

by Ed Groelle

They're still up there in the frozen North, most of them. They rise abruptly from the icy wilderness, a jumble of buildings and platforms topped with giant white domes. A few of the remaining DEW (Distant Early Warning) stations today are rusting hulks filled with obsolete equipment and cases of Danish beer. They look like relics from another time, which in a way, they are. When they were built the primary adversary of the US was communism, not terrorism. Our military's greatest fear was of a sneak attack by Soviet bombers flying undetected over the North Pole.

The DEW Line became a reality in 1954 when Eisenhower approved its construction. When completed, which it really never seemed to be, it extended from the western shore of Iceland, across the top of Canada to the western islands of the Alaskan Aleutians. Over 75 stations spaced so that their aerial detection ability overlapped. It was built at enormous expense and not a few lives. Reportedly, it was the single most expensive military project up to that time. It existed until the mid-1960's when ICBM technology made it obsolete.

For a brief while, we stood on guard like ancients on China's Great Wall. We watched, we waited, and fought the impulse to go nuts. Almost fifty years ago and I still remember the DEW

Line with some affection. Considering that it was located in a barren, inhospitable, region and was an all-male environment, that sentence may sound surprising, but true.

My designated station was FOX-3, located 300 miles above the Arctic Circle in the center of Baffin Island in the Northwest Territories. Of the twenty permanent employees I was one of only two Americans allowed to work on each station in Canada for cryptography support. The remainder came from commonwealth nations; Scotland, England, Australia, etc. It made for an interesting homogenous group.

Whenever I talk about the Dewline I find that most are not interested in the technical aspect of the tons of electronic equipment on each site. Most questions are along the line of, "What did you do with the human waste?" or "Do Eskimos really eat blubber?" So, I'm going to answer some of those questions and tell a few stories instead, like the one about the time a roaming French Catholic priest visited. There were rumors all day about a "Skin Flick" that would be shown that evening at 7:30. Way before 7:30 all off-duty employees were eagerly assembled in the Dining Room. The film turned out to be *The Curing of Seal Skins*. Nobody had the guts to leave with the priest present.

How did I spend my time? Never a problem! As Lead Radician and, for several months, Station Chief, I always had plenty to do. The company (Federal Electric) provided some diversions; dark room, pool table, amateur radio, movie twice a week, and great food. Some diversions were innovative like when a hungry, curious, polar bear would wander near and some of the guys would creep up and attempt to touch the bear's forehead. Although there were bears, packs of wolves, and caribou, the most ferocious beast in the Arctic is not the bear, but the summer mosquito. They are unrelenting and can drive a person insane. Those are never mentioned in travelogues.

Yes, Eskimos do have refrigerators. No, the Northern Lights are not visible … we were too far north. Yes, the sun really does shine at midnight. Yes, the Eskimos do eat blubber and love it. No, the Eskimos do not build igloos like portrayed in cartoons. Arctic snow is quite different than snow here. It does not pack or cut like when building a snow fort. It snows several feet in the fall and then blows around the rest of the year, which results in a sand-like quality. Try building an igloo with sand. You do not shovel or plow it but drive and walk on the surface. Snow really was not a problem because we were outfitted and prepared to deal with it. The biggest weather problem was fog, sometimes unrelenting for weeks on end, totally isolating us from the outside world.

What was it that we found so attractive about life on these cold, remote outposts? Sure, we earned decent wages and the food was good, but was there something more? It's possible we may have kept the "Cold War" cold for our nation and perhaps the world. That may be too altruistic. All things considered, I'd say it was fun and adventuresome along with acquiring a wealth of experience and a hefty bank balance.

The DEW Line may be largely forgotten except for a few like me. I've always considered that The Line gave me back every bit as much as it took. In fact, all it really took was nineteen months of my youth. I had just turned twenty-three when I reported for the assignment after having taken a battery of psychological tests to determine if I was crazy enough to take the job. Apparently, I passed. Some couldn't take the isolation and fled when their contracts were up or even before. Others, like me, remember their time on The Line with fondness.

Oops! Almost forgot! Human waste? Piped a few hundred yards away and forever frozen in the tundra.

The greatest Christmas gift of all

by Kenda Buxton

What's Christmas for a baby boomer if not a nostalgic look back upon the greatest gift of all? That gift arrived, not as a star shone in the East, but instead, just as the leaves were changing colors and Halloween costumes filled store shelves. Although my former Sunday School teachers will likely think now is a good time for me to proclaim the Christ Child as the greatest gift of all, to a six-year-old in 1968, the greatest gift of all had nothing to do with what Mary delivered in a manger and everything to do with what the mailman delivered in early October ... the greatest gift of all that held a kid's greatest gifts of all ... the Sears Wish Book.

Every year between October and December, I devoted more time to the Wish Book than I devoted to any homework assignment or Sunday school lesson. Which is probably why I can still tell you what page the String-Ray bikes were sold on, but can't recite the Declaration of Independence, and why I think that the three wise men arrived in Bethlehem bearing *Lincoln Logs, Hot Wheels,* and a *G.I. Joe.*

If there was a toy the Wish Book didn't have, then it wasn't a toy worth having. As I'm sure Milton Bradley hoped would be the case, I found something I wanted on every page. I'd 'X' the toy, circle it, and then print, "Kenda Wants This" above it. Finally, just to make certain the most important Santa Claus in our house, my mother, knew of my desires, I spent hours lugging the Wish Book around as I followed along behind her. I showed her my pages while she fought to control her enthusiasm by feigning disinterest with comments like, "Uh huh," and "We'll see," and "Maybe," and a really crabby, "NO!" the year I asked for a *Monkees'* drum set. For years, I thought Mom called Santa to tell him what he wasn't supposed to bring me. That encompassed anything you plugged into an amplifier or pounded on with a wooden stick that might someday inspire me to tour with the *Grateful Dead,* or anything that might burn the house down. I never got the *Creepy Crawlers* set I asked for, nor the *Frosty the Sno-Man Sno-Cone* machine, nor that rock polisher on page 262.

Admittedly, some of the toys in the Wish Book were completely useless. The *Etch-A-Sketch* falls into the "Completely Useless" category. Actually, it falls into the "Dumbest Toy Ever Invented" category because all I could draw with mine was squiggly lines. How many hours did my mother think I'd be entertained by something that boring? Not nearly as many hours as a drum set would have entertained me, that's for certain. And then there was the Slinky. Whoever tangled up a wire and made money selling it as a toy was a genius. Whoever thought I'd want something like that for Christmas certainly was not. You can watch tangled wire climb down stairs for only a limited period of time, like once, before the fun is gone and you're wishing Santa had given that Slinky to some other kid and brought you an electric guitar.

Despite the failures the Wish Book held, it contained plenty of successes, too. The Lionel train set I got when I was six tops my list of favorites, followed by the baseball mitt I received at ten. I also enjoyed my *Lite Brite, View-Master, Rock'Em, Sock'Em Robots, Matchbox cars,* and *Jane West* action figure. Of course, it would have been refreshing to come home to a *Frosty the Sno-Man Sno-Cone* after a long day of riding the range with Jane, but as my mother would say, "Little girls with smart mouths don't deserve anything but coal for Christmas." which fortunately, the Wish Book didn't carry.

You can order from the *Sears Wish Book* on-line nowadays. While that's convenient, it's not the same as anticipating the arrival of a toy catalog every fall. Evidently, other baby boomers agree, because a 1971 Wish Book just sold on eBay for $72. While I'm not foolish enough to spend 72 bucks for a 34-year-old catalog, I would like to ask the buyer to do me one favor. Look up that *Monkees'* drum set and put it on my list for Santa.

Dr. Noer's index of new and curious diseases

by Thomas J. Noer

Kenosha News readers may not know that I AM a Doctor. No, not a MEDICAL DOCTOR ... they make lots of money, get the best tables in restaurants, and have cool parking permits. I'm a poor and humble PhD. But, as a Dr., I've noticed that the medical profession has recently found a lot of new diseases that they can charge us to treat. A few years ago nobody had heard of Mad Cow Disease, Attention Deficit Disorder, or Carpal Tunnel Syndrome. I have decided to help my M.D. colleagues by letting them know of some new diseases that I have recently discovered.

Stuffyourfaceus Buffetis - A rapidly expanding disease characterized by an insatiable desire to visit all-you-can-eat buffets and fill as many plates as possible in the shortest time. As it progresses, victims find they can no longer distinguish between Chinese, Mexican, or Friday Fish Fries. Some even begin with breakfast! Those most seriously afflicted have been known to fly to Las Vegas to feed their addiction. A common side affect is 'Bad Chow Disease.'

Exterior Holiday Decorational Disorder - Until a few years ago this bizarre illness appeared only in mid-December when victims were suddenly seized by a strange compulsion to put lights and cardboard reindeer in front of their homes. Unfortunately, recently it has become a year round problem as many sufferers now feel they must place colored eggs in trees in the spring, tack-up red, white, and blue banners in July, and even hang ghosts and witches on their houses in late October. Curiously, the disorder most common in this area is known as 'Christmas Lane.'

Bush and Mouth Disease - Those who have contracted this disorder find they cannot complete a single sentence without major errors in grammar, syntax, or subject/verb agreement. There is strong evidence that it is hereditary, as the patients' fathers also

85

exhibit the same behavior, but at a less severe level. It is most noticeable when sufferers depart from a written text and try to speak off the cuff.

Digital Mania - The major symptoms are an obsession with all things digital; cameras, movies, CD's, television shows, etc. This is potentially a serious illness as there are only three people in the world (all computer geeks in California), who actually know what 'digital' means. The best existing treatment is to lock victims in rooms with 8-track tape decks, 16mm home movies, vinyl records, and old Polaroid cameras.

Packerholicism - This disorder has reached an epidemic level in Wisconsin. Those who acquire it tend to fall to their knees and sob whenever they hear the words, Favre, Lambeau, or Lombardi. Fortunately, many victims let others know they are ill by wearing distinctive green and gold clothing, putting strange flags on their vehicles, or in the most severe cases, placing large pieces of cheese on their heads. This affliction often lasts a lifetime and the public should avoid taverns where it seems to be spread.

Photographic Grandchild Compulsion - This strikes people quite suddenly, usually in their 50's, when they begin approaching strangers with wallet-sized pictures of young children while blurting out words like; cute, smart, or 'she has MY eyes!' Fortunately, this is curable over time and most of those afflicted are harmless, unless they also have the more dangerous *Vacation Snapshot Compulsion.*

Endless Arctic Anxiety - A very common disorder in Southeastern Wisconsin that first appears in February, intensifies in March, and often lingers into April. Sufferers often carry around baseball schedules and gardening catalogues while pounding the frozen ground with snow shovels and licking the salt from their automobiles. Some find temporary relief by watching *Laurence of Arabia* or *Bay Watch* re-runs.

Chronic Basting Disease - Fortunately, this seems to be limited largely to older women and confined to the Thanksgiving/ Christmas season. Its victims seem to derive some strange pleasure by spending hours sloshing butter on roasting turkeys while muttering, "It'll dry out!" Many also have uncontrollable desires to build giant, seven-layer salads and mix walnuts into lime Jello.

Taxic Shock Syndrome - Another seasonal disease that follows a letter from the County Assessor in January and peaks on April 15. Those afflicted have been known to try to sell their spouses on eBay or auction off their internal organs to raise desperately needed funds that they then send immediately to local, state, and national governments. Some relief may be obtained by a dose of 1040EZ.

Columnphobia - This strikes writers for local newspapers on a regular monthly basis as they become increasingly irritable and frantic. They often resolve the problem by putting any sort of drivel on paper and sending it to the mysterious Steve Lund. Symptoms then subside for about three weeks but always reappear. Sadly, there is no known cure.

Reflections at midnight on New Year's Eve, 2003

by Kenda Buxton

As the old year gives way to the new, I, like many Americans, will pause and reflect. Well ... okay, a large percentage of Americans will only be reflecting upon why they drank so much on New Year's Eve, but since the strongest thing I'll imbibe is Hi-C, and since I'll be in bed by eight-thirty, I'll have plenty of time to pause and reflect for all of us.

Reflection One – Now You See Him, Now You Don't. The search for the most sought-after man in the world continues. On September 16th, 2001, President Bush vowed to bring Osama bin Laden to justice. Fifteen months later, we still haven't located a man who apparently excels at fleeing through mountains while wearing sandals and a robe. If only we could lose track of Michael Jackson as easily as we've lost track of bin Laden. Now *that* would be reason to celebrate the new year.

Reflection Two – Old McDonald Had A Farm. It's not Old McDonald's farm any longer with an oink, oink, here and a moo, moo, there. As a farmer, you can make more money leasing your land for a cell tower than you can by feeding the nation. So, Old McDonald had a farm with a cell tower here and a cell tower there. Now ... if we just had a cell phone.

Reflection Three – Receive Him As The Lord With Great Joy. The early Catholic Church condemned New Year's celebrations as paganism. Considering the problems plaguing the Catholic Church these days, a few pagans in their midst would likely be a welcome change.

Reflection Four – Open Mouth, Insert Foot. Trent Lott wrenched his foot from his mouth after endorsing Strom Thurmond's presidential bid on a segregationist ticket. Fortunately, this bid took place in 1948, meaning the hundred-year-old Thurmond won't be our next president. Senator Lott apologized for "a poor choice of words," Al Gore urged the senate to censure Lott, and Jesse Jackson demanded Lott step down. All in all, just another day in politics.

Reflection Five – You Either Get It, Or You Don't. Television can make anyone a star, including a charismatic psychologist named Phil McGraw and an aging British rocker named Ozzy Osbourne. Dr. Phil refuses to feature guests who are taking mind-altering drugs, while on the Osbournes, everyone appears to be taking mind-altering drugs. When it comes to what draws Americans to their TV sets, as Dr. Phil would say, you either get it, or you don't.

Reflection Six – Fly The Friendly Skies. During Thanksgiving weekend, security personnel in airports confiscated 15,982 knives, 98 box cutters, 6 guns, numerous bats, 3,242 banned tools including saws, screwdrivers, flammable items, and meat cleavers. Obviously, large portions of our fellow citizens live in caves and don't take a newspaper. Given the events of September 11th, it's hard to fathom that some people still aren't aware we're supposed to leave our guns and flammable items at home when we fly. Granted, I understand the hardship of being forced to travel without a meat cleaver, but for safety's sake, we all have to make sacrifices.

Reflection Seven - Nothing is sacred. If you're the president of the United States, you can't even undergo a colonoscopy without everyone knowing about your internal challenges. Vice President Cheney came out of hiding for two hours and fifteen minutes when the 25th Amendment was examined, which defines transference of power because, as our president stated in part, "we're at war and I just want to be super ... you know, super cautious." That's what I like. A man who graduated from Yale who wants to be ... you know, super cautious.

Reflection Eight – A New Year's Resolution. New Year's resolutions date back to 2000 BC when the ancient Babylonians celebrated the new year with the arrival of the first new moon after the Vernal Equinox. The most common resolution made by the Babylonians was the promise to return borrowed farm equipment and tools, which might explain why so many of us yet today board airplanes while toting saws and screwdrivers.

There you have them, my reflections of Auld Lang Syne, or 'times gone by' for 2002. I'm still trying to determine why anyone would board a plane with a meat cleaver, but I've got an entire year ahead of me to reflect on that.

Stand out from the crowd, get a life today

by Ed Groelle

I've about had it with retirement. I given it a good shot but I can no longer handle the stress and responsibility. For those of you who are working only for the moment that you will retire I'm going to spout some technical jargon at you … "It Sucks!"

So, after being retired for a few years I'm getting off the shelf and back on the market. To stem the inevitable flood of job offers, I'm listing my criteria of employment. I know exactly what I want; no stress, no responsibility, no defined hours, no routine or repetitive work, and preferably no fellow workers with tedious problems. Some people think I would make a highly effective and history-making mayor but, unfortunately, the field is already choked with overqualified wannabees.

Notice that I didn't specify salary range. That's because I've been doing a lot of volunteering and have become used to working with zero salary. My very first job, back in the dark ages, paid 55 cents an hour and I was perfectly happy with that. Today, many people make that much every minute and aren't content. My knowledge of salaries today is so outdated I consider the minimum wage as a rather respectable compensation. After all, it's over ten times what I started with.

At various times in my life I've been a dairy farm slave, factory drudge, TV antenna putter-upper, hospital bedpan jockey, soldier/trained killer, arctic explorer, broken computer/network fixer-upper, and a Dudley-Do-Right security guard. All were noble and respectable occupations that I wouldn't have missed for anything, but, let's face it … been there … done that … so, any job offers along those lines will definitely not be considered.

Before all you potential employers out there start making offers, I should point out that I am already developing a self-employed profession. I've been reading a lot of obituaries in the past years and find that after a while some of the content appears repetitive. For example: 'He enjoyed rock climbing, scuba-diving, miniature golf, and especially spending time with his grandchildren' or 'She enjoyed sky-diving, skeet shooting, miniature golf, and especially spending time with her grandchildren.' I'm launching an Internet business as an obituary advisor. I'm calling it, Obituary Righter, and my motto will be, "It's never to early to start to finish."

Look in the mirror, and ask yourself, "What can I do, while I'm still living, to ensure that I will be remembered as an outstanding human being?" I can help you to answer that question, and for a small monthly fee, develop an obituary for you that will be the envy of your friends and enemies.

Here's how my service works; First, I'd take the rough edges off of your image. I'll make sure that you are described not as a lifelong, avid, Packer fan and diehard Cub fan but as a dedicated devotee of *International Dance Contest.* Just consider how much more enhanced and interesting this would immediately make your obit.

Getting mentioned in the newspaper while still living is essential for an effective obituary. Your friends must be reminded of your green side. I'll make sure that every unselfish thing you've ever done on nature's behalf gets media exposure including a write-up in the Kenosha News describing how you recycled newspapers for 67 weeks in a row or praising your unselfish donations to Al Gore's, "Sky is Falling" campaign.

I will help you forge a reputation for being the sort of thoughtful, caring individual you definitely would be if you only had a little more emotional depth. I'd get you membership in various lodges, introduce you to the nice people at KAFASI for some volunteer work and possibly snag an advanced degree from Lawsonomy University. With a degree from a prestigious school like that you might even land a lucrative job as a Sunday morning columnist.

Activities like those in your obit will force people to revise their memories of you.

If you are excited about this service, why wait? Subscribe now at a discounted introductory rate of just $99.99 a month. It's easy. Just log onto Obit-Righter.com and click the "Yes, I Want a life" button. Be sure to have your credit card handy.

A look at highlights from the secret Noer letter file

by Thomas J. Noer

As an historian, I spend a much of my time reading old letters, but with the emergence of the telephone and e-mail, the only people who actually write letters anymore are angry Kenoshans who want their picture in the Voice of the People. One of my New Year's resolutions was to start again writing REAL letters and, because you are such nice folk, below are some examples of my recent correspondence.

To: Mr. Donald Trump
    Trump Plaza, Trump Towers, Trump Casino, Trump Jet
Dear 'The Donald',
I was sorry to hear you have abandoned your plans to build the world's tallest building in Chicago and I would like to take this opportunity to let you know of another possible area for development. There is a city just north of Chicago perfect for your entrepreneurial efforts. It is near Lake Michigan, has lots of parking (in fact most of downtown IS parking). I can arrange housing for you and the latest blond babe on your arm in our new condos. Bring a wrecking ball and your checkbook.

To: Mr. Mick Jagger and Sir Paul McCartney
    Various Trashed Hotel Suites
Dear Mick and Paul,
I hope you have your bifocals on so you can read this. It occurs to me that you two rockers have been touring for over forty years and that it might be time to call it a day. I know the problems of finding Metamucil on the road and share your anger that many luxury hotels do not give the AARP discount. So, why not pack it in and consider retirement in a small city near Lake Michigan? My

good friend Donald Trump and I can arrange accommodations and many of our local restaurants offer senior citizen discounts. You'll love that tapioca pudding!

To: Board of Directors The McDonald Corporation
    Chicken Nuggets Road
Do you want fries with this? Just kidding. I noticed that for the first time in your history you LOST money last quarter (and not Quarter Pounder!) and I would like to help you out. There is a vast potential market in a small city near Lake Michigan that you could tap with some small changes in your menu. Might I suggest Smeltburgers, Peppermint Schnapps shakes, and McBeer nuts? My good friends Donald Trump, Mick Jagger, Paul McCartney, and I would be glad to serve as consultants. Lets Super Size together.

To: The Kenosha School Board
    A Secret Bunker in Waukegan
Dear Guardians of Knowledge,
How is the psychotherapy going? Glad to see you may finally have a superintendent. I know I speak for many when I suggest you might consider STAYING in Illinois and letting a new group handle our schools. My good friends, Donald Trump, Mick Jagger, Paul McCartney, and Ronald McDonald have all agreed to serve as your replacements. I hope NOT to hear from you soon.

To: Copy editor, The Kenosha News
    Howard Brown Boulevard
Dear Mysterious One,
There are rumors that your only function is to alter my brilliant columns by re-writing the clever headlines and omitting the bold settings I use so readers can skip along from section to section. I have recently contacted my good friends, Molly Ivins and George Will and have found you NEVER (bold, caps, and underlined!) touch their stuff. Also, what do I have to do to get my photo airbrushed by George Pollard like Liz Snyder did?

To: Sen. Trent Lott

Sons of the Confederacy Estates, Dixie

Dear Senator,

How y'all? I'm sure you know that February is Black History Month and we Yankees are looking for a speaker at the NAACP dinner to talk about the good old days of segregation. We've also arranged a guest gig for you at Twisterz, one of our local entertainment centers, where I'm sure you'll get a warm welcome. I hope you and your good friends, Strom Thurmond and David Duke, can join us. Remember, it is white tie only.

To: Senor Fidel Castro

Avenue of the Sugar Cane Cutters, Havana

Dear Leader of the New Socialist Order,

Buenos Dias! I have observed carefully your forty-four years of guiding the Cuban economy and would urge you to bring your managerial skills to a small city near Lake Michigan. We are having some financial problems that could easily be solved by someone with your vast economic talent. Like Havana, we have lots of cars from the 1950s, a trolley, and soon will have a baseball team. My good friends, Donald Trump, Mick Jagger, Paul McCartney, the Hamburgler, the copy editor of the Kenosha News, Trent Lott, and I would be glad to work on your campaign for county executive or mayor. It that doesn't work out, there always seems to be an opening at the Spanish Center.

Sincerely,
Tom Noer

My no-pain Social Security reform plan

by Kenda Buxton

In the time it takes me to write this column, I'll have my Social Security Reform Plan finished. "Why?" you ask? To prove that a woman can overhaul the Social Security system in less than two hours without it costing you a dime of your hard-earned retirement benefits.

~ First on the agenda: **We're doomed.** This is where I calmly announce that those of us under 55 are doomed to work until we're 102 and drop dead at our jobs because all of the money in the Treasury Department marked, *Social Security For People Under 55* will be gone. Good leaders know that if you announce bad stuff in a calm voice, you prevent the type of revolt that has people stomping on your lifeless body in the middle of the street, since everyone is thinking, "She's so calm. Apparently losing every penny we've paid into Social Security is *good* news."

~ Second on the agenda: **I have a plan.** This is where I announce that I have a plan.

~ Third on the agenda: **Charts and graphs.** Displaying charts with lots of numbers and graphs drawn with colored pencils will make people think I'm really smart, while pondering why they're so dumb that they can't figure out what my charts and graphs mean. To further confuse them, I'll say things like, "I predict a minus 29.652378 change in the inflation rate by 2034, and a debt to income ratio of minus 8267.3 with the possibility of a .65 surplus *if* there's another gold rush in California." And what does this mean? It means if you were planning to retire to a trailer in Florida, buy a plastic flamingo for your yard, and take up lawn bowling, forget it. You won't be able to afford the good life given numbers like these.

~ Fourth on the agenda: **What can be done to save Social Security so we can lawn bowl too?** This is where I outline a few ideas borrowed from President Bush, but claim them for my own, except for the ideas my constituents don't like. As soon as someone starts stomping on me, I'll shout, "Don't blame me! President Bush thought of that one."

~ Fifth on the agenda: **Limiting benefits for wealthy retirees.** It's about time I heard a president say this. And just who's considered wealthy under my plan? Anyone who has more money than me ... that's who. Considering that my boss's favorite word is 'frugal,' most of you won't receive any Social Security dollars under my plan, but I'll happily draw from yours. If you don't like this one, remember, President Bush came up with it first.

~ Sixth on the agenda: **Indexing benefits to prices rather than wages.** This means every time lawn bowling fees increase, we get a raise. I'm not sure where that raise will come from, but once we're retired, who cares about the petty details?

~ Seventh on the agenda: **Increasing the retirement age.** This isn't as bad as it sounds. Under my plan, if the retirement age is increased, I'll take into account that we won't want to work a lot of hours as we age. Heck, we don't want to work a lot of hours now. Therefore, my two-hour workdays should allow us to be productive well into our elderly years. Monday through Friday we report to work at 10 AM. We spend thirty minutes letting our computers power up, getting our coffee, and discussing what happened on *Desperate Housewives, Survivor,* and *American Idol.* We work for thirty minutes, take a lunch hour, then punch out and go home. We continue to earn the same annual salary we currently do, meaning what we pay into Social Security remains the same. Who wouldn't be willing to work until he's ninety on this plan?

~ Eighth on the agenda: Discouraging taking Social Security benefits early. Under my plan, you're only working two hours a day for crying out loud, and talking about TV shows during most of that time! How greedy can you people be?

Well, I've done it. I've overhauled Social Security and it didn't cost you anything. You'll work less, play more, and can sleep soundly at night knowing your benefits will be available to you when you retire. And if for some reason they aren't, don't blame me. After all, it *was* the president's idea to reform Social Security, not mine.

A history of the ascendancy to my rightful throne

by Ed Groelle

News item: *The world of toilets congregated in Beijing, China.*

"The World Toilet Summit was held in Beijing, China from November 17th to 19th, 2004. The theme of this summit was: Human, Environment, & Living. Workshops were organized on such hot topics as; humanized toilet, toilet management and hygiene, toilet designing, and energy-saving measures, etc."

I'm citing this news item to lend some authenticity to the remainder of this article in case you might think I'm writing frivolously or tongue-in-cheek. This is very serious subject! I'm structuring this article from the viewpoint of the evolution of the toilet as it relates to my life experiences using those indispensable contraptions. I seriously doubt that even the inimitable Tom Noer would touch this subject. That reminds me ... I must contact the Pulitzer people and make them aware of his existence.

Let's begin with my childhood. There were no indoor toilets on farms in those days so every farm had the infamous two-hole outhouse. Why two holes? I sincerely hope it was not an attempt to spawn social camaraderie. The really progressive ones had a third smaller hole for children. There were some advantages; the door was always kept open during usage to afford a panoramic view of distant neighbors and Sears catalogs were always available for reading. My most traumatic childhood experiences were when my father would arrive and make use of the second hole. No one needs that level of bonding.

My next level of contact was when I worked my way through school as an orderly or 'bedpan jockey' at a hospital in Chicago and became acquainted with the bedpan. Do they still use those? Caring for the personal needs of patients I got to the point where I could actually carry a bedpan in one hand and eat a sandwich with the other. It's an acquired tolerance, like eating olives.

Then came the Army with its specific regulations on how to set up a slit trench latrine; thirty-six inches deep, ten feet long and twelve inches wide ... perfect for multiple use and for comfortable straddling. The really plush field latrines had a four-foot "modesty" skirt around it fashioned from half pup tents. Very practical, and as trained killers, we would have sneered at Port-a-Pottys anyway.

Troop ships to Europe were not exactly pleasure cruise ships. On-board toilet facilities consisted of a twenty-foot trough with fast running seawater flowing through it and four-inch boards every few feet for body support. No consideration or expense wasted there for sissy comfort or privacy.

The French are great engineers and have given the world some of its most ingenious inventions, but there is sometimes a problem with their ability to bridge the gap between theoretical engineering and practical application, especially in the field of sanitation. Even today, their plumbing would make excellent plumbing school textbook examples of how not to design things. In the area of toilets there sometimes seems to be no thought given to modesty, functionality, or ergonomics. Who else but the French would put a clear glass door on a hotel room bathroom or build a three by six foot, totally enclosed, commode cubicle in a public museum with zero ventilation? There is one very practical device the French designed which, at one time, lent *a saveur de joie de vivre* to the Paris environment ... the sidewalk *pissoir* (talk about the origin of words). They were designed for use only by males and, unfortunately, have gone the way of the dinosaur, probably due to the pressure of feminism or political correctness. They have been replaced by unisex, fiberglass monstrosities, which automatically self-clean after every few uses by completely scrubbing the inside with pressurized jets of water, sort of like an interior car wash. I have never summoned up the temerity to use these for fear of being trapped there during the cleaning cycle.

Then there is the European early version of a toilet in the form of *squats*. These consist of a one-foot diameter bottomless hole in the middle of a room. Embossed footprints on each side of that hole suggested their method of usage. You can still find those in use today in the back "rest rooms" of small cafes. For obvious reasons women really hate them.

The epitome of my throne room experiences came when I once stayed at a five-star hotel in Istanbul, Turkey. The bathroom was the size of my living room, the fixtures gold-plated, and the commode seat heated. I think the flush water may have also have been heated, but I'm not sure of that. My father would have been so proud to see how far his son had come in this area of real life. His only complaint would have been that there were not two commodes side by side so we could "bond."

Taxation with representation ain't so great either

by Kenda Buxton

If life were a story problem, President Bush's Economic Stimulus Plan would read like this: A man named George is in charge of a government and has promised tax cuts for all the people in the land. Another man named George once promised all the people in the land, "No new taxes," but that George lied, and soon the people were paying even more money in taxes than they had been before George vowed, "No new taxes." However, that has nothing to do with our story problem, and is simply a reminder of what bad things can happen when someone invites you to, "Read my lips" and you take him up on it.

The George who is currently in charge of a government, 6.34 trillion dollars in debt, has promised all the people in the land tax cuts that will total 674 billion dollars over the next ten years. If George is already 6.34 trillion dollars in debt, how much debt will George be in after he gives away 674 billion dollars he doesn't have to begin with?

When the Economic Stimulus Plan is reduced to a story problem, it doesn't look so stimulating, does it? Like me, do you get the feeling that eventually someone will be flipping the American taxpayers upside down and shaking the last quarter from their pockets? Since George W. Bush won't be the Commander in Chief in ten years, a future president (a Democrat most likely, since it's a Democrat's job to tell us how his Republican predecessor screwed everything up long before said Democrat got into office) will announce, "George W. Bush screwed everything up long before I got into office. So read my lips ... lots of new taxes." Then he'll inform us that Bush's Economic Stimulus Plan didn't stimulate the economy at all, but rather, has the nation on the brink of financial disaster. After we're done gasping with shock and wondering how this happened, we'll be told we owe the government all the money President Bush gave us back ... with interest.

Let's face it, unless you're amongst those who are considered wealthy in this nation, meaning you have 500 thousand dollars in assets, not including your home, discussing money isn't much fun. That's why I suspect the very people President Bush's plan is supposed to stimulate, the middle class Americans, aren't too stimulated at all. The president starts rattling off big numbers and pulling out flow charts, and we switch the channel to reruns of *The Brady Bunch* because, after all, we are middle class Americans who have learned to appreciate cheap entertainment ... no weekends at Camp David for us, no sprawling ranch in Crawford, Texas that serves as our second home and no mansion known as the White House that we lodge in during the week, largely at taxpayer's expense. Instead, we'll get a tax cut of approximately 1,083 dollars. Since the average family spends 150 dollars a week at the grocery store, that 1,083 dollars will be gone within two months. I don't know about you, but I'll sure be proud to do my part in stimulating the economy by filling my cart with ground beef and Tidy Bowl. What woman needs enough money for a vacation home on a sixteen-hundred-acre ranch, when she's looking forward to making a meat loaf and cleaning the toilet? Which is why it's a shame that just when I was getting excited over spending my tax cut on Tidy Bowl, a new story problem came to my attention.

A man named Jim Doyle is the governor of a state with a 3.2 billion dollar deficit. At his first State of the State address, Governor Doyle said, "Now a storm has broken out and we're left without an umbrella."
I'd offer to buy Governor Doyle an umbrella, but my tax cut is earmarked for groceries. It's just my luck that I live in Wisconsin, where our governor assures us, "Everyone will feel the pain."

On second thought, Governor Doyle, I'll contact President Bush and have him mail my tax cut to you. Somehow, I have a feeling you're going to end up with it anyway.

What to do if your wife runs off with a French waiter

by Ed Groelle

I have some stories to tell, or more accurately, I have bits of napkins, toilet paper, etc. stashed away with stories jotted on them. Accumulated over time, they are treasured with the hope that the Great American Novel will one day rise from them like the Phoenix.

By the way, I do not write fiction. It is never as gripping and unbelievable as the truth.

Kathy Rader who owns and manages *Northside Alignment* relates many customer stories. She once sold a set of Goodyear tires with that brilliant white lettering around the sidewalls. After two weeks the man returned and wanted Kathy to remount the tires so that, when the truck was standing still, the lettering on all four tires would be at the same point of rotation. Kathy, of course, couldn't oblige but she could help another lady customer who returned after having had an alignment on her car. She wanted Kathy to do realignment so the car would pull slightly to the right. The reason given was that if she fell asleep the car would then go into the ditch instead of oncoming traffic. Kathy also says that sometimes she has customers seriously ask if they need to change air in their tires from winter to summer air.

The first day Joni Graham opened the *Standing Room Only* restaurant she was ready with twenty menus. A young boy playing nearby came in and asked what the place was about. He bought a sixty-cent corn dog and left. Then, Joni noticed that all the menus were missing. It was obvious the boy had taken them. Joni and husband decided to just close for the day and celebrate the sale of one corn dog. The next day the restaurant was crowded with customers. Apparently, the boy had distributed all the menus along Third Avenue. Today, that boy is married and has a son of his own. Joni is looking forward to the day she can make a corn dog for him.

Hiring people for restaurant work is always an on-going dilemma for owners. Joni once hired a young man who adamantly insisted that he had a lot of experience cooking in restaurants. Joni took him at his word. She assigned him a twenty-pound sack of potatoes to prepare for deep-frying and then left to do some personal errands. When she returned, she was greeted with a large pile that looked like dirt scrapped from the driveway. The man had cut up the potatoes without either washing or peeling them.

Joni once hired a girl to deliver a noon meal that someone had ordered for a business lunch. Unknown to Joni, there was a zero missing in the address and the girl couldn't find the address. Instead of telephoning Joni, she took the meals home and her family ate it. Joni quickly had to remake the $60 meal and redeliver it. The girl returned and wanted her pay, which coincidentally came to $60. Joni didn't pay her. The mother called later and asked Joni not to be too hard on her daughter since she had neglected to take her medicine.

I need to tell a personal story as well so as not to appear selective. My wife recently told me that she had purchased tickets to a Waylon Jennings concert at UW-Parkside. He is one of my favorite C&W singers so was excited about attending. I did think it strange that a singer of his stature would perform at such a little theater but quickly dismissed the thought. When I picked up the tickets at the ticket window, I was dismayed to find that the show was of the Wallin' Jennies, a trio of folk singers. The show was great, but I still was a bit disappointed. After returning home I Googled Jennings and discovered he died on February 13, 2002. I should have guessed.

As Jimmy Durante used to say, "I've got a million of 'em." but my space is all used up. The sign at the edge of Kenosha says, "Population, 90,320." I figure there are at least that many stories in town. All you need do is listen.

At this point you are probably wondering what this article's title has to do with its content. Nothing really. It was meant to get you interested. Since you read this far it must have worked.

Stocking stuffers: Holiday gifts for the truly needy

by Thomas J. Noer

T. S. Eliot said April was the cruelest month, but December is the most frantic. Not only do I have to deal with alternative street parking (will Santa get a ticket if he parks his sleigh on the street before midnight and leaves five minutes later?), grading final exams, and bad eggnog, but there is also the problem of holiday shopping. Christmas, Chanukah, Kwanzaa ... each year my list grows longer. But, between grading and wracking my brain for a column idea, I managed to find perfect gifts for all those on my lengthy shopping list. Below are Uncle Tom's special holiday presents for those most in need.

I had to find a number of gifts for my friends in the entertainment industry this year. I bought Winona Ryder's, *A Guide to Internet Shopping,* to keep her home and out of any stores. Michael Jackson gets a video on *Effective Parenting* that suggests it may not be correct to dangle a child over a balcony. Both Winona and Michael also will receive large fruitcakes to honor their recent behavior. I'm sending Oprah Winfrey one hour of free career counseling and a subscription to *Bride Magazine* to show to Stedman and Kevin Costner.

There were also a lot of politicians on my list. I ordered George Bush public speaking lessons and arranged a retirement planning seminar for Al Gore so he will not bore us to death by running again. New Wisconsin Governor, Jim Doyle, gets a magic wand to balance the budget and I found Jesse Ventura a job as a commentator on Kenosha's radio station, WLIP.

Many prominent Kenoshans will receive gifts. I bought Bev Jambois a cigarette lighter, set up for outgoing sheriff Larry Zarletti a singing audition with a record company, presented mayor John Antaramian with a life time trolley pass, found Scott Barter a decent sound technician for his TV show, and gave Howard Brown a lovely lime green Ivy League leisure suit.

I also needed to find presents for some of my corporate friends and so bought United Airlines a nice empty tin cup. The Disney Cruise Line gets a big bottle of Lysol and a batch of antibiotics for its passengers, while both Enron and Anderson Accounting executives will enjoy *Fun With Numbers* coloring books, suitable for killing time in jail. I am sending the entire New York Stock Exchange a giant bottle of Viagra and ordered *Krispy Kreme* managers memberships in *Weight Watchers*.

The Kenosha School Board gets a case of Valium and twenty hours of group therapy. Carthage College will receive an underground parking ramp and for downtown Kenosha, I secured commitments for a grocery store, several restaurants, and a large department store. For Twisterz nightclub, I've arranged a special musical appearance from the Kenosha Police Glee Club and Rappers. I'm sending *The Spot* warmer coats for their frozen car hops. Kenosha's beaches get a free consultation from the Environmental Protection Agency and for Tinseltown Theaters, I purchased flashlights so customers can walk up the stairs to their seats without fear of lethal injury.

To brighten the holidays for American TV viewers, I convinced the networks to end those obnoxious Alf commercials, to dump those obnoxious Dell Computer commercials with that nerdy Eddie Haskell guy, and to cancel the obnoxious Anna Nicole Smith! I booked Martha Stewart for a guest appearance on *The Judge Judy Show* and bought Rob Lowe a free return ticket to *The West Wing* to be used when his career collapses.

I sent The Chicago Bulls, Milwaukee Bucks, Chicago Cubs, and Milwaukee Brewers large Garage Sale signs, autographed photos of Vince Lombardi, Bobby Knight, General George Patton, and a very small jar of polish for their trophy cases.

For *Sound-Off!* I found some new, clever, and angry voices. I used my vast influence to arrange for Kenosha News readers to receive *Doonesbury* instead of *Cathy*, editorials instead of *Darts and Laurels*, a book review section, and many more full-page ads so the paper can pay a certain poor, but brilliant columnist far, far more.

Despite all these expensive gifts, there was just a little bit of cash left to buy a few things for myself. So Tom Noer gets a new photo at the top of his column so he no longer looks like a mafia thug or a fascist dictator and some new ideas so he stops raving about Sheridan Road, Packer fans, and alternate parking.

With all my shopping done, there is just time for a quick Happy Holidays to all those friendly readers, because I need to finish this and go outside as I think I left my car on an odd numbered side and it's almost midnight. But wait, maybe it is on the even side. What day is it anyway?

Goodbye winter ...
and good riddance

by Jim Wynne

In a few weeks we will enjoy the glory of the first day of spring. I look forward to spring the way a man with diarrhea looks forward to a restroom ... it just can't come soon enough. This love of the vernal equinox may be traced to my arrival in Kenosha forty years ago this January. It was January of 1964, and we had spent the previous four years in Arizona and California, and the first eight years of my life in North Carolina. I had no idea what serious winter was all about. Oh, it snowed some in North Carolina, but a three-inch snowfall was enough to close the schools and the temperature never got too much below the freezing mark. In California I knew kids my age who had never even seen snow. That rude and abrupt introduction to winter in the upper Midwest has colored my attitude to the extent that I have never since been able to be cold and happy at the same time.

I don't ski, ice skate, or go ice fishing and if I need to be outside in the winter, I make sure that I go back inside as soon as it's humanly possible. Every winter I read with amazement the stories of people who fall through the ice on frozen lakes, some of them on foot, others on snowmobiles, or in pickup trucks. I can't for the life of me imagine what would make anyone, drunk or sober, believe that driving a pickup truck on a lake is a good idea.

The other amazing thing is that many of these people go out on the ice to go fishing, a pastime that requires drilling a hole through the ice, sitting in a little hut using tiny Popeil-like fishing rods, and drinking. Someone is always fishing drunken ice fisherman out of a lake after they've wandered off and fallen through the ice. These people will tell you that you won't really get cold, so long as you dress right. For me though, dressing right would involve so many layers of clothing that it would become impossible to move my limbs voluntarily. I would have to be propped up against the wall of the hut, which is not my idea of a good time, and after only a short time in that position, I would not be very good company. As a small child in North Carolina my mother would make sure I was functionally incapacitated by warm clothing and outerwear before I was able to go outside, and that was in June. She was always cold, so that meant that I was too. "Put on your jacket," she would say, "I'm cold!" So it was either be cold or be uncomfortable, which made it easier to just stay indoors.

I have never gotten along very well on ice ... never able to walk on ice any distance without falling down. I never saw the need for ice skates that would only hasten the process and make it harder to get up again. Every year, my inevitable falls on icy driveways and sidewalks have provided plenty of amusement for my wife and children. They laugh with me and not at me, or so they allege. I approach a patch of ice much the same way that Inspector Clouseau enters a room where Cato is hiding. I know full well that something painful and embarrassing is about to happen, but there's nothing I can do about it. Over the years I have become skilled to the point where I can sometimes regain my balance before falling, but that effort is just as likely to degenerate into a terrible and emotionally draining cycle of slip-regain balance, slip-regain balance, until I get too tired to keep resisting and just give up and fall. When I was younger I was able to sustain the slip-regain balance cycle through perhaps fifteen iterations before allowing gravity to have its way ... and this on a patch of ice only a few feet across. You know what it looks like if you've ever seen the dancers in a Snoop Dogg video.

In front of the building where I work, the tulips are pushing their way up through the mulch, a sure sign that the horrors of winter are nearly behind us. I can see all the grass in my yard for the first time since December. I think back to that first spring in Kenosha in 1964 after the first winter. It was one of the most welcome ever and I can still remember how good those first warm days in April felt. I guess there really is something good about winter after all. It makes us realize how great it is for winter to be over.

A biography set in a world gone dark

by Ed Groelle

You see, I have this friend, well … she is blind and for the past several months I've been writing a biographical book of her life. Actually, I should say, it's really not just me, but both of us who are writing the book. We have two digital recorders, and after she has recorded into one, we swap recorders, and while she is again recording, I listen to the first and convert it into book form. It's time-consuming work and not as easy as it sounds because written English and spoken English are quite different. In addition, many of her sound bytes are random and must be assembled into a logical sequence.

Occasionally, we get together and I read what I have written and then she corrects, adds, or subtracts until she is comfortable with it. I sometimes disagree with her suggestions but I usually try to accommodate her changes as much as possible because, after all, it is her story. Generally, this way of transmitting information is working quite well. I have difficulty comprehending how she does this editing without actually seeing the words but she does it with an astounding memory, which she has developed, coupled with the ability to listen with probably ten times the attention of a sighted person.

Last week we decided to read the entire book as it has progressed to date. The book begins with her early life history up to the point when, as a teenager, she was told she would be blind before she was forty and how she then went into denial by living a normal life. She graduated from college, married, and generally just lived her life as if the diagnosis never existed. Eventually, the ominous symptoms began appearing, first with night blindness and then with missing pieces from random areas of her vision.

The next few chapters describes her effort to accept her inevitable blindness and how she came around to acceptance and then relates her agonizing struggle to lead a normal life and that she came out of this phase with a determination to assist others in dealing with similar life-changing upheavals.

Then come the chapters in which her husband had a tragic motorcycle accident that resulted in multiple fractures, internal injuries, and head trauma that left him without the senses of smell and taste, blind in one eye, no memories, and with a completely changed personality.

The next chapters deal with the totally unforeseen diagnosis of her fifteen-year-old son's malignant brain tumor. It details the intensive treatment of surgery, radiation, and years of therapy. This is the most discouraging segment of her life because there is no assurance that a relapse will not occur. She describes this situation as sitting in the dark, listening to a ticking bomb.

While reading to her of her son's cancer she started to cry. I didn't know what to say or do so I just squeezed her forearm and offered her a couple of McDonald's napkins I found nearby. What could anyone say at a time like that? Something meaningless like, 'God must love you to test you so much.' or 'Whatever doesn't break you makes you stronger?' I don't think so.

She told me she sometimes has nightmares of all this. I asked if she is blind in her dreams and she said that when dreaming she can see perfectly.

Then I said, "But how can you dream what it's like today?"

"I don't. Everything and every one are as they were before I lost my sight."

"You mean no one ever ages?"

"Yes, in my dreams my husband and children look just as they were ten years ago, but my visions of them are fading. Soon, they will have no faces. I will never see my adult children as they are today or ever see my grandchildren. I'll need to form a mental image of them from their voices and laughter."

When and if this book is published, I really hope many of you read it. It is a story of love, pain, courage, and triumph. I hope you won't mind if some of the pages might be tear-stained.

You'll never learn anything by doing it right

by Kenda Buxton

Remember when school field trips didn't involve lawsuits or permission slips with 800 disclaimers of liability? Remember when permission slips were made on mimeograph machines, and every kid took a big whiff of the fresh ink the second the slips were passed out? Remember when field trips took place just once a year, a few weeks before school let out for the summer, and always seemed to involve the Milwaukee Zoo? Remember how soggy your peanut butter and jelly sandwich got after sitting on a sweltering school bus all morning and how the Smucker's grape jelly left purple blotches on your Wonder Bread? Remember washing down those sandwiches with cartons of warm milk stored on the back of the bus in the days before anyone ever heard of salmonella? Remember when permission slips looked something like this: Dear Parents: The first grade class is going to the Milwaukee Zoo. Please provide a sack lunch for your child.

Pretty straightforward stuff. We're going to the zoo, so pack your kid something to eat. No mention of who was liable if the bus driver went bonkers after hearing one too many rounds of *"Cheers to the Bus Driver"* and rammed the bus into a mob of hippies protesting middle class America's fondness for sending their kids on field trips that promoted animal entrapment. While *"Cheers to the Bus Driver"* was a song filled with adoration and praise for the poor sucker who got stuck hauling fifty kids with spring fever to the zoo, it was lacking in any words that went beyond *"Cheers to the Bus Driver"* shouted mile after mile in a variety of off-key melodies. No mention of who was liable if a room mother "accidentally" lost the group of boys that the teachers had been trying to lose somewhere all year long. In that event, the teachers would have hung the woman's picture on the *Room Mother's Wall of Fame* and thereafter uttered her name with the kind of reverence usually reserved for important dead guys.

There would be no mention of who was liable if a kid was swallowed by a lion, mauled by a bear, or yanked into Samson's cage. For those of you who never came face to face with Samson, he was a huge ferocious gorilla housed at the Milwaukee Zoo for 300 years. In reality, he wasn't all that big and the only ferocity I ever witnessed was Samson yawning with the kind of boredom that reflects 300 years of kids on field trips pointing at him, but in legend, Samson was Wisconsin's answer to King Kong.

When I was a kid, I'd have thought it was pretty cool if my mother sued the school because it wasn't willing to take the blame for a bus driver gone nuts, a missing child, or a bear mauling. Similar to the reasons one concerned Kenosha mother brought a lawsuit against the Unified School District that has since been dropped because of changes made to field trip permission slips. Unfortunately, baby boomer parents didn't sue school districts. The philosophy of the parents who attended one-room schoolhouses during the Depression leaned more toward, "Don't come crying to me if you get mauled by a bear because you were stupid enough to stand too close to its cage," than, "I'll sue the school if a polar bear has you for lunch." As evidenced by the warm milk we drank, the soggy sandwiches we ate, and the permission slips that didn't mention any type of liability, our parents believed a school and its teachers could do no wrong, and that if we didn't return home from a field trip, then we must have been screwing off and deserved to be left behind. Oh, how I long for the days when life was that simple.

So, although lawsuits keep kids safer, we now know better than to drink milk that's spent the morning curdling on a school bus and that no health-conscious mom would consider using white bread for her child's sandwich. I'd love to see Samson just one more time while singing another round of *"Cheers to the Bus Driver"* and hearing my mother say it would serve me right to be trampled by an elephant if I was dumb enough to climb into its cage.

What would life be if we only knew things that are true?

by Ed Groelle

A friend recently informed me that she no longer blindly accepted the statements of scientists. After thinking about it for a while, I had to reluctantly agree with her. Perhaps I've become jaded from the vast amounts of information floating about or perhaps I've just become more critical of what I read or hear as a form of self-preservation. It was palpable when only politicians, columnists, and wannabees were disseminating embellished information, but lately it seems that scientists and highly educated persons are joining in the game of doubtful opinions. This upsets my world because I've always had confidence in science that is now being shaken almost daily.

Consider the case of a baby's skeleton being dug up in Ethiopia. Scientists leapt on this discovery and immediately began discussing whether or not it is the missing link and walked upright. It was dated as being three million years old. If you have ever walked among the ruins of Egypt and seen what only 3000 years have done it becomes very difficult to believe. The baby's skeleton is 1000 times older than those ruins and is supposed to have survived no less than five glacial periods, shifts of the earth's tectonic plates, rising and falling of mountains and oceans, several calamitous floods, and many other catastrophic events and survived, just so some enterprising scientist could gingerly dig it up and proclaim it a momentous discovery. With proclamations of this type one can logically begin to wonder about the ulterior motives of some scientists. If I believed this I would probably rush out and buy some land in New Orleans near the dikes because the scientists at the Army Corps of Engineers say it is now safe.

The manned landing on the moon was an exciting event, wasn't it? For me the thrill wore off rather quickly when I realized the moon was no longer mysterious or even romantic. What did the moon mission really buy for us? In reality, all we got are a few rocks, some eerie movies of a guy playing golf, and a map of the far side of the moon. Who really cares? Did we really need or want to know what was on the far side of the moon? We now can no longer pretend that there are alien cities on the dark side of the moon from which extraterrestrials swoop down, create crop circles, start some new religions, suck the intelligence out of our politician's brains, and then swoop back to observe how we handle the resulting situation.

The landing also destroyed a rather pleasant, recurring dream I sometimes had of visiting the ETs who live on the dark side of the moon and discussing with them the artistic possibilities of crop circles and their technique for seeding of the earth with humans about 12,000 years ago. For some inexplicable reason the landing not only destroyed that moon dream, but also my recurring dream of riding a Vespa scooter around Rome with Sharon Stone on the rear seat screaming to go faster. Now all I have left is the horrendous nightmare about me being the toy boy of Hillary Clinton. I wish my dreams and illusions to remain intact. NASA and the astronauts have a lot to answer for.

Everyone loves the runt of the litter, but evidently not scientists. They kicked my favorite planet, Pluto, right out of the solar system. And for what reason? The poor thing wasn't round, it didn't follow an accepted orbit, and generally wasn't well behaved enough to be in this elite group. None of the scientists considered the cost involved in hiring thousands of people armed with buckets of White-Out that will be required to obliterate Pluto from the millions of text and reference books. Also, parents everywhere will need to go up to their attics and cut the planet from their children's Styrofoam model of the solar system. What a terrible waste of resources!

I do not accept creation, evolution, the canopy theory, or alien infestation as facts. They are all theories at best and so I take a rather pragmatic view of all of it. If we ever do discover beyond any reasonable doubt how this all came about it will, like the theory of relativity, be completely understood by only a handful of people.

I accept the universe as it is revealed to me when I lie on my back in a clover-scented meadow on a starry night and allow myself be swept away by the miraculous, awesome, beauty of it all.

Some redeeming thoughts while grousing over medical bills

by Ed Groelle

My mother always told me that I was born a 'blue baby.' I've never been sure of what that meant but the oxygen-starved effect of it probably accounts for my anagrammatical view of the world. As children we were constantly bombarded with the disease of the month; whooping cough, measles, scarlet fever, mumps, chicken pox, etc. We got most of them. Someone from the Health Department often came to nail a 'Quarantined' sign on our front door. The most feared threat was of polio. It always seemed to raise its ugly head in August just in time to prevent us from attending the county fair. Jonas Salk should be canonized for the vaccine.

When I was about twelve years old there was the then obligatory tonsil/adenoids surgery. It's supposed to be a routine, mundane, surgery but was made uncomfortable by the use of ether as the anesthetic. Still, it probably beats out chloroform or a bottle of Jack Daniels and a stick to bite down on.

Somewhere in my early teens I jumped onto a board with a spike sticking up from it. My father took me to our family doctor and I still remember hobbling up to his second floor office with the board and nail still in my foot bone. He looked at it, hummed a couple bars of *Oh Susanna*, and then left, only to return with (I kid you not) a hacksaw and a claw hammer. He said, "This may hurt a bit" and then proceeded to use the hammer claw to pry out the nail. After applying some mysterious white powder and bandaging it, he assured me I would be OK in a day or two. Can you imagine what would ensue if that happened today? There would be shots, blood tests, X-rays, consultations, an orthopedic surgeon and surgery scheduled, and countless bills for months, some from doctors you never have heard of before.

At age seventeen I had an emergency appendectomy. Again with the ether. Ugh!

At age thirty-five I had a spinal laminectomy because I could no longer stand the constant pain. In fact, if I had had a gun the night before surgery I think I would have shot myself. The surgery didn't cure the problem but did take away the pain so I could resume a normal life, within limits.

Some time later I had a two-for-one hemorrhoid/hernia surgery. Don't ever believe doctors when they say, "This won't hurt a bit." Have you ever tried to pass a pumpkin? My night nurse who had four children and also had had hemorrhoid surgery told me that, given a choice, she would rather have another baby. I'm sure she was just being compassionate for my benefit.

During the last fifteen years I've had cataract surgery on both eyes. Now there's a winner surgery. Lie down almost blind and get up with 20-20 vision. It's like a miracle. You aren't even put to sleep. I talked with the surgeon about my up-coming vacation while he worked.

About four years ago I wasn't feeling too well and ended up at St. Luke's Hospital where a couple of stents were installed in my heart. Cardiac catheterization has to be one of God's greatest blessings. It is amazing what they can do today at the tip of a thirty-inch wire.

Gall bladder surgery has gone from a miserable one-week hospital stay to 23-hour outpatient. It alleviated years of chronic abdominal discomfort for me. Some people have had difficulty with it, but I spent the entire night after surgery finishing a jigsaw puzzle at the reception area.

A few years ago I had all my upper teeth capped in one eight-hour session with the aid of about thirty Novocain shots. As you can see from my picture, that resulted in a sexy smile but I don't think I would do that again. Last year I also had two root canals as a Christmas present from a deranged Tooth Fairy.

You people are very fortunate I'm still here to entertain you.

The rusty nail in the foot could have resulted in tetanus or blood poisoning. That's how my grandmother died at age twenty-seven. They could do nothing but watch the deadly blue line creep up to her heart.

The appendicitis, if fifty years earlier, might have resulted in peritonitis. Another lousy way out.

OK, the hemorrhoid thing wasn't life threatening and should best be considered cosmetic surgery.

But, the point and awful truth is, if I had been born 75 years earlier I probably would not have lived this long. If I did make it this far I would probably be attached to an oxygen tank, confined to a wheel chair, eat through a straw, be in constant pain, and probably almost blind. Instead, I'm in relatively good health with almost all my original hair and teeth and can read a newspaper from five feet.

All this generates an entirely different perspective when scanning medical bills. Of course, you can decide not to participate in modern health care. I've heard that aspirin, morphine, and cold packs also work miracles.

Put-downs for use in polite company

by Kenda Buxton

"I expressed myself rather forcefully; felt better after I had done it."

That was Dick Cheney's response upon admitting he cursed Vermont Senator Patrick Leahy on the Senate floor. Personally, I'm glad the vice president felt better after expressing himself forcefully. Expressing yourself forcefully relieves stress, especially when someone accuses you of profiting from a war. Just because Cheney was CEO of Halliburton prior to his latest gig doesn't mean he's profiting from Halliburton's presence in Iraq. Just because he still draws an annual salary in excess of 150 thousand dollars, and holds 433 thousand stock options in the company that's the largest contractor in Iraq, doesn't mean he's profiting, and like the vice president, I curse anyone who claims otherwise.

"Ibbidy-bibiddy, rinkidy-dink, make like a statue and freeze, you fink!" No, this wasn't the curse the vice president used. His curse started with an "f" and ended with the word "off." Grandpa Munster used the "Ibbidy-bibiddy" curse to hold criminals in place until the police arrived.

When someone accuses you of starting a war just so the value of your stock rises, heated exchanges often take place that later make a person wish he'd found a better way of expressing himself. I'm sure the same holds true for the vice president, a member of a political party that campaigns heavily amongst conservative Christians. Since I was scolded for uttering, "Darn it!" in a Baptist Sunday School class (for weeks afterwards, church deacons debated which direction my wayward seven-year-old soul would head if I choked on my Oreos and Kool-Aid at Vacation Bible School), I advise Mr. Cheney to use another phrase when he's upset. Nothing causes conservative Christians to pray harder for you and to find someone else to vote for than not living by Psalm 19:14: **"Let the words of my mouth, and the meditation of my heart be acceptable in thy sight, O Lord."**

To assist Mr. Cheney in his quest for suitable phrases bound to be approved by conservative Christians everywhere, while still satisfying his need to express himself forcefully, I've come up with the following alternatives for the next time some smart aleck Democrat ruins what started out to be a perfectly good day.

"Up your nose with a rubber hose!" A phrase made popular by Vinnie Barbarino on "Welcome Back, Kotter." There's also, "Off my case, Potato Face" if the vice president feels "Up your nose with a rubber hose" isn't befitting a man of his status.

"Stifle yourself!" A favorite of Archie Bunker's that will shut up any pesky Democrat shooting his mouth off on the Senate floor.

"Sufferin' Succotash!" If the vice president says this with the same gusto as Sylvester the cat, it'll come out as, "Thufferin' Thuccotash!" accompanied by a spray of saliva guaranteed to keep anyone of opposing political opinions several hundred yards away.

"Don't have a cow, man!" Bart Simpson loves this phrase, along with, "Eat my shorts!" Either expression will let Senator Leahy know the vice president isn't in the mood to discuss wars, Halliburton, stock options, or John Edwards's charisma, good looks, and full head of hair.

"Kiss my grits!" No episode of *Alice* was complete until Flo said this. It's recommended for Southern Democrats, who will immediately understand Mr. Cheney is cursing them out in a way sanctioned by residents of the Bible Belt.

"Oh fiddle-faddle!" Yes, it's tame when compared to what the vice president usually prefers, but favored by Aunt Bee when Opie walked across her kitchen floor with muddy shoes, when her apple pies baked too long, and when Andy refused to let her learn to drive, because after all, where do women need to go in a car anyway? This expression gets two thumbs up from the Religious Right, suitable for the ears of little old ladies, boys carrying fishing poles, and sheriff's deputies who keep their bullets in their shirt pockets.

So, Mr. Vice President, the next time someone accuses you of starting a war just to increase your retirement fund, cuss him out with, "Kiss my grits!" followed by the newest overused catchphrase, "I'm Dick Cheney, and I approve this message." You might not be expressing yourself as forcefully as you'd like, but oh fiddle-faddle!, it'll get your point across.

You may love these things, but I just don't get it

by Thomas J. Noer

All of my regular readers, Florence, Rick at the post office, and my wife, know that there are many things I dislike, but there is an even longer list of things that other people seem to love but I just don't understand the appeal. Below are some popular things that many of you appear to like but I just don't get!

Sun roofs - Most cars now have air conditioning and heaters ... wonderful inventions to let us close the windows and AVOID heat, cold, dirt, and flying objects while on the road. Why would anyone want to expose themselves to dust, gas fumes, and angry pigeons looking for a moving target? At night, sun roofs become *moon roofs* so people can crash their cars into trees while looking for the big dipper.

Madrigals - I have tried to listen to these songs but can't understand their attraction. A madrigal consists of a bunch of people singing the same word for about five minutes ... Looooooooooooove, followed by other people singing the same word for another five minutes. There was little to do in the 15th century, so they dreamed these up to kill time between plagues. I am sure they are pleasing to some, but to me it is one loooooooooooong root canal.

Sponge Bob - Both kids and adults seem to love *Sponge Bob Square Pants*, but I don't get the appeal. With a young granddaughter, I have grown to appreciate *Blue's Clues*, *Dora the Explorer*, and even the endless whining of *Caillou*, but Sponge Bob's soggy adventures cause me to reach for the remote to try to find *Dragon Tales and Clifford* or even Packer highlights.

Fois Grois - Those of you who dine only in *Family Restaurants* are blissfully unfamiliar with the sight of a slab of greasy duck liver on the plate in front of you that costs more than your monthly mortgage. Regular old cow liver (rich in iron and pesticides) is bad enough, but I can't figure out why anybody orders this concoction.

Some madrigal-singing French chef decided if people will eat brains and snails, why not chunks of duck digestive organs?

Delaware - I know it was one of the original thirteen states, but what of the last 220 years? I can't think of one single person, event, or anything else that you can associate with the place. Don't tell me that in the painting, *Washington crossing the Delaware* wherein he was depicted going from New Jersey to Pennsylvania, that he wasn't trying to get away from Delaware. It is the only state that makes North Dakota look important.

Shaved heads - As one who is follicle challenged, I can't understand why anyone would WANT to look bald. When Michael Jordan's hair started to fall out he went to the shaved look to cover the losses, but I don't understand why eighteen-years-olds want to look like their grandfathers (assuming grandpa had a nose ring and a tattoo on his forehead).

Branson, Missouri - Las Vegas has shows, gambling, warm weather, hookers, and a nice tradition of corruption, but what is the appeal of Branson? It is one of the top three tourist attractions in the nation so lots of people must like it, but I don't get the thrill of going to *The Dancing Chickens Show* (I am not making this up!) followed by a $7.99 buffet with runny lasagna. Well, at least they don't serve *fois grois*.

Pet fish - It may be relaxing to stare at an aquarium full of colorful fish slowly circling all looking for an exit, but I don't get it. You can't walk a fish, play with it, or comb it, so what is the attraction? I guess you do get to feed the fish by shaking a carton of flakes over the water, but eventually one of the kids will put in too much and the fish wind up down the toilet. I seriously suspect those with pet fish also watch *Sponge Bob*.

Ballroom dancing - When public TV wants to raise money, they put on *The Three Tenors*, dog shows, or anorexic women with leather hair named Mimi dancing with men called Raoul in tuxes with numbers on their back, who clearly would rather be dancing with other men. Lots of people must like the *Samba Finals*, but I'm not one of them.

Now, those of you named Raoul with shaved heads who were born in Delaware, love fish and sing madrigals while driving to Branson with your sun roof open munching on a *fois grois* sandwich from a Sponge Bob lunch bucket, don't get mad at me. I am not saying any of these are wrong, only that I don't get them. It is possible you do not grasp the appeal of bow ties, Jello, AM radio, *Designing for the Sexes*, and writing monthly columns about stupid things.

Old men shall dream dreams

by Ed Groelle

Saumur is a small town (Pop: 30,000) in central France straddling the Loire River in what is commonly known as chateau country. I was stationed there at the US Army Saumur Signal Depot for over two years in the late '50's. The depot was built in 1952 as part of the ComZ military zone whose purpose was to establish and maintain a supply line from the Atlantic to the Third Army in Germany in the event the Russians attacked. The Saumur location has miles of man-made caves ideal for storing electronic equipment. The base existed until 1966 when Charles De Gaulle requested all U.S. Forces leave French soil. After all twenty-one bases were emptied and handed over to France, local authorities could do what they wanted with them. Some bases were converted to housing or razed for shopping malls, etc. Some were used as hospitals and one was even converted to a prison.

The Saumur Signal Depot was actually located in the tiny village of Varrains just outside of Saumur. Varrains did absolutely nothing with it for ten years. Today, the small chateau on the base has been converted to student apartments and the two barracks are used for storage and a repair shop. The gym, mess hall, and officer's club are rented for local activities.

Returning twenty-two years after leaving the army post it still looked much like the place I had lived for two years. I have returned six times since and on one of those visits conceived the idea of designing a web site for Saumur veterans. I taught myself HTML

129

programming and developed a web site (http://www.egroelle.net) that has exceeded my expectations. It's a virtual trip back to a place long ago and far away where many of us grew up. It contains 5500 files, 1800 pages, 3500 photos, and hundreds of e-mails, which has resulted in buddies finding buddies, one or two U.S. reunions each year, and an annual French reunion in Saumur for former French base workers.

The Bible, in Joel 2:28, states, "Your old men shall dream dreams, your young men shall see visions." How true! I was homesick for a while when returning to the U.S. and still am, on occasion. I regard Saumur to be my hometown more than the original. It seems that many aging GI's once stationed there now want to relive those days and feel a need for a sympathetic ear for their stories so ... they tell them to me. Here is one of them ... a very poignant story. Dave's daughter e-mailed it to me after she found my Saumur website.

Dave was from a small town in Tennessee and could be described as a naive country boy. He dreamed of seeing the world and so decided to enlist in the Army. The draft was closing in anyway. He received basic and radio training and then was sent to France.

After a few months there, he met Marie and fell hard for her coquettish demeanor.

They were very compatible and made plans for Marie to join him after he returned to the U.S. Returning home, he found his family adamantly against his marrying Marie. His grandmother stated she would disown him if he did. He relented, got a job as a truck driver, and eventually married someone else. The marriage produced three children but was not ideal. After twenty years they divorced.

Eventually, Marie married a GI and came with him to America. Her marriage became shaky to the point of it also ending in divorce.

Over the years, Dave drifted into alcoholism and eventually became morbidly ill with diabetes, kidney failure, and a leg amputation.

When he died in 1991, his daughter, Betty, went through his things and found pictures of Marie. She then recalled how her father had, on several occasions, asked her if she knew how to go about contacting a friend living in France. Remembering this, and with the photos that piqued her interest, Betty began digging into her father's military history. She managed to contact Marie's family in France and was told Marie was living in central Illinois.

She phoned Marie and heard the story of their romance. There was something about the story that nagged at Betty. She contacted the trucking company and obtained the route her father drove three times a week. By carefully scrutinizing the route she discovered the dismaying fact that her father had, for over twenty years, driven within two miles of where Marie lived. He died never knowing it.

If you are reading this article on Feb 18, I will be in France exploring Provence with a rental car. If you are eating breakfast, I'm probably having lunch at an outdoor cafe eating a baguette with a glass of wine watching pretty girls walk by.

Wish you were here.

Has anyone ever actually seen a Number 1 or Number 13 pencil?

by Kenda Buxton

As a kid, I loved this Back-to-School time of year. Or, at least I loved it until about noon on the first day of school. Once I'd met my teacher, found out which kids were in my room, and had dulled the points on all my crayons, my excitement over the new school year turned as lukewarm as the milk they served us at lunch, as I realized 180 long days separated me from another summer vacation.

Getting off the bus at the end of that first day never held the same feeling of anticipation as getting on it had. Instead, the feeling was more like, "I have to do this again tomorrow? You've *got* to be kidding me." That pretty much sums up how I feel yet today whenever I return to work after a vacation. Ten minutes into the e-mails, the phone calls, the voice mails, and the two weeks worth of problems that need solving, I no longer care that I'm wearing a new outfit and that I have a Ho Ho in my lunch bag. About the time when I'm hiding under my desk babbling incoherently while stuffing that Ho Ho into my mouth, is about the same time I'm counting the days until my next vacation. Which just goes to show you ... all those first days of school *did* prepare me for something.

One thing that's changed since I attended school is the length of the supply lists. Actually, supply lists were unheard of in the 1960's. We were too busy trying to win a war, give peace a chance, and put a man on the moon. With noble endeavors like those to pursue, who had time to mimeograph a bunch of stupid supply lists?

Even without a list, every little kid managed to start school with the same things; a package of #2 pencils, an eight-count box of Crayola Crayons, one jar of paste, one pair of scissors so dull that it's no wonder my art projects were never hung on the refrigerator, and a Flintstones lunch box.

And while every little kid started school with the same things, so did every big kid. A few folders, spiral notebooks with yellow smiley faces on them (back when the smiley face was cool, as opposed to being Wal-Mart's logo), a package of Bic pens, a three-ring binder with Bobby Sherman's picture on the cover, a compass, and a protractor. I never did figure out what to do with those last two supplies, but then, I still can't add fractions, so maybe that explains why my compass and protractor never got much use.

Thirty-five years ago, none of us carried backpacks to school either. But then, we didn't lug around 110 pounds of supplies that our parents had to mortgage their homes to buy. Kleenex, glue sticks, hand sanitizer, antibacterial wipes, papers towels, index cards, Post-it Notes, colored markers, colored pencils, highlighters, a ruler with standard and metric measurements (Speaking from experience, kids, the metric part of that ruler is a waste of time, no matter how often you're told that the United States will soon go, 'completely metric.'), and a graphing calculator are just a small portion of what appears on today's school supply lists. And don't ask me to explain what a graphing calculator does. Keep in mind that I use my compass and protractor as cookie cutters.

Amongst the supply lists I studied, one included a kindergarten "comfort kit." Parents are told to pack a kit that includes their child's favorite snacks, along with a family picture, and a note telling the child they'll be reunited soon. Boy, these kids should have started school in Leah Krahn's class like I did. She'd have gotten the little softies over that comfort kit before the first recess hit.

So, whether your new school year starts with little more than pencils and crayons, like mine did, or whether you're forced to unload three store aisles worth of supplies from the back of a minivan, here's to fresh beginnings. If you study hard and listen to your teachers, then someday, you too, can be a successful adult who holes up beneath her desk eating junk food, counting the days until her next vacation, and crying for her comfort kit.

A Parable on Virtue

by Ed Groelle

Long ago in a country across the sea
A king ruled with bare simplicity.
He was a proper king, he even banned the sword
And aroused the good in his subjects with a unique reward.
He pinned metals on those who were supremely good
And flattered their virtues whenever he could.
He thought to exalt the good and the bad ignore
Would prosper his country and never know war.
He didn't know the good, the bad would devour
If the good are good only to please those in power.

Now in this kingdom near the border on the west
Lived a girl who doubtless, was the best of the best.
The epitome of virtue, a teacher's dream in school
She observed with caution every golden rule.
It was a hobby of hers, No, more a reason to live
She gleaned every medal the king had to give.
She wore all her medals with dignity and pride.
They adorned her chest from side to side.
She felt admired but, in truth, was a bore.
Raising envy in some and hate in more.

Now the king was so pleased she had proven him right
He gave a special favor to the girl's great delight.
"You may play in my garden. For a week you may stay
And savor the great beauty of the flower's display.
There is one problem. A wolf lives there too.
You must avoid him and not let him hear you.
If you see the wolf or hear his rustle,
Stop, don't make a sound. Don't move a muscle.
He is completely blind, but his hearing is rare.

134

If you make any sound he will know you are there."

Now, this wolf was greedy and ever probing for food
But this somber fact did not muddy her mood.
She entered the garden minus fear or dread
Musing only of the joy in the days ahead.
Under the summer sun in the perfumed floral air
Her days floated by with no thought of care.
She played mid the roses and hummed a pretty tune,
Danced on the lawns and forgot the wolf very soon.
The chances were good their paths would never meet
In a league-wide garden and twice as deep.

Then, on the last day, she saw the wolf came near.
She froze to the spot through obedience, not fear.
For the king had said plainly in that day
"If you ignore the wolf, he will go away."
Since she was a very good girl, His advice she took
And watched the wolf approach with a disdainful look.
Then a slight breeze arose from out of the west
And tinkled those medals on her breast.
The wolf heard the sound, his ears perked up.
He pounced on the girl and ate her up.

The column writer's lament

by Thomas J. Noer

Each column I write has endless solutions.
This month you get a list of New Year's resolutions.
Politicians and actors and others more near
Have told me their promises for the next year.
Now writing such a list really takes little time
So I put them in couplets and hope that they rhyme.
Kemper's Center's Board vows to be so mild and so meek
That they will keep a director for more than one week.
Pleasant Prairie Planners resolve that they will explode
That hideous brick building on South Sheridan Road.

Kenosha officials are so sick of my endless attack
That they promise to give alternative parking fines back.
The Outlet Mall Owners will not close their doors
But will move all the porno shops into their stores.
Brittany Spears has pledged better songs for her label
And to buy some new pants that will cover her navel.
Michael Jackson informed me he will no longer be 'Jacko.'
His 2004 nickname will be simply 'Wacko.'
Kobe and Rush called and assured me they'd tell
How to be roommates in one tiny jail cell.

The Fab Five of Queer Eye will try to stay sane
When asked to do a makeover of Saddam Hussein.
Bette Midler, Woody Allen, and Cher all agree
To finally retire and join AARP.
Paris Hilton faxed me that her goal for the year:
Is to make that famous video tape disappear.
Tiger Woods is busy preparing for marital bliss
But wants a strong pre-nup before the first kiss.
Ozzy Osbourne confesses that drugs were to blame

And promises never to sing at another Cub's game.

And the Brewers up North vow to stop selling their players
Or to give all that money back to the taxpayers.
The Vikings coaches just called and told me to say
That next year they won't choke to help out Green Bay
George W. pledges a whole year without any lies
And to finally get rid of those ugly blue ties.
V.P. Cheney's resolution is clear and quite certain:
To see all government contracts go to Halliburton.
Howard Dean will stay on the Internet to talk with us
And hope we don't see that he's this year's Dukakis!

Hillary promises to use all the cash from her book
To get rid of the black pants suits and buy a new look.
And husband Bill will explain how it all went so wrong
When he first caught a glimpse of Monica's thong.
Governor Arnold has set-up a buzzer to warn ya
Whenever he tries to pronounce 'California!'
The Kenosha News resolves to stop crying poor
And to pay their columnists a great deal more!
And one of those writers (his picture's above)
Promises a year of nothing but sunshine and love!

No bashing of Packers, no mocking downtown
No criticism of editors or Publisher Brown.
No cynical columns will appear under his name
Only kindness and warmth and words that are tame.
But remember, dear readers, despite what I've spoken,
All New Year's resolutions are made to be broken!

Welcome back to school everybody!

by Kenda Buxton

Unlike the author of "All I Really Need to Know I Learned in Kindergarten", all I *really* need to know I learned in first grade, because at Salem Grade School in 1968, that's where learning began. Salem had no kindergarten then, so my introduction to school didn't include milk breaks or naps, but had instead, a teacher who hacked the erasers off my brand new Number two pencils that I'd brought in my brand new Gumby pencil case.

Leah Krahn had taught at Salem 114 years, and was 137 when I entered first grade, or so rumor claimed. She was a petite, gray-haired, grandmother who wore comfortable dresses and sensible shoes but when she swooped down on your pencils with her switchblade, all comparisons to a grandma vanished. After she'd accumulated a mountain of pink rubber tips, she gave us fat black pencils without erasers that didn't fit in my Gumby pencil case. Mrs. Krahn then declared erasing forbidden, in a tone broadcasting her certainty that the Lord had forgotten to add an Eleventh Commandment, *Thou Shalt Not Erase*, and then a Twelfth, *Thou Shalt Learn From Thy Mistakes.*

Despite her 137-year-old eyes, Mrs. Krahn could detect even the faintest eraser smudge on a worksheet completed at home and would mark the answer wrong, regardless of whether it was incorrect or not. "It's dishonest to erase in this classroom," she'd scold, and then assign the offender to write, 'I will not erase' ten times on the blackboard.

Therefore, **Lesson One:** An honest person admits to her mistakes. Rather than erasing them away, even though I still break into a cold sweat when handed an eraser-less pencil and each time I delete something while writing this column, I swallow a handful of Tums.

Aside from her aversion to erasers, Mrs. Krahn believed in dressing for the weather. If it was raining and you didn't wear boots, you wrote, 'I will wear my boots.' If you forgot your hat on a January morning, you wrote, 'I will wear my hat.'

Lesson Two: Never be in such a rush to leave the house that you aren't dressed for the possibility of wading through a swollen creek or trudging head long into a blizzard.

Mrs. Krahn also had a phobia about children dropping things, or maybe it wasn't a phobia. Perhaps after 114 years of teaching, she could no longer tolerate clumsy first graders. 'I will not drop things' was the sentence we wrote for that offense, and if you tried to pick up a dropped pencil with your feet like I did one day, she'd say, "Be honest when you drop something. Bad things happen to sneaky children."

Lesson Three: If you drop something, yell, "Hey, I just dropped something!" You might get funny looks but at least you're not being sneaky.

The yellow lines painted on the playground defined the boundaries for various grades. One day, Jack Andersen told us we could cross the yellow line and play on the fourth grade side. I don't know why that was such a temptation, since the fourth graders didn't have swing sets or monkey bars, but seven of us bought into Jack's theory that big kids have more fun and crossed the yellow line. Mrs. Krahn caught us, and recesses were forfeited as we wrote, 'I will not cross the yellow line.' To this day, I'm totally useless in a passing zone.

Lesson Four: The grass isn't always greener on the other side of the yellow line. Stay within your boundaries because you probably have better playground equipment anyway.

With the start of school only a few weeks away, I applaud all educators. Many of the biggest influences in my life were the teachers I had at Salem Grade School. Though Mrs. Krahn passed away years ago, I have no doubt Heaven is quiet and orderly due to her presence because no one drops things and everyone stays on his own side of the yellow line. Her methods were 'old school' to us baby boomers, but like every teacher who shines in the classroom, Mrs. Krahn cherished her young students and wanted us to start off on the right foot. All in all, it was a good beginning, although, I'd still like my erasers back.

Welcome to summer and the tyranny of noise pollution

by Ed Groelle

Joseph Pulitzer, of literary prize fame, was blind and a victim of a noise-sensitive disability, which caused him acute suffering. Noises, which could inflict pain upon him, served neither any useful purpose nor gave pleasure to anyone else. Loud talking, whistling, slamming doors, barking dogs, the kick of motorcycles ... these were the noises which made his existence miserable. He complained, justifiably, that his life was made a burden by the utter indifference of a minority of human beings to the rights of others. What right, he asked, had anyone to run a motorboat so noisy that it destroyed the peace of a whole harbor? In an attempt to escape the noise he tried living on the top floor of a tall building in New York. This proved to be inadequate so, eventually, he moved to a yacht anchored several miles off the coast.

OK, perhaps Pulitzer was a tad neurotic but its easy to empathize with him. USA Today had an article recently about suburbs that are enacting laws against noise. The residents claim they had moved to the suburbs in an attempt to escape the noise but soon found it followed them. Specifically, they were in the process of enacting laws prohibiting loud motorcycles and boom cars. I almost stood up and cheered after reading this.

The Census Bureau reports that noise is American's top complaint about their neighborhoods and the major reason for wanting to move. Living on one of the busiest streets in Kenosha near one of the busiest intersections and across the street from a tavern, I certainly can be allowed to empathize with Pulitzer. It has become impossible any longer to sit in my back yard or in my own living room and read a book without earplugs. Harley-Davidson motorcycles are the biggest offenders. Their noise is almost constant, especially on weekends. They are encouraged by the Church which engages in a Spring blessing ritual and are obliquely sanctioned by the city when it promotes motorcycle parades and issues no noise citations. Our police ride Harleys that are whisper-quiet so why can't the others be as well? Isn't it illegal to tamper with the muffling system on a vehicle? If it is, why aren't there tickets being written? I am not anti-motorcycle and fully understand their appeal. In fact, I have owned a motorcycle, off and on, for most of my adult life, always whisper-quiet Hondas.

Then there are the yahoos that ride around town with their million-watt speakers blasting rock and rap music. My windows actually rattle from this audio abomination. I once asked one of these near-deaf boobs why he didn't play Mozart or Beethoven. His response was a blank stare.

Music in commercial establishments may not be a problem for those who can tune it out. I live next to an Osco pharmacy and I find them to be good neighbors with excellent employees and products. But, I have often been compelled to leave because of the type of music they play. Ninety-five percent are vocals by no-talent female singers who screech about love. Why only female singers? I think this is what is so annoying about music in commercial places. Good grief, there are numerous other genre; classical, new age, even instrumentals would be a welcome relief. Better yet, turn it off! Why must we be constantly assailed everywhere by the myopic musical taste of some suit sitting in New York or California when all we really want is to patronize their business in peace? I once complained to the national headquarters of a recently opened chain restaurant about not being able to hold a conversation with my companion because the music was too loud. I was told, in a rather patronizing tone, that the employees are not allowed to turn down the volume or change the source. Isn't that wonderful? There is a recently-opened coffee shop in my neighborhood that only plays music of an Italian flavor at a humane volume. What a pleasure it is to patronize that place.

There are numerous other noise irritations; loud cell phone conversations, auto alarms, talking in movies, laugh tracks, jet skis, construction vehicle beepers, ice cream trucks, barking dogs, blaring radios. Today, the primary purpose of air conditioning in automobiles is not to cool the interior but to facilitate shutting out the noise.

All of this has a common denominator. It is all unnecessary and is inflicted on the majority by a self-centered, uncaring, minority. There are things that make one seethe and wonder why the offending party doesn't have the common decency and sense to know their actions bother, endanger, or trigger a discordant reaction in other people. But then, in a society where individuality is being renounced daily, that just may be the only ego trip remaining.

Strap-up the car seat and enjoy a Happy Meal

by Thomas J. Noer

My daughter and son-in-law are going to Europe for two weeks and my wife and I will be in charge of our beautiful and brilliant four-year-old granddaughter, Sophie. Babysitting grandchildren is an expected duty, but involves some major adjustments. To help, I offer the following tips for grandparents trusted with extended childcare.

Food: Very few children crave a tasty goat cheese salad and a nice glass of Chablis. Instead, you will find yourself dining on purple McFlurrys and encrusted poultry pieces dubbed, 'chicken nuggets.' You will also discover that many foods are 'yucky.' For a real bonding experience, take your grandchild to an all-you-can-eat buffet and count the number of dropped plates. Be sure to leave before they bring in the Shop-Vac to clean up where you sat.

Conversation: You are used to discussing prostrate problems, Social Security benefits, and senior citizen discounts. These topics are not of major interest to four-year-olds. Instead, you will hear the following phrases about 341 times per day: 'Why?' 'Let's all pretend we're cats!' 'Why?' 'My mommy lets me do it!' 'Why?' 'Do ladybugs talk?' and 'Why?' Practice the following responses: 'Because!' 'I don't know!' and 'Your mommy's not here!'

Clothing: Most grandparents have purchased several thousand adorable outfits for their grandchild. You will find kids don't want to wear any of these but prefer to dress as a princess, cowboy, mermaid, or rabbit. You will also discover they take great delight in wearing clothes inside out or backwards and putting shoes on the wrong feet. Accept the fact that you will never find matching socks.

TV: I have noticed very few grandchildren watch *CNN*, *Law and Order*, or the *Golf Channel*. You will have to adjust and learn the main characters on *Dora the Explorer*. (FYI, the monkey is named Boots and the evil fox is Swiper.) You should also know that many kids' programs are 'interactive' meaning you need to yell at the screen during *Blue's Clues* and *Elmo's World*. Finally, the dragons on *Dragon Tales* sometimes speak Spanish. This is not a sign of your senility, but a part of the show.

Travel: You will want to show off your grandchild to everyone in a five-state area, but this means transporting him/her in a car, just slightly more complicated than launching the space shuttle. First, you need to attach the car seat ... a minimum of 3-4 hours. The next step is strapping the kid in not so tight that they cannot breath or so loose they rattle around like coins in the dryer. You will also need a large tarp to catch the cheerios, crushed M&M's, and discarded juice boxes that will soon fill your back seat.

Sleep: It is documented fact that young children fall asleep the exact moment you arrive somewhere and will be groggy and cranky for the next two hours. Conversely, they rarely sleep at night. Don't be alarmed when a small person wanders into your bedroom at 3 AM and asks if you want to play *Puppies and Kittens* or spends an hour or two trying on lipstick and eyeliner while you doze.

Games: I've been unable to convince my granddaughter of the joys of bridge or cribbage. For some reason she prefers *Chutes and Ladders* (a frustrating contest where you slide down the ladder whenever you near victory), *Candyland* that involves avoiding evil chocolate things, and *Hi Ho Cheery-O* that requires screaming out the title endlessly. Kids also like computer games, but they require technical skills absent in anyone over the age of twenty-one.

Bathing: If you are in charge for more than a day or two, parents expect you to keep the kid clean. This means the dreaded 'bath.' A bath for young folk is far different than for adults. First you'll need a minimum of 34 toys in the tub. You also are required to have baby shampoo, baby conditioner, baby soap, baby wipes, baby toothpaste, and 89 other products. Also, one of the major goals of the child is to see how much water can be splashed out of the tub in the shortest time. Bring a raincoat, mop, and rubber gloves.

When the parents finally return and determine their offspring is alive and without major injury, they soon leave, taking your grandchild with them. After you put away the broken toys, clean up the crushed banana slices from the couch, and find all the abandoned color crayons in the kitchen sink, comes the hardest part ... that adorable, remarkable child is gone. The house is strangely silent. You and your spouse look at each other, cry a bit, and desperately start counting the days until the next visit.

When you turn 60, you move to Florida — it's the law

by Kenda Buxton

Some people ask, "Why do men climb mountains?" Instead, I ask, "Why do men spend the winter in Florida?"

In the words of George Leigh Mallory, "There is not the slightest prospect whatever of any gain. We shall neither bring back a single bit of gold or silver, nor a gem, nor any coal or iron. We shall not find a foot of earth that can be planted with crops to raise food. What we get from this adventure is sheer joy."

Mr. Mallory wasn't speaking of Florida as his destination when he said he couldn't plant crops or return with gold or silver. He was, in fact, speaking of mountains. On the other hand, my parents winter in Florida and they've never brought back gold or at least not that they've told me about, nor harvested any crops outside their mobile home, so maybe Mr. Mallory *was* talking about the Sunshine State.

Approximately 1.5 million people winter in Florida. Of those 1.5 million, 850,000 arrive in RV's. In the words of an Ohio man as he was exiting Florida in his 38-foot rig, "I've been snowbirding in Florida for twenty years and I'm sorry to say that Florida has become very commercial and has horrible traffic problems."

Gee, ya' think? With 850 thousand recreational vehicles careening into Florida each November, I'd say horrible traffic problems are a given, not to mention that Floridians are itching to sell you T-shirts that read, 'I'm spending my kid's inheritance in Florida.' Since 850 thousand of you are turning their roads into a commuter's nightmare, it stands to reason they want a chunk of your pension in return for their troubles. No wonder Florida residents say they're glad to see the snowbirds head north each April. I'd be glad to see them head north too, though I wouldn't want to be caught in traffic on the day they do.

So, if it's not for gold, silver, or the opportunity to raise crops that sends people to Florida each winter, what is it? What does Florida have, aside from mild weather that the remaining forty-nine states lack? According to my research, it's ... *restaurants*! Only a small percentage of snowbirds use the beaches or visit attractions like Disney World. A portion play golf and tennis, but the majority cite eating out as their main form of entertainment. I'm amending this last statement because I *know* the majority of snowbirds do four things as their main forms of entertainment; eat out, go to Wal-Mart, attend flea markets, and call their children back home to find out what the weather is like. I'm confident about this because when I speak to my mother each Sunday our conversation goes as follows:

"We've had a busy week."

"What did you do?"

"Went to Wal-Mart five times, went to the flea market three times, and ate out twice every day."

If you're headed to Florida, call me. As evidenced by my parent's daily visits to restaurants, I can give you a list of the best places to dine.

"Have you had any snow?"

"Some."

"How much?"

"An inch maybe."

"Oh."

This is when Mom sounds disappointed, as though nothing would give her more pleasure than finding out a blizzard has brought Kenosha County to a standstill. Evidently this would justify her expenses as a homeowner in two states.

"Is it cold?"

"Not very."

"Oh."

If I don't tell her it's sixty below zero, this also elicits disappointment. Apparently, you're entitled to bragging rights when you flock with your fellow snowbirds for breakfast, if you can claim to have snowbirded from the coldest state in the union.

This answers my question as to why people winter in Florida. It's not for gold, silver, or crops. It's to eat out, shop at Wal-Mart, and call their kids for a weather report. If you think traveling to Florida is a long way to journey to pursue such mundane activities, just be thankful there aren't 850 thousand RV's clogging Wisconsin's roadways.

So, the next time you talk to snowbirds tell them it's sixty below here. Even if that's not true, they'll have something to brag about when they eat out which, after all, is the *real* reason why people go to Florida.

What is, is. What isn't, isn't.

by Laurie McKeon

It's not as if I didn't realize that I am poised between youth and old age, but just in case I thought otherwise, life, with all of its characteristic lack of subtlety, has recently taken great pains to underscore the point.

My daughter impatiently waits for her college acceptance (rejection?) letters, eager to know what her future holds, full of hopes, plans, and dreams for a life now unfolding. While she is feeling an understandable anxiety, "What if I don't get into any college?" she is largely filled with an excitement and confidence that only the young can hold and "can't wait to go to college!" While it's so gratifying to watch my girl take that necessary next step toward adulthood, I would be deceiving myself if I did not acknowledge the tug at the back of my throat every time I think of her going away.

At this same time, my father sits in a hospital bed, kidneys failing and liver deteriorating. His health, gradually waning over the last few years, starts to noticeably and rapidly decline. His latest episode of kidney disease has left him permanently on dialysis and unable to walk. While his current condition has stabilized, his long-term prognosis is not good. In contrast to my daughter's verbalized desires to leave the nest, all my dad wants is go home.

As I help my daughter find the right college, pick a major, navigate dorm life and meal plans, I am calling social workers, visiting rehab facilities, dialysis centers, and nursing homes looking for the best long (short?) term solution for my father. As my daughter finishes off a last-minute essay, applies for scholarships, updates her applications, and constantly assesses her chances of getting into her top choices, I try to persuade my father to sign over a power of attorney, put our family home on the market, stop resisting the medication, and face the indignity of asking for help to the commode. Trust me, the full frontal irony of this situation has not gone unnoticed. Lately I find a black-humored amusement at my ability to negotiate with nursing home administrators (finding an available bed in a top notch rehab facility right now is WAY harder than getting into any Ivy League school) and college admissions offices with an equal fervor.

While I am reassuring my child that she will end up in the right place, will make the friends of a lifetime, will meet the challenges ahead, is fully prepared to take on a life full of promise, and attain her wildest dreams, I am reassuring my father that he will end up in the right place, will be well taken care of, can work hard in rehab, should be able to walk again, and just may be able to come home but, in my heart, I know that I am lying to at least one of them. For both of them, I just pray that we ask the right questions, gather the best information, and make the best decisions and choices given the knowledge available. I hope that I am giving solid advice that is helpful, comforting, and not totally misleading as they both face the unknown.

From my perspective, sitting squarely in the middle of these two lives, one at the beginning of adulthood and one at the end, I look back somewhat wistfully at the journey I know my daughter will take with all of its joys, challenges, heart break, and wonder. I look somewhat fearfully ahead at the place where my father is now poised. I know that some day, I too will be old, I too will be scared, and as much as I hate to admit it, I know too, that he and also I, will eventually die.

With this bird's eye view, still able to recall with utter clarity the anticipation of heading to college, yet gleaning a clearer vision of what the future may well hold, I've gained a realization and acceptance that despite my desires, I can't live the lives of either one of them. I understand the need to gently guide my daughter, allowing her to make her own mistakes, forging her own path, and learning to trust her own internal compass. Likewise, I need to respect my father's choices, his fears, and desires while easing him into this last phase of his life with some dignity and decency. I can't erase the pain and fear my dad has felt any more than I can stop the hurt and sorrow that I know my daughter will inevitable experience.

I do take comfort in knowing that my father had a life full of family, children, friends, and laughter and that my daughter has all that to look forward to and more. Children grow up, parents die, and somehow it is those of us in the middle that act as the fulcrum, balancing the beginning, the end, and all that is in between.

Let's start a Lydia Pinkham bandwagon for president

by Ed Groelle

Have you ever noticed the similarity between political campaign promises and the claims of medicines in TV ads? This led me to think about not only their similarity, but also of the surprising fact that neither has changed very much during my lifetime. Out of curiosity I began do a "Whatever happened to ...?" study into some potions from the past.

In a splendid leap of logic, about a hundred years ago, doctors identified the cause of violent crime, suicide, nervous exhaustion, insomnia, fatigue, headaches, confusion, bad skin, baldness, tuberculosis, gum disease, cancer, poverty, and spinsterhood. The culprit was poor blood and/or constipation. Slightly nefarious entrepreneurs recognized the potential and marketed their home remedies.

Serutan was an early Metamucil-type laxative that was widely promoted in the media and was marketed until the 1960's. The advertising slogan was, "Read it backwards" ... as though that somehow verified its effectiveness.

Carter's Little Liver Pills was touted to cure headaches, irritability, constipation, and bad complexions. It also claimed clear eyes, clean tongue, and perfect health. Government nitpickers forced the manufacturer to remove the word 'liver' which made the pills less appealing to the public and the brand just faded away.

Hadacol was marketed as a vitamin supplement. Its principal attraction to many was that it contained twelve percent alcohol making it quite popular in southern dry counties. The developer, Louisiana state Senator Dudley LeBlanc, was not a physician or a pharmacist, but that was not an obstacle for him. When Groucho asked LeBlanc what Hadacol was good for, he answered, "It was good for five and a half million dollars for me last year."

Toothache Relief - I don't remember the name of this product but do remember having it in our family medicine cabinet. It consisted of a tweezers and two tiny bottles. One bottle contained tiny cotton balls and the other oil of cloves. You would pluck a cotton ball with the tweezers, dip it into the clove oil, and then push the ball into your tooth cavity. It actually worked and postponed the visit to our dentist who used the spit sink as much as his patients since he chewed tobacco. I was amazed to find a very similar product still being sold over-the-counter today.

Lydia Pinkhams Vegetable Compound was a medicine for *all those painful complaints so common to our female population,* meaning mostly menstruation. Many regard her as a crusader for women's health in a day when doctors, more often than not, scoffed at womens' ailments. Lydia was a teetotaler, but she also understood human nature, so cleverly added twenty percent alcohol, thereby alleviating many health problems for her customers.

Laetrile is the only product here whose demise I can empathize with. It was made from crushed apricot pits and was aimed at curing or alleviating the ravages of cancer at a time when few cancer treatments existed. Many users swore to its effectiveness and some claimed a complete cure. When the pharmaceutical companies realized it was cutting into their line of potions they successfully sued the government to declare it illegal. Its manufacture was then moved to Mexico making it, possibly, our first industry to go offshore. Sound familiar?

We like to assume these entrepreneurs were snake oil salesmen and took advantage of people's medical innocence. However, didn't they just provide people with some hope, respite, and escape from whatever ailed them? In fact, isn't what they claimed for their medicines almost exactly what our politicians are promising us now, a quick fix for whatever ails us, real or imagined? Both give me the uneasy sensation of being taken for a ride. Both products are alive and well but in much slicker packaging and lacking the alcohol. Watch some TV medicine ads or walk down any pharmacy aisle and it is obvious that not much has changed in one hundred years. At least medicine ads, unlike political ads, have the decency to warn us of the side effects.

Ed Groelle

It's too bad Lydia and Dudley are gone. They could form a desperately needed third-party presidential slate. Now, there's a winning idea. Lydia Pinkham for president and Dudley LeBlanc for Vice-President. Campaign slogan: "You're going to get exactly what you paid for."

Don't spam my blog or I might go Tyson on you

by Thomas J. Noer

I was blogging some metrosexuals when I was ginormously spammed and everything cometised. I went completely Tyson and wanted to Swayze those netizens!

Confused? Well you haven't kept up with the language of the 21st century. Many of us in the older generation are unaware of new terminology. Just when we learned the verb "to network" and what "outsourcing" means, along come more new words. Making up new words is called "neologism" (a nice cocktail party term). Below is a quiz of ten new words I have created to see if you are "krunk." Answers at end.

BTW, *blogs* are Internet journals read by bloggers. *Metrosexuals* are straight guys who go to hairdressers and spas. *Ginormously* is a combination of gigantic and enormous. *Spam* is unwanted e-mail and *cometized* is when Netscape crashes (named after the little star on the screen). To go *Tyson* is to lose control like the boxer and to *Swayze* someone is to beat them up (after Partick Swayze in the movie Roadhouse). *Netizens* are Internet junkies (net citizens) and *krunk* means awesome. Now, don't you feel smart?

1. Kerryoke:

   A. A large tree. "We should plant a kerryoke in the backyard."

   B. A new flavor of Coke. "Try a glass of refreshing kerryoke!"

   C. Someone who bores us with old slogans. "He's just kerryokeing that issue!"

2. Martha:

   A. A scenic island near Massachusetts. "We stayed at really a nice resort on Martha."

   B. A convenient store. "Run to the Mart-Ha and get some milk."

C. To blow everything for a few dollars. "Man, he just marthaed his career!"

3. Cellannoyic:

A. A severe allergy. "She had a cellannoyic reaction to the seafood."

B. A biologist. "He's in college studying to be a cellannoyic."

C. An annoying phone user. "Tell that cellannoyic to take it outside!"

4. Idolist:

A. A lazy person. "He does nothing all day, a real idolist!"

B. To worship an image. "The ancient Romans idolisted at the temple."

C. One who is addicted to bad reality TV. "I'm so idolistic I want to have Simon's baby!"

5. Bushmentalized:

A. To plant shrubs. "She bushmentalized her yard."

B. To be fatigued. "I was up all night and am really bushmentalized."

C. The inability to speak clear English. "I don't understand what he is saying. It's all bushmentalized!"

6. Cub:

A. To hold a child. "He cubbed the cute baby."

B. To spit up. "I cubbed that piece of candy when it got stuck in my mouth."

C. To fail at the end. "I was doing fine but I completely cubbed the final exam!"

7. DaVinci:

A. To add spices to pasta. "I DaVincied the lasagna with oregano."

B. Name of an Italian guy. "Hey! It's my man, da Vincie!"

C. To search a bad novel for religious significance. "I have been DaVincing that book for a year and still can't figure out Mary Magdalene!"

8. Gasly:

A. Something terrible. "That movie was just gasly!"

B. Indigestion. "Eating that garlic and perch pizza made me gasly."

C. Rage after fueling your car. "I paid $35 to fill-up and went totally gasly!"

9. Starbuck:

A. A small deer. "Oh, look at the darling little star buck!"

B. A special dollar bill. "Mom gave Suzy a star buck for her allowance."

C. To pay way too much for a cup of coffee. "$4.00 for an espresso? You got starbucked!"

10. Noer:

A. Stunningly handsome. "That Brad Pitt is a real Noer!"

B. Incredibly brilliant. "Einstein sure was a Noer!"

C. To write something of absolutely no significance. "That column was a complete Noer."

Answers

1. Kerryoke: C: In Honor of John Kerry, to kerryoke is to offer unoriginal ideas in a way to put us to sleep.

2. Martha: C: Named after Martha Stewart, to martha means to destroy everything for a few dollars.

3. Cellannoyics C: yak endlessly in their cell phones in airports and restaurants. It is OK to Swayze them.

4 Idolist C: People who watch *American Idol* and think it is real are clearly idolists.

5. Bushmentalized: C: Named after George W. Bushmentalized and can lead to words like "misunderstandingly."

6. Cub: C: To recognize the futility of a certain Chicago sports team. To cub is to always fail in the end.

7. DaVincied: C: Readers of *The DaVinci Code* who seek enlightenment in a book that reads like a bad chase movie have been DaVincied.

8.Gasly: C: To feel gasly is a natural response to paying more for a tank of unleaded than you did for the car you put it in.

9. Starbucked: C: To be starbucked is to overpay for a cheap product. (It also applies to bottled water and trolley rides.)

10. Noer: C: Also, a combination of any or all of the above! If you don't agree, I will go Tyson on you!

As a child your parents forced you to eat What?!

by Ed Groelle

What is patriotism but the love of the food one ate as a child? ~Lin Yutang

For twenty years my mother baked twenty-two loaves of bread a week in a wood-fired stove. We were allowed to eat the new batch only after the old was eaten. As a sympathetic concession she always made a tiny loaf we could eat immediately, right out of the oven. This, inevitably, raised a *dispute* among her five sons particularly over who got the crust ... the best slices. At butchering time we also made scrapple, which was made from the pig's ears, nose, and anything that fell on the floor. This was formed into loaves with cornmeal, then sliced and fried in lard. Delicious, especially with that homemade bread. If interested, you can still buy frozen scrapple at Woodman's.

Children hate liver but if they are lucky they will grow into it, provided they are not forced. It's especially delicious next day when you have it cold between two slices of Italian bread with raw, sliced Vidalia onions and mayo, washed down with a cold Michelob beer. That's as close as heaven comes on earth.

Never liked olives until I discovered the open markets in Greece with twenty-foot long tables of olives ranging from white to black, sweet to sour. Loved them ever since. There should be a law in this country prohibiting the stuffing of olives or removing the pit. That borders on sacrilege.

A long time ago, in France, I went with three friends to a restaurant where we ate ten dozen snails accompanied by a bottle of Cognac. I've loved snails ever since. Unfortunately, snails only taste as they should in France. Here in the US they take them out of cans and as an additional indignation, serve them on a porcelain plate with individual indentations. Serving snails without their shells is just as sacrilegious as removing the pits from olives.

Not picky about food, but there is one dish I simply can't stand ... potato pancakes. Potatoes are a lot like bread dough, form it differently and it always tastes differently depending on its shape. Leave out the leavening from bread and you've got fish food or communion wafers; boil it in water and you've got dumplings; add caraway seeds, etc. and you can proclaim it an ethic delicacy. Very metamorphic, bread and pasta.

Plum pudding usually pops up at Christmastime on English television programs. It's a lot like our fruitcakes, i.e., best used as a doorstop. If an attempt is made to eat it, first put it on a bed of vanilla ice cream and douse liberally with rum. If you can ignite it at this time, try a bit. If not, give it another good rum soak.

From a distance, the odor of Taiwanese stinky tofu resembles that of sewage or a garbage dump. It consists of tofu that has been marinated in brine with fermented (read rotten) vegetables for as long as several months. In spite of stinky tofu's smell, the flavor is surprisingly mild. It tastes a bit like blue cheese and the more it smells, the better it tastes. It is sometimes served with goose blood soup.

Egyptian and Israeli falafel is made from fava beans or chickpeas. The beans are soaked, skinned, ground with the addition of onions and spices, and then deep-fried. To me, it has no taste. If you are going to sample it be sure to have a McDonald's ketchup packet with you. Just don't let any Egyptians see you applying it. The Israelis won't care.

Norwegian lutefisk is made from air-dried whitefish prepared with lye in a sequence of treatments. First, the fish is soaked in cold water for a week, then soaked in a solution of water and lye for two more days. They are then perfect as emergency repairs to your shoe soles. I have a better word for it, which is unprintable here.

Smorgasbord is the Swedish word for hodge-podge. A true Swedish smorgasbord will usually produce a quizzical look on the face of most Americans. American smorgasbord and Swedish smorgasbord are very different. In Sweden it consists mainly of a variety of lumpy, fishy things usually covered with a mysterious yellow sauce. To enhance the disappointment there are seldom any desserts.

Haggis is a traditional Scottish dish. It is made with sheep's heart, liver, and lungs, minced with onion, oatmeal, suet, spices, salt, stock, and then boiled in the sheep's stomach for about an hour. Let's call it what it is ... stuffed sheep guts. You'll need to go to Scotland for this one. It cannot be imported because the USDA has declared it "unfit for human consumption." Yep, internal organs of sheep boiled inside its stomach. It's either fanatically loved or reviled by the Scots.

Some of the items I've denigrated should really be tried before taking my word for it. If you are reluctant consider that, at one time, the French thought hamburgers and corn on the cob to be primeval. New tastes can be delightful travel experiences and you too may like some of these. The natives all appear to, but then, they just might also spit out my scrapple. Philistines!

My nemesis — inanimate objects. They hate me

by Jim Wynne

It appears that I owe the readers of this column an apology and an explanation. The reaction to last month's column, judging from the VOP contributions, was such that I've come to the conclusion that I must have been wrong. In case you missed the column in question, I opined that Conservatives were well on the way to canonizing Ronald Reagan even before his death was announced and that they seemed to be overlooking some aspects of his presidency that might cast a more negative light on His legacy. The extent of the hoopla over Reagan's passing was such that one would have thought that a truly great American had died … someone like Hugh Hefner, for example. One irate letter writer flatly stated that most of the piece was wrong, and although he offered no counter arguments in support of that contention, it appears that he might have been right.

In trying to determine what could have possibly made me think such obviously wrong thoughts, such as that the Reagan administration produced indictments and felony convictions on a par with Richard Nixon's, it occurred to me that just prior to writing the column I received a substantial blow to the head from a renegade bungee cord. I was in the back lot at Menard's trying to secure a new storm door to the top of my van. I hooked the rubber bungee on one side of the vehicle, then went around to the other side to stretch it across and secure it when it let loose and snapped back with the metal hook striking me squarely between the eyes. The description of the event is based on the evidence at hand and conjecture, as all I'm really sure of is that I found myself flat on my back, my glasses smashed to bits, and blood all over my face. I suppose it's possible that some unseen assailant, possibly an irate letter-writer, knocked me arse-over-tin-kettle with a large blunt object, but I don't think so.

This was one in a series of blows to the head that I've received from inanimate objects over the years, the cumulative effect of which might further explain my difficulty in understanding the Conservative way of thinking. I was once, for example, attacked by the hood of my car. I stopped at a gas station one blustery morning to get fuel and check the oil. The car was a 1988 Chevy Sprint, a tiny vehicle with a three-cylinder engine and body panels made from sheet metal so thin that without paint they were probably translucent. I opened the hood, set the prop rod in place, and then proceeded to pull out the dipstick to check the oil. A sudden and violent gust of wind came up, pushing the hood up and back, off of the prop rod. The force of the backwards motion (i.e., towards the car's windshield) caused the hood, after it had traveled as far as its hinges would allow, to rebound and start back towards the closed position and my head. At that very moment there was another gust of wind, opposite in direction from the first that sealed my fate. The hood latch struck me in the middle of the forehead before I realized what was happening. Once again I found myself prostrate, dazed, and bleeding. All the aforementioned activity took place in the space of no more than a second, so that I was scarcely aware of what was happening and had no chance whatsoever to get out of the way. The effect was the same as if a large person had picked the hood up, held it over his head, swung it down, and slammed me in the face with it. I assume, again, that that's not what happened, especially since I didn't write an op-ed column at the time.

There was also an incident several years earlier involving my cranium and a steel stop-sign pole, but space doesn't allow me to tell about it in the detail the story deserves. Suffice it to say that the pole leaped into my path as I was crossing a busy Chicago street trying to avoid an oncoming car, and my injuries would probably have been less severe and far less embarrassing had I just let the car run me over.

So, to any readers who were offended by my less-than-reverential treatment of the passing of St. Ronald of Trickle-Down, I apologize, and I do so not so much because I really believe that I was wrong, but because The Voices told me to, and they are the same ones who told me I needed a new storm door.

New Year's resolutions go in one year and out the other

by Kenda Buxton

Supreme Court nominations, the war in Iraq, the identity of Deep Throat, and Michael Jackson (yet again) are just a few of the subjects that made news during 2005. While I try to come up with a resolution for 2006 that I haven't already made and broken during some past New Year, let's bid farewell to the year gone by.

"You want a friend in Washington? Get a dog." **(Harry S. Truman)** By the time she'd finished answering the 57-page questionnaire entitled, "Why I Want to be a Supreme Court Justice," only to have Senators Arlen Specter and Patrick Leahy return it with a big red "Incomplete" stamped across the top, Harriet Miers was desperate for a friend in Washington. With Republicans attacking Miers for being too liberal, and Democrats attacking her for being too conservative, the beleaguered and undoubtedly confused woman withdrew her nomination. If Ms. Miers hasn't heeded Harry Truman's advice, maybe she should. After all, a dog doesn't care whether you support abortion or oppose it, and he'll never ask you to fill out a questionnaire about anything when you could be taking him for a walk instead.

"It's like *déjà vu* all over again." (Yogi Berra) During 2005, Michael Jackson was once again accused of child molestation. Only the eccentric Jackson would arrive at a courthouse dressed in pajama bottoms and slippers, while claiming back problems had hospitalized him. Given Mr. Jackson's wealth, you'd think *someone* on his payroll could have brought him a pair of pants and some shoes before he was discharged. Since his acquittal, Jackson has moved to the Middle Eastern nation of Bahrain. While I'd like to think this relocation means we've heard the last of Michael Jackson, based on past experience I have a feeling that, where Jackson is concerned, it'll eventually be *déjà vu* all over again.

"I really don't believe in magic." (J. K. Rowling) The author of the popular Harry Potter series may not believe in magic, but her books and the movies based on them, seem to continuously generate it. During its opening weekend in U.S. theaters, *Harry Potter and the Goblet of Fire* grossed 101.4 million dollars. Regardless of whether or not you believe in magic, that's nothing to shake your wand at, or your Nimbus 2000 broomstick, either.

"I am not Deep Throat and the only thing I can say is that I wouldn't be ashamed to be, because I think whoever it was helped the country, no question about it." (W. Mark Felt, Sr.) Thirty years after he claimed not to be Deep Throat, Mark Felt, now 92, announced that he was, in fact, the man who fed information to Washington Post reporter Bob Woodward about the Watergate break-in. Debate is still on-going as to whether or not Felt's identity as Deep Throat *did* help the country, but if nothing else, it inspired this famous quote by Richard Nixon, "Well, I screwed it up real good, didn't I?" followed closely by, "I hereby resign this office of president of the United States."

"I liken it [Medicare Prescription Drug Law] to quantum physics ... expect I understand quantum physics better." (Mark Fuller, Executive Director, Biotech Medical Management Association) 2005 found senior citizens confused and uncertain over the new Medicare prescription drug program. With some states offering 65 different plans to choose from, it's no wonder a guy can figure out quantum physics easier than he can figure out which drug plan to sign up for.

"Old men declare war. But it is the youth that must fight and die." (Herbert Hoover) Regardless of whether you support our presence in Iraq or oppose it, President Hoover was correct. As the conflict continues, it is, unfortunately, the youth who must fight and die.

And so, 2005 leaves us with the knowledge that a dog is often our only true friend, a good book can inspire an abundance of magic, quantum physics is easier to understand than most of our government programs, and sadly, the cost of war is our youth.

As 2005 now makes way for 2006, I'll quote Oprah Winfrey by saying, "Cheers to a new year, and another chance for us to get it right."

Merry Christmas, everyone
Your American cornucopia is
overflowing and waiting

by Ed Groelle

Recently, I had no bananas for my cereal. Panicsville! I went to the store assuming it would have bananas. I was right. This set me thinking about how American food production and distribution has evolved to a point where I can go to any store and expect to buy bananas at any time; winter, summer, day, or night. I know nothing about banana production but am familiar with the production of milk. My experiences may be a bit dated but probably still valid.

Let's pretend you've decided to become a dairy farmer. You've always admired those picturesque black and white animals leisurely grazing in fields. How difficult could it be? With the price of milk at $3.50 a gallon it must be very profitable. So, you buy a farm, eighty acres for $500,000 ... a steal; $100,000 down scraped from friends and relatives and the farm as collateral.

The farm has a dairy barn but checking with the County Agent reveals problems. The milking arrangements are hopelessly out of specs. Milk cannot be exposed to air or contact anything but sterile stainless steel and polyethylene. There must be refrigerated holding tanks and equipment rooms as sterile as an OR. Ok, just a bit more expense than you had planned, but it doesn't dampen your dreams. Anyway, you are certain that money will soon be rolling in faster than you can count it.

Buying heifers (virgin cows) turns out to be a tad more involved than you thought. That cute metal tag or tattoo in a cow's ear is not a bovine personal statement. Those numbers refer to a record containing every detail of its life. For the records you'll need to name each cow ... Elsie and Daisy are particularly popular. Don't laugh! As a conscientious dairyman you will know your cows more intimately than your in-laws.

You cough up about $10,000 for six top-of-the-line heifers from the heifer broker. Hopefully, you have harvested your farm for their food. If not, you will find the cost of feed roughly equivalent to that of noble metals. Cows must give birth to produce milk, so you'll need to engage a cattle artificial breeder for his expertise. His services will cost approximately $50 per pop and a cow requires two pops to ensure success. The heifers must be watched carefully for a sign of being "in heat." They can conceive only for about a ten-hour period each month so you must be on the alert twenty-four hours a day, every day.

OK. So far, so good. You now have six pregnant heifers that will become milking cows in nine months when they give birth. You want only female calves that you can raise to replace cows that have reached their milking age span of about eight years. Use this waiting period to buy a PC and set up your record keeping. This is crucial for building a good herd. Also, take a vacation. It'll be the last one for a long time. Cows are creatures of habit and demand milking at the same times, twice a day, every day. They don't take sick days or holidays and neither will you. To help with maintaining a dairy farm you put a veterinarian and a tax consultant on retainer.

After the calves are born you will need to watch for a time when the milk is clear so you can begin shipping it. Selling the milk turns out to be not such a get-rich-quick endeavor. Farming is one of the few industries in which the buyer dictates the price. Take it or leave it. The only way you can affect the price is to develop high butterfat content.

You will never be alone in your dairy endeavors. You will be on a first-name basis with your banker, veterinarian, county agent, and a host of inspectors whose visits will be unannounced. Your milk will be tested and retested, not only by them, but also by the truck driver who picks up your milk. Any hint of medicine or foreign substances will result in kissing your 1000-gallon tank of milk "Goodbye!"

Fast-forward twenty years. The conglomerates haven't put you out of business and you have developed a first class, pedigreed, milking herd. You are content and proud of the success but still deep in debt. If there is any justice at all, you will now have a son who will take over when you retire, assuming he doesn't want to be a rock star or Packer lineman.

Tomorrow, when you belly up to the table for Christmas dinner, reflect on the above scenario and be grateful for the multitude of workers and systems that are working to bring you this cornucopia of great eating. Enjoy it and have a Merry Christmas.

Advanced technology seems a lot like magic

by Laurie Mckeon

About a month ago, absolutely unsolicited and without any warning or fanfare, a little blue rectangular box started appearing every now and then in the upper left corner of our TV screen. The box contained a name and seemed to arrive just as our phone rang. How very curious. After a while, (not the sharpest knives are we) we figured out that this blue rectangle was in fact, wonder of wonders, caller ID displayed on our TV! It was like witnessing the invention of fire.

At first the blue box kind of freaked us out. How dare someone usurp a portion of our new 42-inch flat screen with a name and number? Then, we sort of got used to it. It was kind of nice to know who was calling us before we went to pick up the phone. Now, we are in love with the blue box and cannot live without it. Until we had this amazing, vital feature I had no idea just how much effort it took to peel my eyes away from the TV screen, actually get up, lift the receiver from the cradle, and answer the telephone. It's exhausting just thinking about it. Now, if the phone rings during *Dancing with the Stars*, I know exactly who's calling without having to so much as shift my retinas and miss one second of Jane Seymour's eye popping jitterbug. Caller ID on TV (we're not quite sure what this life-altering device is called) allows me to ignore a ringing phone with full knowledge of the person I'm ducking. That's some real innovation. "Oh, it's just dad, we can call him back during a commercial." How did humanity ever survive without this cutting edge technology?

I love modern conveniences. Seriously, I'm glued to my cell phone, go gaga for Google, and would be totally lost without my car, dishwasher, water heater, microwave, iPod, vacuum, and every other twentieth century invention. I'd rather give up a kidney than lose electricity. And I'm not even kidding when I say that I am way more attached to my two front-loading washers and my commercial dryer than I am to any and all of my first cousins. I must admit that I have an enormous fondness for any business that has a drive-thru (I'm still waiting for the drive-thru gym) and any innovation that saves me time, money, or both.

I'm plenty old enough to remember life before PC's, CD's, DVD's, ATM's, GPS, and TiVo. When I mention to my kids that we used to make popcorn and bacon on the stove they act like I'm describing a Victorian taffy pull. They can't believe that I used to wash dishes by hand, devote hours to make a party tape, and talked on a phone tethered to a wall. But, the real killer for them is that people used to get up from their chairs to change the channels on the television. This is beyond their comprehension. Heck, I still refuse to watch TV with my dad as I spent most of my early childhood years acting as his manual television remote control in the pre-clicker era.

So, I am fully aware of all the benefits that modern engineering has produced and am vocally thankful for every one of them. But, I also realize just how quickly modern innovations become everyday necessities and take hold of our lives. Remember when only doctors and drug dealers had pagers and cell phones? Now, every self-respecting seventh grader is sporting a Razor and lobbying for an *iPhone* for Christmas. Lately, technology has gone beyond making life easier to making life just plain lazier. Let's face it! As a society, we invent, mass produce, and purchase in bulk just about anything that keeps us from having to break the seal between our backsides and the sofa, *Barca* lounger, or driver's seat. (it's not called a *Lazy Boy* for nothing)

There are robotic floor vacuums, hands free phones, voice activated grocery lists, the car that parallel parks itself, and who can forget the *Clapper*? I recently read about a machine that automatically turns your ice cream cone as you lick it. C'mon … if eating an ice cream cone is too taxing, then you might as well just pack it in. The survival skills so carefully honed by our hunter and gatherer forbearers are atrophying by the minute.

Although most of these conveniences purport to save time or make the world safer, we are really just kidding ourselves. It's not like anyone is using the time saved by clapping off the bedroom light to cure cancer or alleviate world hunger. Hardly! I must confess I'm fully wasting any extra time that I might have saved just sitting on the sofa, hoisting my remote, and ignoring our ringing phone because I have the mother of all inventions ... TV Caller ID.

Searching for Tarzan on the Dark Continent

by Ed Groelle

I just returned from a 24-day trip to Africa. Easy folks! I can hear your groans from here so I promise that this will be more entertaining than the usual Bush-bashing or school overcrowding. I went to find the dark continent of my youth, the comic book land of Tarzan and Jane. Africa is huge, 2 ½ times the size of the United States so it would be very presumptuous of anyone to claim even minimal knowledge after such a short and limited trip, but here are my impressions anyway.

The first step was to get my yellow immunization card up to date with six shots and a couple of take-along prescriptions. Some countries will not let you in without that card and some will not let you out. I didn't mind doing this because I like my doctor. She has seen me naked on several occasions and still likes me, and more importantly, she didn't laugh.

The next step was to get a South African airline ticket for a twenty-seven-hour brain and butt-numbing flight from Chicago to Cape Town, Africa on planes designed to accommodate persons no taller than five feet. This experience reaffirmed my conviction that all airplanes should have their seats welded in to the upright position so the numbskull in the seat in front of you cannot put his seat back into your lap.

South Africa is the most similar to the U.S. of any country in Africa but the arrival in Cape Town is still a shock since the route from the airport to town goes through some of the most appalling slums in the world. But, Cape Town is a gleaming city with fierce nationalistic citizens who are still struggling with a turbulent history and are very proud of their race relation advances. The high point of this visit was standing with the baboons on the very tip of the African continent, where the Indian and Atlantic oceans meet, and watching the whales frolicking and blowing their top. To me, South Africa is a first-world country on a third world continent.

On to Kenya, a complete cultural change from South Africa and full of pleasant surprises. You will not see any white faces anywhere except for the tourist areas and everyone seems to speak English, even the Maasai people. Looking into the crater of Mt. Kilimanjaro is a thrill, but the main reason people come to Kenya is to safari and to experience animals in the wild. Animals seem somehow different when viewed without bars in their natural habitat. In what zoo can you see a baby elephant showing off to its mother or watch a warthog settle a dispute with a zebra? I will always now feel empathy for animals kept in a zoo. To stand on the Serengeti Plain and be surrounded by thousands of elephants, giraffes, zebras, etc. as far as the eye can see in all directions is almost a religious experience.

My next and last stop was Egypt, a major force in Africa and the Middle East, where few speak English and there are more AK-47's than Christians seen the streets. This was my second visit to Egypt and the increase in tourism was striking. Where before I had stood with a handful of tourists, now there were hundreds. The tourist boats on the Nile had increased from twenty to over three hundred. Where before there were twenty people watching the night laser show at the pyramids, there is now seating for a thousand. There is a spot where you can get a perfect camera shot of the Sphinx and if you turn and face the opposite direction, you can also get a perfect shot of a KFC/Pizza Hut. You gotta love progress.

Everyone comes to Egypt to see the Sphinx and the pyramids, but the real treasures of Egypt are in its streets and markets along with the slow, pleasant trip up the Nile to the Aswan Dam where the beautiful Nubians live. The cruise alone is worth the trip.

African has a major HIV/Aids problem (22% in South Africa), but everyone I talked with was much more concerned with the scourge of malaria, which kills millions every year. The hum of a mosquito is more feared than the roar of any wild animal.

Everywhere the people were friendly and anxious to show us their lifestyle and homes, even the Maasai who invited us into one of their villages with houses made entirely from cow manure.

No, I didn't find the land of Tarzan. Edgar Rice Burroughs had it all wrong. Africa is no longer the Dark Continent, if it really ever was. Everywhere they are turning up the lights against overwhelming difficulties. To many travelers, Africa is off the beaten path. It shouldn't be.

An innovative way to make newspapers more entertaining

by Ed Groelle

Once a week at Gateway Technical College I read the Racine Journal on WGTD radio for the benefit of vision-impaired people. It's a volunteer job that requires me to search the newspaper for local items and news that couldn't possibly make the commercial broadcast news reports. In the past year, for my own amusement, I've taken to thinking up my own comments to some of the articles. Sometimes they will also trigger a remembrance of a joke I have long forgotten. It's too bad I'm not allowed to air them. Here are some news item examples. My ad-libs are in italics.

~ A commentary on the increasing interest of metal detecting as a hobby. *This summer I'm going to the beach to bury metallic objects with, "Tag, You're it!" written on them.*

~ According to official statistics one-third of all workplace accidents go unreported. *How could anyone possibly know that?*

~ A want ad asking people to help in recovering a lost dog complete with a detailed description. *Wouldn't it be less expensive to just buy an ad in the paper that reads, "Here boy!"?*

~ A Canadian psychologist advertising his video that will test your dog's IQ. *If you send for that video isn't your dog's IQ really higher than yours?*

~ A report on how countries around the world are preparing their entrants for the Miss Universe pageant. *Why is the winner of the Miss Universe contest always from Earth? Why aren't Mars and Venus ever invited?*

~ A man tried to kill himself by taking 1000 aspirins. *After taking two wouldn't he feel much better and just abandon the idea?*

~ This article described the affects of excessive video game playing on the development of children. *This is nonsense! I played Pac-Man and if I were affected I'd be running around in labyrinth, munching pills, and listening to repetitive music.*

~ I read a couple of articles one day of Winnie the Pooh and Alexander the Great. *Isn't it unusual that two such diverse people would have the same middle name?*

~ A financial article reporting on the trials and tribulations of the extremely rich. It appears many complain that there is nothing left to do and no more interesting acquisitions to be attained. *And you thought you had problems.*

~ A very well written article detailing the discomfort of a woman who was in labor for thirty-six hours. *Good Grief! I can't even think of anything that feels good I'd want to do for thirty-six hours.*

~ An article on the popularity of the martial arts movies and the extensive training needed by the actors. *Is any training really required to make some of the worst movies in the history of the world?*

~ A medical report of both the advantages and complications for men using the almost "soon to be released" male birth control pill. *It does make sense to take the bullets out of the gun rather than to wear a bulletproof vest.*

~ Macabre, maybe, but this old joke sprang to mind while reading the obituaries. A woman called the newspaper and wanted them to insert a death notice for her husband. She was a miser and just wanted the words, "Angus Dead" printed. When informed that the minimum was five words she said, "OK. Use Angus Dead, Volvo for sale." *If she exists and we can find her, we should get her into political speech writing ASAP.*

~ A commentary on the appeal that professional wrestling has for some people. *Isn't it strange we live in a country where a significant portion of the population think professional wrestling is real but the moon landing is not?*

~ An article which stated that one in five people in the world are Chinese. *I have four brothers and I tried to figure which one was Chinese. It could be my older brother John or my younger brother Ho-Chan-Chu, but I'm almost certain it is John.*

~ One of the 2008 presidential candidates said that he wants every intelligent person in America to vote for him. *That won't be enough. He will need a majority.*

You get the idea. Try it sometime. You'll find the news much more palatable.

Burning books isn't easy. They're hard to light

by Kenda Buxton

All true Christians (as opposed to untrue Christians, I'm-Only-Here-Because-My-Wife-Made-Me-Attend Christians, and the I-Only-Go-To-Church-On-Major-Holidays Christians) have been called upon to decrease the number of Harry Potter books circulating in America.

On a website devoted to the supposed dangers of Harry Potter, one minister is quoted as having said, "We're giving True Christian children the Biblical authority to remove these evil books from their libraries, bookstores, and anywhere they find them. All they need to say is, "Jesus wants me to take this book!"

I have my doubts that, "Jesus wants me to take this book!" will keep a little *Warrior Against Harry Potter* out of jail when he's caught stealing. I also suspect someone has put a Memory hex on that minister, since he's apparently forgotten the Eighth Commandment; Thou Shalt Not Steal. If, by chance, the child does escape detection by hiding beneath an *Invisibility Cloak*, which works great for Harry, then he can ignite the Holy Ghost fire the minister recommends for burning those pilfered Harry Potter books, unless someone puts an *Extinguishing Spell* on the blaze. In that case, he'll have to find another way to rid the world of the infamous boy wizard. Personally, I recommend the *Library Book Spell*. Why go to the trouble of banning Harry Potter from your school's library and risk being unpopular with your neighbors, who may put a *Twitchy Ears Hex* on you, when all that's needed is for the Hogwart's school librarian, Madam Pince, to put a curse on the books so they scream, "Keep your grubby little paws off me!" if any child gets within thirty feet of them.

As an avid reader since the age of eight, it's difficult for me to comprehend burning books, banning books, destroying books, or in any way discouraging a child from reading. I don't fault parents for making rules for their children, even rules that prevent their kids from reading Harry Potter. Every parent has that right. I don't, however, agree with anyone who attempts to govern what other children can check out from their school's library. That deserves nothing less than the *Silencing Charm*, which shouldn't need an ounce of explanation, regardless of whether or not you're a fan of Harry Potter. Since I have yet to see hoards of children walking down the streets carrying magic wands, or congregating on playgrounds dressed in wizard robes, or gathered around a steaming cauldron while attempting to perfect the *Vanishing Teacher* potion, I believe I'm safe in saying that the majority of kids reading Harry Potter can distinguish between the fantasy that dwells within a work of fiction and the reality of the world we dwell in. In my opinion, Harry Potter is just good old-fashion fun and not laden with secret messages meant to lure young minds to the dark side. J. K. Rowling's only message is that she is a talented storyteller who pens riveting fiction that makes the reader ache to turn the page and find out what happens next.

There's no denying that some children are easily influenced by what they see, hear, and read, and no denying that parents must monitor what their kids are exposed to. However, I doubt most children believe they can put a *Jelly Legs Jinx* on the schoolyard bully any more than I believe I can put a *Scouring Charm* on my bathroom (despite an attempt that left me dizzy, and with Comet in one hand and a sponge in the other). Nor do I believe Harry Potter encourages children to practice witchcraft any more than *Charlotte's Web* encouraged me to marry a hog farmer ... well, all right, bad example. How about ... any more than *Bible Stories for Children* made me think I could build an ark, slay a giant named Goliath, or part the Red Sea. The real "magic" in Harry Potter has little to do with fictional witches, wizards, spells, and hexes, but instead, has everything to do with the magic of a good book and how, when we open the world of reading to a child, we open a world of enjoyment, a world of make-believe, a world of new people, places, and experiences, but most of all, we open a world of knowledge.

And if you don't believe me, all I can say is watch out for that *Cross-eyed Reading* curse.

The coming generation will do just fine

by Laurie McKeon

St. Joseph High School is celebrating its Homecoming this weekend. (Go, Lancers) Homecoming is always a big deal, but this year, St. Joseph's Fiftieth Anniversary year, Homecoming is a REALLY big deal. Many, many alumni came back for the parade, the game, the tailgater, the race with the big sausage (?!), and the alumni dance.

Three out of six of my kids currently attend St. Joseph High School. We've got one still in the Junior High and two more waiting in the wings. When we moved here from Ohio we actually chose to live in Kenosha rather than a northern Illinois suburb because we wanted our kids to attend a Catholic High School that was an integral part of a community, a school with a local history, a visible tradition, and a bar across the street. (Just kidding about that last part.) Seriously, while we were slightly taken aback by those two bars (in Ohio, it's illegal to have a bar anywhere near a school), we really liked the close-knit, down-to-earth feel at St. Joes. Despite our status as newcomers we've been warmly welcomed at the school and quickly drawn into the fold.

St. Joes has gotten a fair amount of press lately. The Kenosha News Supplement has highlighted the Fiftieth Anniversary, the Mass with the Archbishop, the Lady Lancer Lakeshore Conference Tennis Champs, and especially, media coverage of the varsity football team. Due to persistent injuries, a thin roster and a lot of bad luck, the varsity season at St. Joes was cut short. I have no doubt that the administration of St. Joes made the right decision when they chose to protect their kids, call off the remainder of the varsity season, and replace it with some non-conference games against squads that matched up better in size, depth, and experience.

I know for a fact that this decision is not in any way a reflection on the coaches, the athletic department, the viability of the football program, and most certainly not on the players on this season's team. Those players, only one of who weighed over 200 lbs, suited up every week during their regular season knowing they were facing teams who were bigger, stronger, and deeper. These kids never backed down, never flinched, and always came to play. As impressive as that was it is even more impressive to me, as a parent, a fan, and a St. Joes supporter that when their season was cancelled these kids understood. They didn't pitch a fit or hire an attorney, hold a press conference, or transfer schools. They accepted a tough decision with the same maturity, responsibility, and insight that they showed on the field. These players, especially those seniors who knew that this would be their last opportunity to play organized football, have continued to be leaders, making the best of a rough situation knowing that it is their job to set an example for the younger players on the team.

Being the parent of way too many teenagers and having first hand experience of the self absorbed, myopic, thoughtless, and histrionic behavior that is endemic to the species, I cannot convey how much these kids have impressed me. But I must admit, the St. Joseph High School students that I come into contact with (and that's pretty much all of them, given that we have a senior, sophomore and freshman this year) have often exhibited a levelheaded thoughtfulness, a sense of decency, and genuine kindness that seems inherent in their nature.

Two weeks ago Elizabeth Clark, a St. Joe's junior and the number one singles player on the varsity tennis team, was seriously injured in a car accident. She is still hospitalized in Milwaukee but is making steady progress. When her teammates heard of Liz's accident they quickly spread the word making sure every student knew about Liz and kept her in their prayers. In just a few short hours the students relayed the message that the next day's 7:15 daily rosary service would be dedicated to Liz. By 7:00 the next morning, the St. Joseph High School parking lot was full. Over 300 students and faculty packed the school chapel, lining the aisles, and streaming out the door. The St. Joseph student body, to a person, prayed with one voice for their friend in need. These students on their own time and of their own volition with their own community, immediately and instinctively joined together with an awe-inspiring gesture of faith and love.

I'm not saying that St. Joe's kids are perfect, that they have a lock on good behavior, or haven't snuck into one of those fine establishments across the street at some point in time during the past fifty years but, St. Joseph High School does have richness in spirit, a devotion to others, and an innate faithfulness that is so much bigger, deeper, and broader than any one team, season, or sport. Welcome back, St. Joseph alumni! Your alma mater still stands strong.

Find something you like to do and then do it for life

by Ed Groelle

When I was in high school, my Quantity Cookery teacher called me aside one day and informed me that the class had too many students and not enough stoves. She also happened to mention that I was in danger of flunking the course. Evidently she couldn't picture me reaching the culinary expertise of Chef Boyardee or Julia Child. She suggested I switch to a one-semester psychology class as a flunk-preventive substitute. I was intimidated enough to agree to her recommendation.

So, entering the psych class already in process for a few days, I soon found the course was basic, but rather interesting. I learned, for example, that there are three types of intelligence; abstract, mechanical, and social. As a project of self-awareness every psych student took an IQ test. This ostensibly would give each of us a vague measure of our abstract intelligence.

On the day the results were handed back to us, face down with a suggestion that we not discuss the results with any fellow students, I was asked by the teacher to remain for a minute after class. I immediately thought to myself, "Oh! Oh! I'm going to be asked to switch to the woodworking class."

That didn't happen, but he did want to know why I had one of the highest IQ's in the class and also the lowest grades. I sort of shuffled about a bit, looked down at my feet and suggested that since he was the psychology expert perhaps he could explain it to me. That didn't get me any points, but I couldn't tell him the probable reason was that I got up a 6 AM, helped milk twenty-five cows, ate breakfast, got ready, and then rode a bus an hour to school. After school there was the same routine again, resulting in a later than 7 PM quit time. There just wasn't much energy or time left for homework.

After high school, I landed a job installing TV antennas on homes. I'd come back to the shop after sliding around on icy roofs only to see the technician contentedly sitting at a bench studying an oscilloscope display. I started thinking, "Why can't I do that?" So, I left home to attend an electronics school in Chicago. I worked six hours a day and went to school six hours a day but after the farm it seemed like a vacation. Electronics didn't seem very daunting to me. To me it consisted of formulas and common sense more than anything. It was mathematically provable and just plain logical. If you run a current through a resistance you get a voltage drop. What else could possibly result, peach fuzz? I loved it and graduated top of the class.

Why am I writing this? Because, at the time, I felt some smugness in my test score but today, I consider IQ testing to be of little value. It doesn't measure the much more important attributes like interest and motivation. If someone gave me a full scholarship to Harvard business school, I would have to turn it down.

A high IQ with no aptitude, interest, or motivation is useless. It is all relative, isn't it? I once met a person who could learn a foreign language in 24 hours but couldn't tie his own shoes. I sometimes wonder what his IQ might be. If anyone out there would like some IQ points I'm willing to trade some for the ability to tell a joke well or fix my tin ear so I could play the violin.

I don't know what value is placed on IQ tests in today's education system. I hope very little. It is much more important to find out what you love and are good at doing and then making that your life's work. Work will then feel like play. I was fortunate. I found my vocational niche early and spent my entire career in electronics, first with military equipment and then over forty years in computers. I have never dreaded going to work in the morning or ever considered calling in sick.

I once discussed IQ testing with my manager, whom I admired. Her comment was right on the mark when she summed it up by saying, "It's all horse puckey."

Noer for president:
Vote early and vote often

by *Thomas J. Noer*

My fellow Americans ... as I look across this great land in this election year, I see over 200 million citizens BORED OUT OF THEIR SKULLS! Yes, it is six months before we vote and we are already tired of both parties and candidates and badly in need of an exciting alternative. That is why I take this opportunity to announce my candidacy for the Presidency in 2004. Given the other choices, that should be enough to get your vote, but candidates need to reveal their platforms so here is my agenda for America:

Rent Out the White House - If elected I will stay in Kenosha so I can read *Darts and Laurels* and go to Cohorama. This means the White House will be vacant and can be rented to visitors. Bill Clinton put contributors up in the Lincoln Bedroom, but I propose even stronger measures. Spend a day in the Oval Office for only $50,000. Take your friends on a tour of the War Room and pretend to bomb countries you hate for $25,000. Admit it, you have all seen *The West Wing* and would like to be waited on by staff and servants, well now you can! You can also book the presidential retreat at Camp David for a poker party that includes a helicopter ride from the White House lawn.

Abolish Most of the Cabinet - OK. I guess you have to keep Defense, State, and Homeland Security. But what do the rest do? Can anybody tell me who is in charge of the Department of Commerce? The duties of the Secretary of Labor or Agriculture? I thought not! So let's just abolish them and make their offices into high-rent condos. I will create a new Department of Dress and Language (headed by Miss Manners) that IS desperately needed, but the rest can just close their doors.

More Holidays - Do you realize that Europeans have 20-30 paid holidays a year? I will close this dangerous holiday gap with a

MINIMUM of ten new holidays so we can go to the beach, drink wine, and eat snails like the French and Italians. Let us begin with *New TV Shows Day* when we all get a day off to recover from the junk the networks trot out each fall and a *Storm Window Removal and Dandelion Dig Day* in the spring. Of course, there will be *Brett Favre's Birthday* and *National Alternative Parking Day* when every American stays home to move their vehicle.

Get Rid of Alan Greenspan - I am sure the Federal Reserve does something important, but aren't we are all sick seeing this guy come out of hibernation every six months to pontificate about interest rates followed by Wall Street going bananas or into the tank? If we have to hear this stuff, let's have someone younger and better looking. Wouldn't you rather listen to Nicole Kidman or Brad Pitt tells us, "Inflation is a still a threat, but production seems in a moderate growth mode?"

Impose a Stupidity Tax - With rent from the White House and the end of most cabinet positions we can get rid of that annoying income tax. To pay the modest cost of the new Noer government, I will tax stupidity. This can take the form of actions (be careful Paris Hilton, Michael Jackson, and the Kenosha School Board), statements (we should get a lot of cash just from George Bush, John Kerry, and Ralph Nader), or just appearing stupid (people with cheese stuck on top of their head or underwear sticking out of their pants). Not only will this free most of us from paying taxes, but also will dramatically improve the quality of life in the nation.

A Lottery for Running Mate - I spend many hours thinking of who would add dignity and experience to the ticket (Jessica Simpson, O. J. Simpson, Homer Simpson), but remembered that the vice president does nothing much except keep track of the health of the President. One of Franklin Roosevelt's VP's said, "The vice presidency isn't worth a pitcher of warm spit!" Well, he didn't really say, "spit." So, why not give everyone a shot and raise some money for the increased salary of President Noer by having a vice presidential lottery? For only $1 you have a chance to get your name in the history books and cadge free meals from the White House cafeteria, if it is not being rented that day for a PTA bake sale.

So I pledge to you a New Deal, a Great Society, a Thousand Points of Light, and a low-carb chicken in every pot. And if that is not enough, if elected I vow to never write another column. That ought to get your vote.

In today's world, invention is the mother of necessity.

by Ed Groelle

There have been some really neat, innovative, and useful inventions in the past couple of years. One is *TV-Be-Gone* and, like the name implies, will turn off any TV from twenty feet away. It's only about the size of a Zippo lighter. One surreptitious click and, poof, the TV is off. It's cooler than a hobo's mittens. Its usefulness is really appreciated when I wait in a doctor's office while one of my volunteer riders is at an appointment. No more am I forced to watch Jerry Springer or inane football player interviews while I wait. As a bonus activity it's also a lot of fun turning off all the TVs at Wal-Mart. In case you are interested, it will also turn the TV back on when leaving. $20 off the Internet and worth every penny. When first being put on sale, the inventor had such a heavy response he had to shut down his web site for a few days to upgrade his web servers.

There is another invention, which I don't think I could use with a clear conscience. About the size of a cigarette pack, it can be magnetically attached to any moving object, like your teenager's car. In constant contact with GPS satellites, it will record every movement and time. Just retrieve it, plug it into the USB port of your PC and a map pops up that shows where the vehicle has been and how long it has stayed at each location. It's perfect for tracking your teenagers, but I don't think I'd want to use it. It smacks of wire-tapping and invasion of privacy.

The *Select Comfort* mattress deserves an award of some kind. The firmness is separately set on each side by a remote control. It will dramatically enhance your quality of sleep life. Purchase a *panini* maker, HD TV, and a small refrigerator at the same time and you will never again have any reason to leave your bedroom.

I have some suggestions for aspiring inventors: How about some total noise-canceling earphones that would be available for rental at any movie theater? No more having to listen to people talking, coughing, munching popcorn, or crunching candy wrappers. Not only would the earphones have the movie sound track piped in but it should also have several channels of various music that you could select instead being forced to listen to that awful music, advertisements, and previews before the main feature. For those who prefer to read a book there would be a tiny focused reading light. Good idea, although it would probably never get past the people who sell theater advert time.

A noise-saturated world really needs a *Boom Car-Be-Gone* and a *Harley-Davidson-Be-Gone*. I e-mailed the *TV-Be-Gone* inventor suggesting that he start work on these, but he never replied. I'll wager Fords to Ferraris he is working on those ideas right now, and if successful, won't share any of the profits with me.

Please, please, please invent a reliable, cheap, and tool-free way to open this new indestructible clear plastic that is now shrink-wrapped around just about every product. It's very inconvenient, time-consuming, and not to mention dangerous to have an acetylene torch and chain saw hanging in the kitchen.

Let's get this medicine bottle cap problem solved once and for all. Develop a method of sealing medicine bottles so children can't open them but arthritic seniors can. So far, everything tried has failed miserably. For Pete's sake, how hard could it be? Maybe the problem could be given to the people who designed that plastic wrap stuff.

I'm surprised no one has ever come up with this idea before. Design a cylindrical cell phone tapered on one end so when you tell some users where you'd like to see them insert their cell phone it would be silenced with a minimum of pain. Pure genius!

A lot of inventive creativity is being wasted on already over-engineered products and really should be diverted to solving the problems above. Toothbrushes and razors come readily to mind. None of them can do the job any better than the 49-cent toothbrush your dentist gives you free or the 39-cent throwaway Bic razor. Some are now battery-operated and can vibrate, rotate, and play

MP3 music. For humanity's sake, they should give it a rest and go work on the medicine bottle problem.

I think I've given out some very valuable ideas here to potential inventors and entrepreneurs. I don't expect any compensation for putting forth these ideas. Just go down in the basement or out to the garage and get cracking. They are desperately needed!

My job is done.

Popular board games updated for the 21 Century

by Thomas J. Noer

Back in the B.C. era (Before Computers) families actually played games. Not bloodthirsty, blow-up-everything-that-moves video games, but games that had boards, cards, dice, spinners, and little figures that you moved around. Adults and children actually played together and sometimes even talked with each other during the game. I know it is hard to compete with the intellectual challenge of shooting pimps in Grand Theft Auto but maybe if we updated some older games they would have an appeal even today. Below are some contemporary versions of classics designed to make you turn off your Game Boy.

Candyland, The Healthy Version - Given current concerns about obese children, we can't have a game with lollipops, fudge, and chocolate drops. In the updated version, cheerful but scrawny dieticians lead children through the Tofu Forest, past the Carob Castle, towards Soy City while evil Cruddy Carbs tempt them with bread and pasta and Fast Food Freddy tosses onion rings at them. Winners receive 2.5 ounces of broccoli coated with wet wheat germ to bring to their exercise class.

Clue for the 21ST Century - No more Prof. Plumb or Miss Scarlet. No knifes or candlesticks. No library or conservatory. Now the suspects are Martha with the spatula in the kitchen, Koby with the basketball in the bedroom, Rush with the pillbox in the radio studio, and Michael with the glove in Never Never Land. Each player is a celebrity lawyer and whoever negotiates the best plea bargain and charges the highest fee gets the O.J. bobble-head doll.

Hide and go Chic - A wonderful chance for the whole family to become young and beautiful by enduring a little pain and spending a lot of money. You move miniature plastic surgeons around the Big Botox Board to Liposuction Lounge, Tummy Tuck Tower, and

Dick Clark Crowfeet Corner. When anything starts to sag you have to go back and start again. Be careful of the dangerous Side Effects Slide that sends you back to looking like a normal person.

Twister: The John Kerry Edition - Hilarious fun as you struggle to take different positions on political issues without falling on your face. Laugh as contestants put one foot on either side of the Gay Marriage and The War in Iraq spots. See if you can cover both sides of Medicare while keeping one hand on the Prescription Drug mark. The winner gets a waffle.

Go Fish in Lake Michigan - The children's card game in a contemporary setting. Players sit in a cardboard charter boat, the cards are dealt, and they try to make matches. "Do you have any alewife?" "No, they are all dead on the beach. Go fish!" "Do you have any perch?" "No, the Asian carp ate them all. Go Fish!" "Do you have any Coho?" "No, they are all radioactive. Go fish, but don't eat them!" The winner hosts a smelt fry.

Kenosha Monopoly - The classic board game set in our city. Buy property in Allendale, White Caps, Forest Park, or Uptown and when you have a monopoly you can collect alternate street parking fines. Bargain hunters can buy all of downtown for $8 or corner the transportation business by purchasing the trolley line. (Unfortunately nobody ever lands there.) You get $200 every time you cross Sheridan Road alive.

Chinese Checkers for the Unemployed - Players try to avoid being outsourced to China by working for lower and lower wages in America. When you can't compete, you are sent to Shanghai to make underwear, Christmas ornaments, and coffee mugs. Engineers will want to order the special version, Living in India on 200 Rupees a Day.

Presidential Scrabble - This word game is both fun and challenging as players try to explain our President's words and sentences. What does *interspacedness* mean? Can you explain *misunderstandingful*? Use *Hispanically* in a sentence? There is a bonus for successfully translating, "For every fatal shooting, there were roughly three nonfatal shootings. This is unacceptable in America and we're going to do something about it!"

Password - A Game of Memory and Confusion. Players try to remember the passwords for their computer, e-mail, phone messages, ATM card, their pager. Watch them put their computer name into their ATM machine and it eats the card. Laugh along as they try to use their phone password to login to their e-mail and their computer crashes. The last two players have to recite their money market account, social security, and cell phone numbers while punching in the code to turn off their security alarm system.

Unless you are dying, a hospital is the last place to be if sick

by Jim Wynne

I am currently recovering from a surgery I had a few weeks ago. While I won't bore you with the details of the affliction that occasioned the subcutaneous intrusion, I will say that it is not the first time I have been cut, and in fact I have been cut so many times now that I consider myself an expert in the general area of inpatient surgical procedures. As a public service for those who are facing their first experience with surgery and a hospital stay, I thought I would offer a few tips that might make the experience less stressful.

Don't go into the hospital thinking that it will be a restful experience. Hospitals are full of people whose job it is to keep you awake. How they know when it is that you actually fall asleep I don't know, but I can assure that as soon as you drift off, no matter what the time of day, someone will come in and wake you up. One time I was awakened from a sound and much-needed sleep by a nurse who informed me that it was time to take a sleeping pill, and I'm not kidding. If it's not a nurse, a phlebotomist, or some kind of technician, it will be a housekeeping person who believes that he or she can change your bedding while you are still in the bed. You might be awakened at 2:00 AM by a nurse-assistant strapping a blood pressure cuff on your arm, then go back to sleep and be awakened twenty minutes later by the same person, now wanting to take your temperature, having forgotten to do so when she was taking your blood pressure.

If the hospital staff somehow fails and allows you to get to sleep and you are in a semi-private room, the other patient in the room will be charged with the responsibility of keeping you awake. My favorite experience with a hospital roommate occurred after I had been kept awake all night by the incessant gurgling of a machine that was pumping a viscous brown fluid out of the roommate's stomach into a glass receptacle on the floor. Apparently he had some sort of upper-gastrointestinal problem that had been aggravated, if not caused by, excessive consumption of alcohol. Early the next morning a nurse came in and mercifully turned off the gurgle machine. She was followed soon by my roommate's physician. I heard him tell the roommate that he (the doctor) was going to let him go home that day, but with an ominous warning, "If you leave here and go out and buy a six-pack and drink it, I guarantee that you'll be back here within twenty-four hours of drinking the sixth can. Do you understand that?"

The roommate anxiously agreed.

A short time later, the roommate was on the phone, giving the good news of his release to a friend. "I'm going home today," he said, "but the doctor says I'm probably going to be back here pretty soon."

If you are unfortunate enough to be confined in a teaching hospital, you will be subjected to the morning rounds of attending, resident, and student physicians. They roam the floors of the hospital in packs numbering upwards of sixty or seventy individuals, all of whom will try to squeeze into your room at 5:00 AM. If a terrible mistake has been made and you were actually allowed to go to sleep, the pack of roaming doctors will set things straight by suddenly pulling the bedclothes off of you and poking you wherever they think the poke will cause you to shout the loudest. The group won't leave the room until you have cried out in pain at least once. You will never have any idea what the group is actually supposed to accomplish other than making you yell because they speak only in polysyllabic, Latinate, medical terminology. For example, physicians are not allowed to use the word 'armpit', they must say 'axilla.' When they are finished speaking in gibberish, poking you, and making you scream they will abruptly leave the room. Then another group will come in fifteen minutes later and start the process again because the first group was actually supposed to be poking the patient in the next room.

While I don't want to make it seem that staying in a hospital is not a good idea for people who really need to be there, my own experience has been that if you need to have a fairly routine procedure done, such as an appendectomy, amputation, or some sort of neurosurgery, you will probably be better off if you fill yourself full of rotgut whiskey and take care of the operation yourself. At least you won't have to worry about post-operative sleep deprivation.

I don't care if it is in Webster's dictionary. I'm tired of the f*** word.

by Ed Groelle

While in another town, several weeks ago, I went to a fast-food restaurant for one of their "gourmet" fish sandwiches. The place was crowded, and while waiting in line, a young man about senior high school age stepped in front of me just as though I wasn't even there. I tapped him on the shoulder and pointed out that the line formed behind me. What happened next came as a total surprise. He started cussing at me and calling me names in a loud voice. Every other word from his filthy mouth was the f*** word. I seriously doubt that he even knew any other adjectives or adverbs.

I've been in the Army and worked in the Arctic so I am no stranger to raw words of men living away from the constraints of society but hearing teenagers use the f*** word routinely always makes me feel vaguely uncomfortable. It seems so flagrantly unnecessary and accomplishes nothing but to demean the speaker.

He didn't appear to be drunk or under drugs but his eyes looked like he had gone berserk. I decided the best action would be to not react, but just to watch him along with the other astonished patrons. As he continued to shout and rant I took a step back from him. If he took a menacing step towards me and, even at the risk of creating further brain damage, I fully intended to inflict a swift kick to the groin area. At my age, fighting fair is no longer an option.

Thinking it over later, I made an effort to understand his actions. I ended up feeling sorry for him. Here was what appeared to be a clean-cut-looking, young man verbally attacking someone who was three times his age. He didn't seem to care that he was making a fool of himself and frightening everyone around him. He was completely oblivious to any effect he was having on others.

Perhaps, our evolving society had, in some respects, cheated him out of a proper boyhood by never allowing him a sense of accomplishment and self-worth. He probably had never made a model airplane cut with a razor blade from balsa wood and powered with a rubber band. He had never built a radio from scratch or assembled a Heathkit device. Of course not! Building Heathkits requires time, patience, and the ability to follow directions. These qualities don't appear to be a valued any longer, possibly due to instant gratification of iPods, cell phones, and video games.

He has witnessed no-talent musicians earn big money and adulation by acting like animals. That may be what inspired him to start a rock band but was frustrated to find that the good band names like Purple Vomit and Ptomaine Tonsils were already taken.

Cars have evolved to the point where all he can do is to wash and polish it. Routine maintenance and experimentation have been eliminated. Even changing the oil requires a special tool. No modifications or tinkering allowed except for installing resonators on the exhaust for the sole purpose of irritating as many people as possible.

He has lost his innate sense of adventure after seeing idiots on TV chase themselves around the globe to places with implied adventure or romance in their names like *Tierra del Fuego* and *Timbuktu*. That would stifle anyone's dream of exploring foreign countries. Why dream when it's already been done for you comfortably on TV?

He sees his fellow citizens thumbing their self-absorbed noses at the law by running stop lights, speeding, and irritating as many people as possible with superfluous noise and bad manners. He has noted that the authorities don't see scofflaws, so why should he be concerned about decorum or acceptable behavior or even following rules?

He has concluded that without confrontation no one will notice him. I would have liked to point out to him that random confrontation of strangers is a stupid, fool-hardy action and could result in a whole lot of pain. He doesn't realize that there are certainly thousands of ex-Special Forces and Frogmen out there who have been highly trained to inflict lethal pain very effectively.

When leaving the restaurant a teenaged employee was having a smoke break just outside the door. She said to me, "Have a nice day." and then added, "I'm sorry you had to listen to that."

I asked her, "What is wrong with him? Is he on drugs?"

She just said, "No, they're all crazy."

Apparently, she was a lot smarter than her nose ring suggested.

What being an American is all about

by Kenda Buxton

Virginia Gazette, July 18th, 1777: "Thus may the 4th of July, that glorious and ever memorable day, be celebrated through America, by the sons of freedom, from age to age till time shall be no more."

Independence Day commemorates the signing of the Declaration of Independence on July 4th, 1776. Taxation without representation was the issue that unified our first thirteen colonies when their citizens were forced to pay taxes to Britain's King George III without proper representation in parliament. Although 229 years later we're still forced to pay taxes without proper representation, we're considerably less rebellious about it than our forefathers, since we don't have to pay those taxes to a guy with a funny accent, wearing a powdered wig and knee britches.

Asking Americans to unite and bear arms means asking us to get off of the couch and miss *Fear Factor.* When given a choice between paying taxes and the physical exertion it would take to charge Bunker Hill, most modern-day Americans would gladly write a check to Uncle Sam. If our forefathers had only known Life, Liberty, and the Pursuit of Happiness would eventually give us TV shows with bikini clad women eating rancid cow intestines, they might not have been so willing to risk their lives by throwing all that tea into Boston Harbor.

Speaking of life, liberty, and happy pursuits, have you noticed that every time a major holiday rolls around some stick-in-the-mud feels it's his duty to remind us of how little we know about their own history? Evidently, it's not enough that we can name every member of the Partridge family, recall who shot J.R., and sing the *Gilligan's Island* theme song. Someone always has to come along and spoil the Fourth of July cookout by telling us how stupid we are. This year, that someone is a law association with numerous concerns about our lack of historical knowledge that are sure to keep us studying from now until the next Fourth of July.

~ **Nearly half of all college seniors surveyed do not know basic, general information about American democracy and the Constitution.**

However, 100% of college seniors know how to transfer music to an iPod. What would you rather listen to when you're studying? Some guy reciting the Constitution or David Cassidy singing, *I Think I Love You*?

~ **Only 20% of college seniors surveyed could identify James Madison as the Father of the Constitution.**

The good news is that 95% of all Americans can identify the Dolly Madison Bakery as the maker of Zingers, Donut Gems, Pecan Rollers, and Dunkin Stix.

~ **40% of Americans do not know that the Declaration of Independence was signed in 1776.**

But 98% of Wisconsinites know that the Packers won the Super Bowl in 1967, 1968, and 1997.

~ **One-third of those aged 18-29 years do not know that America gained her independence from Britain.**

Possibly because they're still waiting for us to gain our independence from Iraq.

~ **85% of Americans could not identify John Hancock's role in the Continental Congress. (John Hancock, president of the Continental Congress, signed his name to the Declaration with great flourish so, "King George can read it without spectacles.")**

And when polled, 55% of Americans did not know what spectacles were.

~ **"The British are coming! The British are coming!" 28% of college seniors could not identify Paul Revere as the speaker of these famous words.**

But all college seniors know it was Donald Trump who first uttered the now famous words, "You're fired!"

~ **62% of Americans could not name the thirteen colonies that made up the United States at the time the Declaration was signed.**

And 62% of Americans can't name all seven dwarfs, either.

Although some of us may be lacking when it comes to our knowledge of U.S. history, Americans are grateful for the freedoms we have and appreciate the men and women who have fought to attain and protect these freedoms. So what if we don't know when the Declaration of Independence was signed, or who James Madison was? The important thing is, we know who makes our Zingers. And as 100% of us who were surveyed said, that's *really* what being an American is all about.

The philosophy of pain

by Ed Groelle

Philosophers talk, poets rhyme
To justify their claim
That fear and pity could not exist
Without the taste of pain.
But pity seems a shabby wage
For years of painful life.
I've paid too much this fickle guest
Who fled before the surgeon's knife.

The lesson then is more than that.
Pain must cloud the lives of men
For who loves this life too much
May not go home again.
Still I clenched and raised my fist
And denied to play His part
To resurrect within my soul
The forgotten beat of child's heart.

I long to tear the veil apart
And see the other side,
But faith must answer all the doubts,
Revelation is to death denied.
I do not know what form to take
Within God's mold of love.
But now I know my fist must unclench
To fit His predestinate glove.

Please don't Ill-annoy me

by Laurie McKeon

Five summers ago, after spending fifteen years in Ohio, the McKeon family made the pilgrimage into the land of cheese and beer. Because my husband was taking a job in Waukegan, we had the option of living in either Illinois or Wisconsin. Since we both grew up in Illinois and both of our families were still firmly rooted in the Land of Lincoln, it was quite a big deal when we chose to cross the border. While I don't think we qualify for official cheese head status yet and we still have a few cultural barriers to cross like cheese curds (I will never eat them because I can't get past the name), and the Packers (sorry), we have gained a real appreciation for living in the Dairy State.

When my sisters start talking smack about how Illinois has it all over Wisconsin, I like to put them in their place by listing the Top Ten ways that Wisconsin kicks Illinois' ass.

10. Lakefront Property - It's the same Great Lake, but in Wisconsin you don't have to be a Rockefeller to enjoy it. I must admit, our heads were turned pretty darn fast when we realized that regular people actually own property right on the beautiful shores of Lake Michigan. The only affordable lakefront property left on the north shore of Chicago is right next door to the nuclear power plant in Zion.

9. Politics - Madison may seem nutty at times, but Illinois invented the crooked politician. George Ryan, Dan Rostenkowski, Operation Greylord, Operation Safe Road, the Hired Truck scandal, and the always-colorful Daley Dynasty truly exemplify Illinois politics. While Wisconsin may have a dodgy alderman or two, the last honest politician in the state of Illinois was Abraham Lincoln.

8. Beer - Somehow it goes down just a little bit smoother knowing that you are supporting the local economy while tossing back a few cold ones. In a state with a professional baseball team named the Brewers drinking beer is your civic duty and not to be taken lightly.

7. **Vacations** - If Illinois is so great, why does everyone hightail it to Wisconsin the minute they get a day off? We've got the Dells, Door County, Lake Geneva, and Kohler. You're welcome.

6. **Big Ten Football** - Since the inception of the BCS system, neither the University of Illinois, nor Northwestern, has been to a major bowl, while Wisconsin has been tearing up the Big Ten. Moreover, you don't see any badgers picketing outside Camp Randall protesting a politically incorrect mascot.

5. **Traffic** - Sure, there's some construction on I-94 heading into Milwaukee, but I swear to God, they have been working on the same section of the Chicago Sky Way, that part right after the toll booth, since the early '80's. When I die and go to hell, I'm pretty sure I will be spending the rest of eternity driving behind a semi trying to merge onto the Dan Ryan.

4. **Chicago** - Here in southern Wisconsin we are close enough to the city to enjoy all its perks without suffering through the ownership hassles. As I point out to my Chicago based family, if it's not rush hour I can get from my house in Pleasant Prairie to the Bloomingdale's parking garage in just about an hour. I can shop myself silly on Michigan Avenue, ship my purchases home, and avoid the exorbitant city sales tax. Somehow, this seems like a big plus to me. For my husband, not so much.

3. **ACT scores** - Every single year, Wisconsin tops Illinois in average ACT scores. This just kills my sisters. Since the beginning of time Wisconsin high school students have aced the ACT, consistently scoring hirer than the national average. It's a fact, look it up. I'm only hoping the McKeon progeny do not spoil this fine academic benchmark.

2. **Cicadas** - We don't have any, they do. My bug-a-phobic sisters have been pulling cicadas off their cars, clothes, and kids all summer. My house, car, hair, and children are all cicada free. I'm trying really hard not to gloat about that.

1. **Attitude** - The very best thing about Wisconsin is that people aren't copping attitude. Illinois, particularly in the northern and western suburbs, can be slightly full of itself. Everyone is keeping

score and sizing up your house, cars, kids, and bank account. People in Wisconsin don't seem to be caught up in it. Raising six kids is hard enough. Raising six kids in the midst of hyper competition and blatant materialism is almost impossible.

I'm not ripping on Illinois. I know it's a really great state. I just like messing with my sisters. In fact, Illinois and Wisconsin, especially in our part of the world, have way more in common than not. We share schools, churches, stores, banks, parks, and sports teams. And, most importantly, we share the undying relief that at least we're not Hoosiers.

A $400 X-Box under the Christmas tree? Bah! Humbug!

by Ed Groelle

An old-fashioned Christmas. Does that phrase conjure up Rockwellian and idyllic visions for you? Don't fall into the trap of thinking that the past was somehow better than the present. There are many people of my vintage who do not look back on Christmas as something they'd want to relive. For example, my mother-in-law was not someone who waxed nostalgic for the good old days. She would tie into anyone who did, like a bum on a bologna sandwich.

My Christmases as a boy went something like this: For several weeks I'd meticulously pore over the Sears catalog making lists of anything I'd like Santa to bring. I'd show these lists to my mother but she never reacted with much interest.

I attended a parochial grade school and for two weeks before Christmas every grade would practice for a Christmas Eve program in the church jammed with parents and relatives. The church was decorated with a twenty-foot tree but my primary interest focused on the paper sacks stacked around its base. Each child was given one as they left church after services. The sacks were filled with candy. Actually, I lie. The sacks contained an apple and a hefty amount of unshelled peanuts. There was some hard candy throw in and one candy bar. OK, that's the parochial method of teaching children that life is a veil of tears, full of disappointments, and anything you get for nothing is probably worth the price. My church's tenet was that it's never too early to burn that philosophy into a child's psyche.

After church we'd visit my childless aunt for a few hours, and in the days when children were expected to be seen and not heard, this was a fidgeting, torturous, visit somewhat tempered by her homemade eggnog. I thought it was the nectar of gods.

Riding home, I doggedly clung to the expectation of an Erector Set with which I could build a steam shovel capable of digging a septic tank hole but, alas, my parents considered Christmas as an opportunity to buy us some new socks and shirts and a game or two to be shared with siblings. So much for my list making.

I don't remember what we did on Christmas Day but we did own a horse-drawn sleigh that was used in winter to harvest trees for the woodpile. I know what you're thinking, but no, we didn't use it to go over the hills and through the woods to grandma's house. That's way too much work for a rare day when we expected to do only minimal work. Just as well, since I don't think my father much liked my grandmother anyway.

Don't get me wrong. I'm not complaining. My parents did the best they could coping with the depression, war, and farm obligations. Mine was a typical Christmas as it was for most of our neighbors. I'm painting this picture to contrast between those times and to when I had daughters of my own and tried to develop an interest in the holidays. I found that if this isn't experienced as a child it is difficult to capture as an adult. Even today, my contribution to the festivities is only to set up the tree and string the lights.

We did enjoy selecting Christmas presents for our daughters. A visit to a large toy store resulted in our searching elsewhere, anywhere else. We found and bought many Swedish games and toys that we still have stashed away somewhere in our attic. They were educational and durable. The dolls even had (Gasp!) buttons for eyes. But the best present ever was a playhouse I constructed from cardboard shipping containers.

Recently, a friend asked for ideas on Christmas gifts for her granddaughters, so I gave her the benefit of my vast experience. I advised her to go to a furniture store, bat her baby blues, and beg for a couple of refrigerator shipping boxes. Then go to a hardware store and buy a box cutter. Next, take both boxes to the basement and cut a door in front, a couple of windows, and a connecting door between the playhouse rooms. Use an old shag rug as flooring. Get the cat involved ... they love cramped spaces. I assured her that her grandchildren would treasure the memory of this gift from grandma for the rest of their lives. My children do.

Dr. Tom's Tax Preparation Guide: A 1040 quiz

by Thomas J. Noer

Spring is in the air. The snow has melted so we can see all the Christmas decorations that are still up; the salt is gone and we can find out if there is any chrome left on our cars and the geese are organizing to take over the city. But, the real indication of spring is that it's TAX TIME when we go through the annual agony of finding forms, digging out receipts, and trying to follow the "simple" instructions of the IRS. To help you through the ordeal I offer a simple Tax Preparation Quiz:

1. To secure the 794 forms you will need to complete your taxes:
   a. Download them from the Internet. (Be sure to include the dozens of pop-up ads for breast enhancement with your return.)
   b. Go to the library and look on the shelf labeled, "Horror."
   c. Go to the IRS office but use a fake name so the angry man wearing a green eyeshade won't order an audit.
   d. Get some crayons and construction paper and make your own.

2. When you finally find copies of your W-2's in your glove compartment you:
   a. Will be stunned to learn how little you made last year.
   b. Will try to figure-out what "FICA" means.
   c. Will get your fingers dirty from the carbon paper.
   d. Will discover they are from 1983.

3. If you write a column for The Kenosha News you can deduct:
   a. The cost of a map to find the Sunday Editorial page.

b. The cost of an answering machine to avoid angry Packer fans.

c. The cost of gifts to Howard Brown.

d. The cost of bourbon.

4. To use the Child Care Credit:

a. Subtract the number of children you have by the number of your ex-spouses.

b. Multiple the number of your children by their average monthly Gap bill.

c. Divide the number of children you have by the number that still talk to you.

d. Temporarily adopt a Boy Scout troop.

5. Form 1040 EZ:

a. Is only for left-handed people who live on the even-numbered side of the street.

b. Can only be used by people who have an adjusted income below mine.

c. Is designed for people who have lost all their receipts.

d. Is badly misnamed.

6. You should use the standard deduction if:

a. You failed math in high school.

b. You gave nothing to charity, do not own a home, were never sick, and do not own a cell phone.

c. You shredded your receipts into confetti for that New Year's party.

d. It is 11:50 PM on April 15.

7. Be sure to mark the following $1 "check offs" on your tax form:

a. Presidential campaign fund. George W. and John K. really need the money.

b. Save the timber wolf fund. (They EAT geese!)

c. Buy the Badgers a decent quarterback fund.

d. Tom Noer retirement fund.

8. To complete the math required for IRS forms you should:
a. Find a calculator that still has batteries in it.

b. Get a PhD in advanced calculus.

c. Build an abacus (you can deduce the cost!)

d. Just estimate. The IRS will be happy if you are sort of close.

9. If you owe the government money:
a. Put it on a credit card that you have recently canceled.

b. Call them up and ask if you can work it off in Iraq.

c. Offer them your childrens' souls.

d. Stick dollar bills together with old gummy bears. (The IRS loves a good joke.)

10. The Tax Table is:
a. The one in the kitchen where you spend 436 hours preparing your returns.

b. The one in the basement you claimed as a business expense.

c. Designed by sadistic accountants who failed their CPA exam.

d. Impossible to read it without bifocals and a ruler.

11. If you get audited, you should call:
a. Your lawyer and your accountant.

b. Your mommy.

c. The tailor who makes prison jump suits.

d. Tony Soprano.

Scoring:
   Take the number of a.) answers and multiply by .05. Subtract one half of the number of b.) answers and divide by the age of your youngest pet. If you have no pets, subtract your gambling losses and add the number of c.) responses. Find the square root of the number of d.) responses and subtract the largest of either

your oil depreciation allowance (Form 878333Z) OR the average of your past five homestead credits. If you are over 65, stop here and take your Metamucil. If you are under 65 and the number is less than zero, or more than zero, immediately send $25 to: Tom Noer, C/O The Kenosha News. Keep your receipt, as it is deductible next year.

Our family was once host to royalty

By Ed Groelle

One day our oldest daughter asked if we would keep a kitten for a few days until she got settled in a new apartment. I'm a cat person but had never really considered getting involved with a cat, but we agreed. A few days later she brought the kitten promising to pick it up in a week or two. That was fifteen years ago.

The kitten was only a few weeks old... a beautiful apple-faced Siamese wearing a fur coat with colors gently varying from gray to brown to white, accented by its black ears and piecing blue eyes. Cats have the uncanny ability to sense a real sucker softie, so it immediately jumped on my lap and leisurely strolled up to my nose with a look on its face that said, "Well? I'm here! Get used to it." Then he sealed my fate by licking my hand with his warm sandpaper tongue.

His name was Klondyke and was a pedigreed Siamese, but his papers had been lost. That was not a problem for Klondyke. His attitude about that was, "Papers? Who needs papers? I'm Siamese so I'll expect to be treated as royalty anyway."

Klondyke turned out to be a very affectionate cat and immediately assumed that our house was his home and we were his family and, more importantly, his staff. He watched TV with us and slept in our beds. He instituted some changes like the one about 6 AM being a perfectly reasonable time to get everyone up and that at

3:30 every day he would be served one shrimp. Of course, it had to be the jumbo size or he would turn up his nose and indignantly walk away.

He certainly was a very pleasant, well-behaved roommate. He never broke anything and never missed his cat box. Once a day we'd harness him to go outside to terrorize the field mice and squirrels and chew on his catnip plant.

A couple of months ago we noticed he avoided putting weight on his left front foot. X-rays were taken and blood tested, but they were inconclusive. The vet said it might be arthritis or perhaps his body functions were shutting down and to prepare for the worst. His walking ability worsened and one day he jumped from the sofa to walk toward me but only got half way before his legs collapsed under him. It was obvious he was in pain and I realized that it might be time to consider a compassionate goodbye.

The thought of doing this brought back a childhood memory I'd rather forget. When I was about eight years old I had found the nest in the barn of four baby kittens mothered by one of our feral cats. I'd rush home every day from school to play with them. One day I came home to find the kittens missing. The next day I found them dead, lying next to the cement silo with a sack nearby. My father had put them into the sack and bashed it against the silo wall. He had decided the farm could not sustain any more cats. I was shocked at the sight and it felt as if my father had killed something inside me. Now, it seemed that I was contemplating doing the same thing under very different circumstances but still akin to that experience many years ago.

The next day we offered Klondyke all the shrimp he wanted, wrapped him in a blanket and took him to the vet. He sat on the table and looked at us with, we hoped, some understanding and forgiveness. The vet gave him a tranquillizer and we watched him slowly fall asleep. She then injected him and in a few seconds his little heart stopped beating. We wrapped him, brought him home and buried him near his favorite catnip plant.

Sometimes now, in the middle of the night, I think I still hear him racing around the house. His favorite place to sleep was the linen closet and when I go to take a towel, I half expect to see him still sleeping there.

We are left with a cat-sized hole in our home and hearts that will never be filled. But, thank you, Klondyke, for fifteen years of love and laughs.

Hunger never finds any fault with the cooking

by Laurie McKeon

Every evening around 5 PM, a Greek chorus shows up in my kitchen asking that age-old question, "Mom, what's for dinner?" Every single night for the last sixteen years, (ever since my oldest could eat solid food) I've been expected to provide an answer along with some sort of hot, balanced, nutritious meal, at what is legitimately the busiest time of the day. I must tell you, I'm getting a little tired of it. I'm not quite sure who started this whole healthy dinner presumption, but I'm pretty sure that it wasn't a mom. I know for a fact that it wasn't me because, honest to God, I hate to cook.

Despite all appearances to the contrary and the nine million meals I've cooked over the years, I would be the happiest woman alive if I never had to enter my kitchen again. I know there are people who love to cook, who find it relaxing, therapeutic, and even enjoyable to whip up a béarnaise sauce, who don't mind spending three days assembling a chocolate ganache cake, or who actually own a collection of spring form pans. I can respect these people. In fact, I hope that one of them asks me over for dinner, but personally, if I didn't need to feed my family, I wouldn't even bother having a stove.

Back in the day, BC (Before Children) I never cooked. Ever! When I married, I had an amazing repertoire of exactly three dishes; chocolate chip cookies, guacamole, and hot dogs. That's it! That's all I knew how to make. In my world, that's really all I needed to know. I had an appetizer, a main dish, and a dessert. I was covered. Before I had kids, I used to work ninety hours a week and went out for lunch every day. (Man, I still miss those lunches.) I was perfectly happy with a bag of microwave popcorn or a bowl of Special K for dinner.

Then I had a kid, and then I had a lot of kids, and suddenly, all these little people were expecting to be fed real food, actual meals, every single night ... by me. While I could fake it through breakfast and lunch with cereal and sandwiches, come dinnertime, I had to come up with the goods and operate an appliance. Since eating out every night wasn't really an option, out of pure necessity I learned how to cook. Now, five nights a week, fifty-two weeks a year, I begrudgingly exercise these hard earned culinary skills. (Friday night is pizza night, and Saturday night is date night.) You do the math. That's a lot of buttered noodles.

I'm not saying I'm a good cook. All I am saying is that I do cook. The fact that my children are all still alive and relatively healthy bears this out. My limited menu has expanded to about twelve dishes that fall into one of two categories: meals that can be made in a little over ten minutes (pasta from a box, sauce from a jar, salad from a bag) or meals that I can throw into the oven and ignore while I drive the kids to soccer, basketball, and play practice, that still remain edible when I pull them out two hours later (roasted chicken, standing rib roast, or lasagna).

Truth be told, it's not just the actual cooking that I hate. It's the planning, the shopping, and the thinking about it that sends me over the edge. I can't tell you how many nights I forget to take the roast out of the freezer, fail to buy the key ingredient for some recipe, or just plain ignore the fact that dinner time inevitably arrives. (BLT's anyone?) Then, to add insult to injury, once I've spent all the necessary lead time, prep time, cooking time, and serving time, if all goes right, my family eats what I've made and I've got nothing left to show for it but the dirty dishes. That's the real killer and the part that I still can't quite get passed. I put in all this time with the sole and absolute purpose and then the end product gets devoured in about ten minutes. Then, I have to do it all over again the very next night. It just seems like a great big waste of time to me.

So, when my kids are lying on an analyst couch one day whining that I never really loved them, (you know that day will happen as soon as they get a job with decent health insurance coverage) I am keeping a running tally of all of these meals as proof of my eternal devotion. Because honestly, it's not the pony rides, the trips to Disney World, and designer jeans that reflect maternal love, it's the twenty years of tuna noodle casseroles that really show how much I care.

Renewing special memories on a sentimental journey

by Ed Groelle

A couple of weeks ago I diagnosed myself to be suffering from wanderlust, so my wife and I roamed the Internet panning for cruises. We studied trips up the Nile, down the Ubangi, and across the Atlantic. After a couple of hours I leaned back and asked, "What would you really like to do as a vacation get-away if there were no obstacles in place?" With no hesitation, she said that she would like to visit Petra.

Petra was one of our exchange students from Berlin, Germany who lived with us for a year almost forty years ago. We had visited each other over the years and last year, when her Berlin home became an empty nest, she and her husband immigrated to Nova Scotia and built a house.

Now, with digital telephone we can visit with her for free every week. She had hinted to my wife that she could use some help with the house and an art show she was planning. We ended up buying an airline ticket for my wife to Halifax for a week in October.

I sat there for a while thinking that my wife had her vacation but I still had none. That was definitely not the intent of the exercise. I shifted mental parameters to only think of activities I had had in the past that I enjoyed. Maybe I could recapture those moments in a sentimental journey. I came up with some experiences I'd like to relive again. Here are two. I don't think I fully appreciated them at the time.

As a boy, one activity I always enjoyed was going to the garbage dump. That needs a bit of explanation. Our family created very little garbage. My mother canned from the garden so we had few cans, paper was used to start the kitchen stove, bones were fed to the dog, anything else edible was fed to the pigs, and anything flammable was burned in a bonfire. Like most families during the depression and WWII we were a very self-sufficient and make-do family. I remember my mother even washing and drying the paper plates. There were no garbage bags and no preservation type plastic or paper products except for wax paper that was also reused.

Anyway, to make the story short, hidden out of sight, behind the woodshed we had three 55-gallon drums which would fill with garbage every three months. My dad and I would load them up and go to the garbage dump, which was a valley or depression that the farmer wanted filled. Anything could be dumped; paint, oil, anything at all since there was no EPA or supervision of any type.

There were no garbage bags so trash was all out in the open, a veritable treasure trove to a young boy. While my father emptied the barrels, I'd scour the dump looking for broken toys or any material I could make into something with a little imagination. If I could summon up the innocence and anticipation of a ten-year-old again I'd like to do that one more time. Maybe not a true vacation, but certainly a renaissance step back to a time when life seemed to be full of discoveries and possibilities.

When I was about eighteen I lived in Chicago for a while. I was usually broke, but every Saturday night I'd manage to scrape together enough money to take the subway downtown to the Loop. Before the dubious convenience of shopping malls the Loop was the place to be on a Saturday night. It was a shoulder-to-shoulder mass of humanity.

If I had enough money, I'd go to a movie in one of those then movie palaces decorated with a gaudy Chinese motif. I'd really like to experience that excitement again. Please don't suggest that I could visit a shopping mall for that experience because, believe me, it just isn't the same.

These are sentimental journeys and do nothing to ease the wanderlust. Perhaps, like Claude Monet, I've reached the age where I just want to be left alone to raise flowers in a quiet garden. I could name it, Giverney II. No doubt, like Giverney I, hordes of sentimentally deprived tourists will come to see it when I'm gone.

Every day should be Father's Day

by Kenda Buxton

"I felt something impossible for me to explain in words. Then, when they took the baby away, it hit me. I got scared all over again and began to feel giddy. Then it came to me ... I was a father." (Nat King Cole)

Father's Day never garners the whoopla Mother's Day does. Hallmark commercials fade away as May turns to June, and no one reminds you to send Dad flowers or to serve him breakfast in bed. Dad's supposed to be grateful for the Mother's Day leftovers, a backyard cookout that he grills himself, and whatever family members can manage to gather between vacations, weddings, and Little League games. And with good grace, fathers always seem satisfied with these leftovers, which is all the more reason on this Father's Day to remember what Dad means to us.

"Fatherhood is pretending the present you love the most is soap-on-a-rope." (Bill Cosby) For years, soap-on-a-rope ranked as the second most popular Father's Day gift. Not necessarily popular with the receivers, but extremely popular with the givers. I don't know if that's because we baby boomers lacked imagination, or because we all wanted to use Dad's soap-on-a-rope on the sly, or because every neighborhood had an Avon lady desperate to make a sale. What I do know is that some guy made a fortune out of carving bars of Zest into fish, cars, and baseball mitts, and then stringing a ten-cent piece of twine through them.

"My father taught me to work; he did not teach me to love it." (Abraham Lincoln) Considering I've been counting the days until retirement since I was 25, I'd say I've got more in common with our 16th president than I ever thought possible.

"It is a wise father that knows his own child." (William Shakespeare) Whether he took you fishing, taught you how to ride a bike, or made popcorn, and watched *Bonanza* with you every Sunday night like my father did with me, I bet some of your fondest memories are of times spent with your dad.

"All fathers are invisible in daytime; daytime is ruled by mothers, and fathers come out at night. Darkness brings home fathers." (Margaret Atwood) Today's involved parenting by so many fathers makes this quotation outdated. But for those of us born before 1970, how well we remember the excitement of waiting for Dad to come home, and then running to greet him as though he were a superhero who'd been gone for weeks slaying dragons and ridding the world of all evil.

"May all your days be smooth as silk, may all your nights be restful. May all your cereal stay crisp in milk, may nothing clog your cesspool." (Otto E. Turner Jr.) Twenty-nine years after his passing, I wish I could say my father left me with advice that made me rich and famous, but let's face it, how far can a girl get in life when all her dad ever told her was to keep her cereal crisp and her cesspool flowing freely? Although, admittedly, soggy cereal and a clogged cesspool can sure start a woman's day off on the wrong foot.

"When I was a boy of fourteen, my father was so ignorant I could hardly stand to have the old man around. But when I got to be twenty-one, I was astonished at how much the old man had learned in seven years." (Mark Twain) It's amazing what time, maturity, and distance will do for a person's perspective. You only have to live on your own for about three weeks before discovering that Dad and Mom aren't so stupid after all.

"It doesn't matter who my father was; it matters who I remember he was." (Anne Sexton) As someone who has had only memories of her father for almost three decades now, this statement rings so true. It doesn't matter who my father was to anyone else. What matters is who his child remembers he was.

On this Father's Day, I hope you're able to see your father and not just remember him. And when you do make that visit, wish dear old dad a "Happy Father's Day," and tell him that you hope his nights are restful, his cereal crisp, and that nothing clogs his cesspool.

Get some insight when sight is not a requisite

by Ed Groelle

Ever had one of those days? Ever feel that life never gives you a break? Enjoy wallowing in self-pity and cursing the darkness? I'd like you to meet a neighbor and friend of mine, Terri Gilliland. I first met Terri two years ago while volunteering with the *Kenosha Area Family & Aging Service's Driver Escort Program.* As we drove to Twin Lakes to meet with one of her clients we chatted about various subjects and she would give me directions and tell me where to turn at intersections.

"Big deal!", you're thinking, "I could drive to Twin Lakes with my eyes shut."

That's just what Terri was doing. You see, she is blind; not just legally blind but totally blind. No bits of light or occasional shadows ever pass before her eyes.

When first meeting Terri I was surprised to find her an attractive lady in her early forties. She has a distinct resemblance to Teri Garr, the movie actress, and could easily pass as her sister. She was a change from most of my passengers who are elderly and sometimes with obvious infirmities. Of course, I was told beforehand of her vision impairment, but soon realized that it didn't seem to make any difference. Terri exudes so much confidence within her environment that much of the time I simply forget she is blind. She looks you in the eyes while speaking and will touch your arm when making a point. She has a confidence and an awareness about her surroundings that constantly astounds me. She winces when anyone thinks of her as handicapped. She is a trained and degreed psychologist who worked as a crisis counselor before losing her sight ten years ago through a rare retinal condition medically known as *Retinitis Pigmentosa.* There is no known cause, no cure, and no procedure for retarding its insidious progression. Three out of five of her siblings are also afflicted. Her parents and three children are not. It is one of those myriad "bad things that happen to good people."

When diagnosed, she retreated to her sofa for six months and struggled against an overwhelming feeling of hopelessness. Terri eventually became resigned and began to realize that perhaps her sight loss had given her a useful insight and understanding into the trauma of progressive vision impairment in others experiencing a similar agony. She established a program for aiding and counseling others with life changing conditions such as macular degeneration and diabetes and appropriately dubbed it "Insight." Last year she also began employment with the state representing the '*Southeast Wisconsin Office of the Blind and Visually Impaired*' program that deals only with persons experiencing vision loss.

I have watched Terri on many occasions give her presentation or, more accurately, I have watched the faces in her audience as they change from despair to hope. I have seen them gather around her after a presentation to excitedly ask questions and attempt to detain her a little longer. Terri is good at her work and could justly be described as a miracle worker.

I wish this story ended here but there is more ... Terri's husband, Tracy, was struck by a DUI one night returning home from work on his motorcycle. He was flown to Froedert Hospital on the *Flight For Life* helicopter and was hospitalized for several weeks with multiple internal injuries and fractures. The worst injury was the crushing of his skull on one side. It left him blind in one eye and a loss of all taste and smell. Terri jokes that when they tell their children, "We're keeping an eye on you," they mean it literally.

I wish this story ended here but there is more ... two years ago Terri's son, who is now 17, was diagnosed with a brain tumor. Surgery was performed but the prognosis for full recovery is poor. The tumor was partially excised and then radiated, resulting in further physical and psychological complications. It has instilled a sense of fatalism in the boy which Terri must deal with on a daily basis. Terri describes her situation as one of sitting in a totally dark room with a ticking bomb never knowing when it will explode.

I wish this story ended here but there is more ... last year Terri's daughter, age fifteen, developed severe abdominal distress, perhaps as a result of family stress, with symptoms similar to that of a defective gall bladder. She was fully tested but there was no definitive diagnosis. Daily medicine is keeping it under control.

Everyone has a cross to bear. If you need help carrying yours, contact Terri Gilliland. You'll be glad you did.

How do you drink tea wearing a gas mask?

by Kenda Buxton

When it comes to trends, I've always been a day late and a dollar short. When everyone was doing the Macarena, I was still learning the Hustle, which explains why I wasn't Al Gore's dance partner at the '96 Democratic Convention.

When it was fashionable to drive SUV's, I was still in a compact car. Now that I'm contemplating the purchase of an SUV, I discover Jesus wouldn't drive one, and according to Christian environmentalists, I shouldn't either.

More recently, when my fellow countrymen were reinforcing rooms with plastic and duct tape, I was reading a booklet found in my mother's home entitled: *Prepare for a Nuclear Attack – Build a Bomb Shelter*! Evidently, the underground bunkers of the 1950's are now out in favor of confining your family behind Visquine.

For a change, I want to be a trendsetter. Rather than wrap my home in plastic, and stock three days worth of tuna fish long after people are laughing over how foolish we were to think duct tape could protect us from biochemical warfare, and that we'd actually *want* to eat tuna fish for three days, I'm implementing the following tips, some of which were found on the government's Homeland Security website, so I'll be prepared the next time we're put on Orange. That's another example of what a trendsetter I wasn't. Everyone at work was concerned about being on 'Orange' and I thought they were playing Twister on their lunch hour.

1. Be alert for freshly shaven men in ill-fitting uniforms.

I pity the UPS man who's gained weight this winter. Not only is his wife nagging him to lose his beer gut, the public will tackle him over it. As far as freshly shaven goes, I'm trying to figure out how I determine if a man is freshly shaven, short of asking him, "Are you freshly shaven?" which likely foils the element of surprise.

226

2. When creating your safe room, start by sealing air conditioning units.

There won't be air conditioning in my safe room? Hell will be cooler than a sealed room in Wisconsin during August.

3. To improve chances of survival set up a small tent within your sealed room. Be cautious though, air supply will rapidly dissipate in these tight quarters.

Air supply in the confines of a small tent will dissipate even more rapidly when my husband and I throttle one another. If God wanted us to co-exist with our spouse in a tent, he wouldn't have allowed Adam and Eve to roam a garden.

4. Follow all instructions for gas mask usage, and NEVER let anyone sleep in his gas mask.

Good advice. Heaven forbid the neighbors should see you dressed in pajamas while wearing your gas mask.

5. Keep a supply of Chamomile tea on hand. Chamomile tea is a mild, herbal sedative.

In other words, when in a sealed room with your family, sedation is recommended. Also recommended … something stronger than Chamomile tea. In a situation like this you can never have too much Valium.

6. Comfort and Sanitation. Kitty litter, a scoop, and garbage bags will be needed for human waste if the sewage system isn't available. Don't forget, you may need to store your 'garbage' inside for a while.

I don't consider kitty litter and a scoop comforting or sanitary for a cat or me. And, as far as storing my garbage inside, I'll need more than Valium to get through this. I wonder if Glade offers discounts on cases of air freshener?

7. Use bleach for decontamination purposes. Be mindful of the vapors though.

If you're in a sealed room, embarking on a spring-cleaning spree with bleach is probably not a good idea.

8. Most important … practice. Spend a weekend with your family in your safe room without utilities.

This *is* important, because after spending a weekend confined with your family eating tuna fish and guzzling Chamomile tea, you'll realize why standing outside during a biochemical attack is worth the risk.

Now that I've reviewed my bioterrorism preparations, tackling UPS men and sealing rooms sound like too much work. The next time I decide to be a trendsetter, I'll just shop for an SUV while wearing a gas mask.

I jog every day, just for the health of it

by Laurie McKeon

In the highly commercial and somewhat dramatized style of James Frey, Jimmy Swaggart, Barbara Walters, Elliot Spitzer, and every other whining exhibitionist, I have a confession to make ... I am an addict. It's a sad and awful truth. I have an absolute obsession and I fear that I will never shake it. I have pursued my addiction in the early morning before dawn and late at night when no one else is around. My addiction has taken me to all kinds of places ... dark and lonely streets, parking garages, bike trails, and urban roadsides. I rarely go a day without indulging my habit and if I miss a dose, I get more than a little twitchy. I have engaged in my obsession in front of my kids and lately have been coercing my sons to join me.

Before you go searching my recycling bin for empty vodka bottles, checking my arms for track marks, or making an anonymous phone call to DCFS, let me fill you in on the details. I am a runner (using the term quite loosely), and have been for the last twenty-five years.

I started jogging in college when I gained the obligatory freshman 'ten' and wanted to take it off. Because I never met a cookie I didn't like, I decided that exercise rather than food depravation was the route for me. I started small, just a mile or two, but quickly got hooked. By the time I entered law school I was running thirty miles a week with the occasional ten or twelve miler thrown in. As my life became more stressful, I found that I ran not to maintain my weight, but to maintain my sanity.

Before anyone gets the wrong impression, let me quickly set the record straight. Although I am a dedicated runner, I will never in any universe be a good runner. I swear to you that I could not run a six-minute mile if someone was chasing me with a gun. However, like millions of other quiet, steady runners, I get up every day, put one foot in front of the other, and hit the streets. I can't seem to stop. I've run pregnant, sick, on vacation, in parking lots, hotel stairwells, pushing baby joggers, and dragging rollerbladers. During last winter's deep freeze I ran around and around my basement. I've run in the sub zero temperatures of Duluth, Minnesota wearing Sorrel boots and a ski mask, and in the steamy humidity of a Philadelphia summer not wearing much at all. I realize that there is an obvious scientific explanation for my addiction ... endorphins and all of that, but all I know is that I am a much nicer, calmer, and saner person when I run. Despite the fact that I've run six marathons over the years (one after every baby,) I'm not a racing kind of runner. I rarely run for time, pace, or a set goal. I run simply because it makes me feel better. It's pretty hard to have a bad day when just about every morning starts with me watching the sunrise over Lake Michigan as my feet rhythmically hit the pavement.

After I had my first child, I found that an early morning run taken while my family and most of the sane world still slept, allowed me time to organize my thoughts, plan my day, and have an entire hour all to myself. Draw whatever conclusions you want, but the more kids I had, the more I ran. With my first five kids born in a little over six years I couldn't get out the door for a run fast enough. Whom are we kidding? Leaving my kids with a sitter for three hours because I was doing a twenty miler to train for a marathon was a lot more socially acceptable than, say, leaving them to toss back gin and tonics at seven in the morning. In all seriousness, running takes the edge off of the unavoidable chaos and stress that life with six kids brings. I like to think of my daily mileage as my personal contribution to child abuse prevention because as long as I get in a decent run everybody in my house breathes a little easier.

Last month, after seeing yet another one of my sons lying on my sofa in baggy sweats messing around with a cell phone, I hit my limit with adolescent boys and instituted the McKeon Brothers Running Club. Four days a week my four sons hit the pavement at the crack of dawn to slog out their mandatory two miles and keep their mother off of their backs. They all pretty much hate it right now, but I can only hope that they will come to appreciate the self-discipline, order, strength, and calm that regular running can bring. I really hope that one of them becomes an addict.

No more classes, no more books, no more teacher's dirty looks

by Ed Groelle

It's very probable this article will have many senior citizens nodding their heads and probably a lot more readers of the younger persuasion, especially teachers, shaking theirs. It concerns a one-room brick school.

Yes, Virginia, at one time there really were one-room schools. If you doubt that, take a hike to Hawthorn Hollow's meadow area where one has been moved for the benefit of posterity. Unfortunately, the folks who moved it there neglected to bring the two outhouses and the merry-go-round with it, so it looks uncomfortably naked to the experienced eye.

Welcome to Whittier Grade School, District 7, Newton Township, Manitowoc County. It always seemed somehow appropriate to me that the school was named for a 19th Century Quaker poet who gave us lines like, "Blessings on thee little man, barefoot boy with cheek of tan." Certainly appropriate to its locale, which was on a small plot in the corner of our farm that my grandfather had deeded to the school district in 1894.

Since there was no kindergarten or legal starting age, I was sent to first grade at age four. I was considered "too young to be of any use around the farm" so, why not? You may think this would be an advantage, but think again. It resulted in me being a high school senior at age sixteen. Academically, that worked, but socially it was, at times, very traumatic since most of the girls had reached maturity and I still had five years to go. I still remember a couple of girls asking me to the senior prom and I reacted like a deer caught in the headlights. No, not so good.

The campus consisted of the schoolhouse, garage/storeroom, and two outdoor privies. I didn't figure out why the boy's outhouse was twice as big as the girls until fourth grade. Think about it.

The interior of the school was indeed one large room with two small anterooms at the entrance for storing outer garments before entering. These were necessary because all the children walked to school in all kinds of weather and needed a place to take off their snow pants, buckle galoshes, etc. For furnishings there were blackboards, lift-top desks, a cantankerous furnace that needed to be coaxed into life first thing each morning, and all the other basic accouterments necessary to ensure a quality education. A mechanical wind-up RCAVictrola for playing old bakelite 78's stands out in my memory because it had the then RCA logo of a dog looking at the sound horn with the slogan, "His Master's Voice."

Our teacher was Mrs. Polster, a capable, dowdy, 50-ish, neighbor who presided over thirty plus students and eight grades in that one room. Her teacher training consisted of eighteen months at County Normal school.

There were some advantages to one-room schooling. If you were the only student in one grade, being the valedictorian was a shoo-in, and if you were bored with your study assignment, it was easy to "audit" the grades ahead. The curriculum was what you could justly label, Reading 'Riting and 'Rithmetic.

The school didn't own any of the excellent McGuffey readers but did use the equally effective Dick and Jane textbooks. As a result, every student became very competent at reading and writing. I don't remember the arithmetic textbook but do remember learning the multiplication tables from flash cards. If that method is not used today it should be. It was fun and, more importantly, it worked.

There were a couple of recesses and lunchtime when we all ate our bag lunches and then played games like *Pom Pom Pull Away, Annie Annie Over,* and *Kick the Can.* These games all had some commonality in that they could be played by mixed ages and genders with no equipment other than a ball or can.

The district allocated $5 per student each year for new books, not frivolous game equipment. There was also a large merry-go-round mounted on a concrete base that today's insurance and safety experts would regard with stunned horror. As I recall, no one ever got hurt on it even though a favored activity was to get it spinning as fast as possible with the intention of losing some riders. Parent "volunteers" maintained the school by a once-a-month janitorial party, which doubled as a social event. Parents had an interest in their school and did their best to maintain it like it was their home. They also participated in any disciplinary activities.

Today, that schoolhouse is still standing as a private residence. The belfry, outhouses, and merry-go-round are gone and the buildings have been modified by additions. Kind of sad, really. It should have been kept in its original state as a museum.

We didn't have any bloated administration, ESL classes, hot meals, bilingual teachers, Ritalin, counselors, or any of today's other "progressive" initiatives. But you want to know a well-kept secret? The one-room school system worked, and worked beautifully.

Perhaps the parents who are home schooling their children have discovered this secret.

It's really not plagiarism, it's called 'research'

by Kenda Buxton

Sometimes it's not enough to do our best, we must do what's required. On the other hand, it's better to be quotable than honest. Although, well-done is better than well-said, and if a man does his best, what else is there? But while the secret to success is to know something no one else knows, no one can earn a million dollars honestly, and few things are harder to put up with than a good example. However, the price of greatness is responsibility, and we should live our lives as though Christ were coming this afternoon. And four score and seven years ago, our fathers brought forth on this continent, a new nation, conceived in liberty and dedicated to the proposition that all men are created equal. No matter what happens after that; it ain't over till it's over.

I swear on a stack of computers that I didn't plagiarize any of the above, although I must thank Winston Churchill, Benjamin Franklin, George Patton, Mark Twain, Aristotle Onassis, William Jennings Bryan, Jimmy Carter, Abraham Lincoln, and Yogi Berra for their words on honesty, dishonesty, and conceiving things in liberty. The latter having nothing to do with honesty or dishonesty, but hey, when you're copying and pasting from the Internet, sometimes things get included that make no sense within the context of your article, but big whoopee doo. As one high school student recently said, "Cheating is kind of a sin, though it's low down on the list. I mean, it's not like you murdered anyone."

No, I didn't murder anyone. Most of the men I quoted were dead before I started this and actually, I didn't copy and paste either. I typed in all of those quotes myself, which was a lot of hard work, let me tell you. If my editor submits that first paragraph to the turnitin.com website, like many teachers do now with students' written assignments to see how much of it's original, only ninety-five percent will be red lined. I'm proud to say a whopping five percent of that paragraph contains my own words ... "on the other hand," "although," "but," "however," along with the use of "and" in several places.

Since seventy-four percent of students polled admitted to cheating on an exam at least once during the past year, and the Internet has made plagiarism as easy as toasting Pop-Tarts for breakfast, all newspaper articles may soon look like my opening paragraph. A little borrowing from one source, a little lifting from another, a copy and paste command, along with a few "and's," "but's," and "what's it to ya's" thrown in just so the writer can take credit.

Forty-three percent of the students also said that sometimes a person must lie or cheat to get ahead. Sometimes? Boy, kids, have you got a lot to learn. Which is why you should be listening to your teachers, instead of text messaging your friends for answers to the history quiz. Soon enough you'll discover that any retiree who can afford medical care without hocking half the stuff in his house on eBay, has lied or cheated to get ahead. As the old saying goes, and I'm plagiarizing this, the rich get richer. The rest of us get nothing. I didn't plagiarize that. I just know it's true, since I have nothing but an old car, an old dog, and an old husband.

Stephanie Feldstein, a high school junior, observed, "In my experience, little things like copying a stupid homework assignment doesn't count as cheating." If he were alive to respond, Mark Twain might repeat one of his famous quotes of, "Denial ain't just a river in Egypt, Stephanie." While Dr. Seuss might say, "You have brains in your head. You have feet in your shoes. You can steer yourself any direction you choose."

As for myself, I have this to say to students contemplating cheating: We the people of the United States, in order to form a more perfect union, establish justice, ensure domestic tranquility ...

Oops! See what can happen when you copy and paste instead of writing something original? Oh well, to quote Richard Nixon, "I am not a crook." When all is copied and pasted ... um, I mean said and done ... it's not like I murdered anyone.

Modern dancing is really old-fashioned

by Laurie McKeon

My two younger sons are going to Cotillion School. You know, the manners and dancing class that is offered to sixth, seventh, and eighth graders at Kemper Center in the spring. They weren't exactly begging to go, but I convinced them that it would be in their best interest to slap on a tie and a smile and put their best foot forward, literally, for the next four weeks.

Boys are kind of a hot commodity in the cotillion world as my two sons are discovering. In the Crystal Cotillion class of 2008, nine of the twelve students are girls, leaving my two boys and one other stalwart young gentleman (way to step up, Ryan Rafferty) to mingle with several lovely, well mannered, young ladies as they learn how to politely introduce a friend, answer the telephone, reply to an invitation, write a thank you note, and do a mean fox trot. A few of my friends wondered why I would spend the money to send (read: force) my boys to a manners class. I've got to tell you, in my honest opinion as the mother of four sons ages 11-16, it's because they **need** it.

In a world where "What up, Dawg?" and "Hey, B****!" serve as common and acceptable salutations, I think a little coaching in the appropriate way to greet a friend or acquaintance is not a bad thing. Manners are, in many ways, a lost and dying art. Our lives are hectic, meals are eaten on the fly, corners are cut, and the opportunities for etiquette instruction are lessening. (What is the proper fork to use when eating a crunchy gordita out of a paper bag in the back seat of the car?) Your average fifth grader can text message, instant message, email, and voice mail without missing a beat, but he has no idea how to look an adult in the eye let alone offer a firm hand to shake. Removing a cap indoors, holding open a door, posting a timely *Thank You* note, and maneuvering a soupspoon may seem to be anachronisms, quaint antiques from a distant time, but in many real world instances, manners mean something. They not only smooth the rough edges off of most social and business situations, but taken in the best possible way, manners show a respect for others, an effort made, and time taken to extend courtesy above and beyond the norm. As my youngest son pointed out, quoting his cotillion handbook, "You know, Mom, manners really are just a fancy version of the golden rule."

Most parents think nothing of dishing out hundreds of dollars on sporting goods, travel teams, athletic camps, and private coaching. I know tons of families who spend every weekend on the road playing in some tournament or another and forking out major dough for hotels and meals. Parents are intimately aware of their kids' batting averages, free throw percentages, and shots on goal yet often overlook their children's social demeanor. While many families are researching the very best sporting summer camps for junior, no one is beating down the door to send their kids to 'nice' camp, and frankly, lots of kids, including mine, could use it.

While kids can learn a lot of great life lessons through athletics, very few of them will be earning a living playing professional sports. I know for a fact that none of my kids will ever be cashing a big league paycheck. Nevertheless, every one of my kids will have to interact with others, whether it is a teacher, friend, boss, or co-worker for the rest of their lives. So, when it comes to allocating resources to teach my kids some skills that they will need when interviewing for colleges, dining with clients, or just sucking up to their prospective in-laws, I don't mind writing the check to give them a leg up in the hand shake and manners department.

Let's face it. In our society today, golden rule role models, particularly those for boys, are few and far between. Our kids merely have to turn on the television to see the selfish, outlandish, degrading, and generally poor behavior of professional athletes, politicians, and media stars. Taking some time to emphasize positive, thoughtful behavior with a verbalized regard for others seems like the least I can do to prepare my boys for a very long future as men. While I totally realize that knowing how to correctly address an invitation will not insure a lifetime of goodness and success, I believe enough in social skills and the underlying message that they send for me to make the boys keep going to cotillion class every week. Moreover, as my boys are finding out, learning the proper way to pass the condiments may seem like overkill, but the ladies go crazy for a man who can dance.

National columnists weigh in on Kenosha casino

by Thomas J. Noer

The Kenosha News is conducting a search for Friday columnists and entrants are asked to submit a piece dealing with a local issue. I have decided to have my own contest and have asked the newspaper's national columnists to submit a sample of their work on the pressing local topic of building a casino.

First up is noted humorist **David Barry**: "An alert reader has informed me that Kenosha (which means Frozen Alewife) is considering a casino at a dog track. It is a little known fact that greyhounds make excellent blackjack dealers. (Wouldn't Casino Dogs be a great name for a rock group?) Well, recently my daughter, Sophie, and I went to the toy store (men in toy stores are like Janet Jackson at a bra boutique) and bought a Barbie Casino for $498.99! It would be cheaper to buy the one in Kenosha (which means Burned Bratwurst). Here in Florida, we bet on when the dew point will drop below 90. (The Dew Points would be a great name for a rock group.)"

Thanks Dave, but let's try **Miss Manners**: "Dear Gentle Local Columnist. Visitation to a casino requires one to consider several elements. First, the proper dress for a woman at a casino includes white gloves (those chips are dirty) and, of course, designer sunglasses so the dealer cannot view your eyes. It is also necessary that all bets be recorded in black ink on watermarked white paper so you can send a hand-written 'Thank You' note within 24 hours of winning. At the 'all you can eat buffet' avoid the macaroni salad and be sure to start with the fork on your left."

I'll keep it in mind, but I need to hear from conservative intellectual and baseball fanatic **George Will**: "In ancient Rome gambling was strictly *sub rosa* as the motto was, of course, *cravat emptor*. With the ceaseless expansion of an all-intrusive government, the quality of entertainment has eroded or, as Cicero, observed,

"Never double down on a pair of sevens!" If only Ronald Reagan were still in office. Fortunately, the annual ritual of regeneration known as 'spring training' will soon begin and there is some hope for the republic. As noted philosopher Pete Rose used to say, "Bet on it!""

George and I both like the bow tie, but let's listen to my favorite homemaker, **Heloise**: "To remove stains from clothing stained by the free drinks at casinos, simply place the garment in a mixture of six parts chlorine, four parts distilled water, and seventeen parts onion juice. Soak for eight days and put it in the oven at 450 degrees for two hours. Good as new. Also, to clean dirty poker chips, just put them in your microwave, cover with olive oil, and heat for fifty seconds. Not only clean, but a tasty snack."

You are always good, Heloise. How about **Ray and Tom Magliozzi** of Car Talk: "If your car won't start in the casino parking lot it could be that you left the lights on. Or, you are so drunk that you are at the wrong car! Either way, open the hood and stick your tongue on the battery. If it shocks you to the ground, there is nothing wrong with it!"

"Yeah, Ray, then you might try using your car key to start it! Seriously, just dismantle the cooling system, run a hose into the gas tank, and blow. It won't do any good, but you will impress your friends! Remember, don't bet like my brother."

"Oh yeah? Well don't bet like MY brother!"

I'll remember the tip. Now for the Texas Tornado**, Molly Ivins**: "Y'all are talking about gambling? Well that shrub in DC is gambling with your future. I don't give a hoot or a holler about casinos, but we've got to do something about George W! As we say here in Texas, "Never draw to an inside straight, never eat a chicken-fried steak before noon, and never vote for anybody named George. Remember the Alamo!"

Take a Valium Molly. It's time to hear from the **Editors of the Kenosha News** for their take on this controversial issue: A laurel to those in favor of the casino as it will create jobs and lower taxes. A laurel to those opposed to the casino as it will lead to crime and other problems. A laurel to those in favor of a referendum on the casino. You are right. The people must be heard. A laurel to those against a referendum. You are right. The people have already spoken on the issue. Wait a minute! You seem to be in favor of both sides and unwilling to take any position on the issue! A dart to Tom Noer for revealing our editorial policy.

Wisdom to tape to your refrigerator door

by Ed Groelle

I've lived long enough to have found solutions to some of life's rich pageantry of minor problems. I feel a heavy responsibility to pass them on to future generations. After reading these, the *Helping With Heloise* column will appear amateurish by comparison.

~ **Refrigerator light doubts** - You suspect the light in your refrigerator doesn't turn off when the door closes. You are cheap and don't want to pay Wisconsin Electric a penny more than is necessary, so it must be verified. This problem stymied me for a long time but with diligent mental effort came up with a simple solution. Take a digital camera, turn on the ten-second delay, and turn off the flash. Click it, put it in the fridge and wait twenty seconds. Then, preview the photo. If it is all black the light is turning off. If there is a photo of your leftovers, the light is still on.

~ **A mouse gets trapped in the toilet bowl** - Immediately put weights on the lid ... a spouse is perfect. If you don't have one, borrow someone else's ... the heavier, the better. Use a turkey baster to add a pint of chlorine to the water without lifting the lid. Wait until there is no movement or squeaks. Then, move about ten feet away and ask the weight to get up and raise the seat. If successful the mouse will be comatose. If not successful, see next paragraph for further action.

~ **How to handle an irate spouse** - Appear remorseful, keep your mouth shut, and your head down.

~ **Razor burn** - Take a ten-inch length of duct tape and apply it across your lower face. Stand in front of a mirror and using colored Marker pens, paint your face features on the tape. If done well no one will probably ever notice the razor burn.

~ **Senior moments** - We've all had them. If yours is in the form of Right/Left confusion, wrap a rubber band around right wrist remembering that rubber band starts with an R = Right. Wrap a shoelace around your left wrist remembering that lace starts with L = Left.

~ **Toothbrush falls in the toilet bowl** - This is similar to the mouse thing but here you want to rescue the victim. Remember, you are very cheap and the dentist appointment when he gives you the free toothbrush is several months away. The easiest solution is to boil the brush in one part alcohol to ten parts water for an hour. If you are then still skittish about using it, take it along when visiting relatives and swap it with one of theirs.

~ **Mid-life crisis** - If you are contemplating quitting your job, dumping your spouse, buying a red convertible, or wearing clothes appropriate for a twenty-year-old, you are probably suffering this affliction. There is no known cure but not making any important decisions and keeping your mouth shut as much as possible until it passes can minimize symptoms. The more you talk in this condition, the sillier you will appear.

~ **Tattoo Pain** - If you think getting a tattoo is painful think of the anguish you will suffer when you are sixty and forced to look at it every day in the bath mirror. To get a preview of that pain get a temporary tattoo and then go to any circus fun house and stand in front of a distortion mirror. That's what it will look like then. That's real pain!

~ **Filling time during retirement** - You could religiously follow and keep meticulous records on the Chicago Bears, meet at McDonalds every morning, or write brilliant, witty, and educational Sunday articles for the Kenosha News. But, that really isn't enough, is it? Consider annoying other people as a time-consuming activity. Here are some suggestions:

Wait five seconds before starting when the traffic light turns green. To enhance this annoyance take your TV remote with you and hold it to your ear like you are using a cell phone. You will learn many new hand gestures and colorful words doing this.

Drive around town at the posted speed limit in the left lane. You'll also feel righteous to be setting a good example for other drivers.

When checking out at a grocery store never have your store card, credit card, checkbook, or wallet out until the final total appears on the screen. Then fumble for these items, pretend to not know how to scan your card, and ask what the date is. Also, just before paying, ask the cashier to get you a pack of Marlboro light, mentholated, slims in a hard pack. If you pay by cash always carry a dozen pennies and laboriously count them out.

   Any gratitude for these solutions is not expected. Just don't cut my photo off when posting this article to the refrigerator.

Mother is a verb, not a noun

by Kenda Buxton

"Nobody knows of the work it takes, to keep the home together.
Nobody knows of the steps it takes, nobody knows but
Mother." (Author Unknown)

~ ~ ~

Mother's Day was first called, "Mother's Work Day" when
Appalachian homemaker, Anna Jarvis, organized the day to raise
awareness of childrens' health conditions in her community.
Needless to say, most Appalachian women felt they worked hard
enough *every* day, and therefore weren't too crazy about only one
day designated as 'Mother's Work Day.' Which just goes to show
why a good marketing strategy that includes flowers, Hallmark
commercials, and dinner cooked by someone else, is often the
key to success for what would otherwise be an unpopular idea.

As time passed, Anna's daughter, also named Anna, wanted
to publicly recognize her mother's years of community service,
so lobbied Presidents Taft and Roosevelt to set aside a national
day honoring all mothers. The younger Anna was astute enough
to drop the word "Work" from the day, and in 1914, President
Wilson signed the bill that recognizes the second Sunday in May
as Mother's Day.

Although it hasn't been called 'Mother's Work Day' in over a
century, is there ever a day when a mother isn't doing her job in
some way? My mother is 77, and while she retired 25 years ago
from the career she earned a paycheck for, she's never retired from
her job as *Mom* to my sister and me. Evidently, she plans to keep
going strong in that regard for quite a while yet, because as my
sister put it once, "When we're both old and feeble and in a nursing
home, Mom'll still be around to tell us the best way to mix our
Metamucil so it doesn't splash on our lap robes."

When it comes to her children, my mother is concerned about a
lot of things besides just Metamucil spills, even though the children

are now 53 and 43. She's told us how to recognize the symptoms of small pox, that we should never use our cell phones while pumping gas, and which Christmas tree topper was recalled because of fire hazards. I wanted to ask her if it was okay to use my cell phone to call 911 while pumping gas if:

(a) A rogue terrorist at another pump sprayed me with small pox, or

(b) I suddenly realized I owned the fire-starting tree topper and had left it plugged in. Unfortunately, my sarcastic humor is wasted on my mother, who long ago learned to ignore it.

She gives me cosmetic tips on a regular basis, like how I should put a little blush underneath my eyebrows. Blush? Do I even own any of that? She tells me to use a piece of chalk to clean my silver jewelry. The day I clean my jewelry with *anything* is the day I'm in a home for the criminally insane where jewelry cleaning is part of Arts and Crafts Hour. She still reminds me to wear a hat when I run during the winter, and she recently told me not to put Vicks up my nose because you can inhale it into your lungs, even though I haven't had Vicks up my nose in thirty-five years. Mmmm ... come to think of it, the last person to put Vicks up my nose is the same woman who's now telling me I could die from doing this. She keeps me current on other health tips too, like taking a baby aspirin to prevent heart attacks, and how the mercury levels in fish will likely kill us all if we're not careful.

As my mom's proven with her many motherly tips, a good mother never stops working for the sake of her children. Although 'Mother's Day' took the place of 'Mother's Work Day' years ago, I think every son and daughter blessed with a loving mother will acknowledge that, as much as Mom deserves a day off, every day is 'Mother's Work Day' for the women who put the needs of their children ahead of their own, no matter how old those children are.

And don't worry, Mom. Now that I'm done writing this column, I'll unplug my tree topper, wipe the Vicks out of my nose, and start cleaning my jewelry.

Teaching is the profession that teaches all the other professions

by Laurie McKeon

WANTED: *Mature individual with youthful spirit, willing to work with untrained, unresponsive, unruly, and uncooperative groups. Expected to communicate with the masses, elevate the average, and eradicate ignorance every single day. Strong managerial and leadership skills required, able to work in hectic, busy environment, coordinate group activities, while providing individual attention and reassuring overbearing supervisors. Enthusiastic, personable and willing to repeat yourself without loosing your mind. College degree required and continuing education mandatory. Knowledge of science, math, English, art, music, history, health, spelling, and technology a must. Diplomacy, counseling, and first aid skills helpful. Not afraid of runny noses, glue eaters, bad attitudes, slackers, suck ups, truants, and the occasional pants wetter. Be prepared to come in early and stay late. Also expected to work at home. Long hours, low wages.*

School has started and once again my kids' teachers amaze me. First of all, I'm amazed that they keep showing up every year. Think about it. How many times can you explain fractions and really care? As a parent, even just hearing about the same lessons year to year numbs my mind, not to mention having to construct a 'City of the Future' every time I've got a third grader. Teachers just keep coming back. They are the worlds' greatest optimists. They must truly believe in what they are doing or they'd find a different profession because they sure aren't in it for the money and the perks.

Every year teachers are randomly assigned a group of students and then are expected to teach something valuable, positive, useful, and permanent to every single kid, every single day. They get the gamut from the bright and eager kid to the reluctant, belligerent

247

one. They get the kid whose parents can barely find the classroom and the kid whose parents will never leave, the smug kids who think they're smarter than they are, and the quiet kids who are afraid to even try. By law, they're not allowed to leave a single one behind. Teachers do this year after year after year. That's the part that blows me away. Remember teaching your kid to tie his shoe, ride a bike, write his name, or drive a car? It's kind of interesting the first time, but by my third or fourth kid, I just let them figure it on their own or let an older sibling do all the heavy lifting. I actually told my fifth child that I'd give him twenty bucks if he taught himself how to ride a bike without involving me in any way. He did. I paid. Teachers don't have that option and I don't think they'd want it.

All of the teachers I know find a real joy in the process of teaching and live for the moment when the penny finally drops. Last year, on *Grandparents and Special Persons Day*, I was sitting in my fifth grader's math class listening to a lesson on least-common multiples. These kids just weren't getting it. As I sat there, dying to blurt out the answers, the teacher patiently and gently guided the lesson, engaging every student until they could all solve the problems. You could see her mastery of the subject and her subtle ability to instill this knowledge. It was like watching performance art. When she finished I wanted to stand up and applaud.

Through the years my kids have had literally hundreds of teachers and, while they've liked some better than others, I can honestly only think of one dud. (Don't worry, he taught in Ohio. I think he sells insurance now.) Sure, some were nicer, kinder, more effective, but every single one of them taught my kids many valuable lessons and not just academically. Teachers can challenge and motivate students in ways that parents envy. Every parent knows that their kids will perform Herculean tasks for a teacher they love that they'd never do at home. It's often the teacher who is the hardest on your kid that teaches them the most.

As this school year settles in there may be a teacher your kid doesn't like or one who doesn't do things the way you would or has yet to recognize the potential genius that is your child. Be patient and remember that teacher is doing an invaluable, demanding, and exhausting job, not just for your child, but also for every child in the class. Your kid will be okay, he will learn much more that you can imagine, and he'll end the year infinitely better off than when it began.

My brother's third grade teacher was an eighty-five-year-old nun who seriously could not speak English, but she was dead on accurate with a flying eraser from twenty yards out. Maybe the only thing he learned that year was how to duck but he turned out just fine. He graduated from Northwestern, has a Masters in Education, and is proud to be a teacher. To all the teachers out there ... thanks, and have a great year.

Give us seniors a break, but please, not the hip

by Ed Groelle

I recently had lunch with a friend who brought up the subject of bibliotherapy. I had to admit I'd never heard of it. Simply stated, the purpose of bibliotherapy is to assist someone in overcoming the emotional turmoil related to a real-life handicap by having him/her identify with characters in books or the media with similar problems.

What a splendid idea! But it got me to thinking that there seems to be very few characters for seniors on TV to identify with any more. Those seniors, especially the grandmothers depicted on TV, are not typecast and can easily be mistaken for post-graduate college students. Not at all like the real-life grannies I had with ankle length, flour-sack dresses, orthopedic shoes, and a cane that served as a chastisement tool. At one time there were some realistic TV seniors like the father in *Everybody Loves Raymond* and especially *Becker* who was the epitome of an astute senior curmudgeon. All gone.

It's not news to any anglophile, but there are a few British rerun shows featuring seniors; *As Time Goes By*, *Waiting for God*, *Miss Marple*, and *One Foot in the Grave*. These can still be seen on the PBS Channel every Sunday evening. The longest running sitcom in TV history was a British comedy featuring a trio of odd, whimsical, old duffers who roamed a backwater English village getting into mischief with a variety of socially challenged characters. *Last of the Summer Wine* ran for over thirty years and all the episodes were written by one man, Roy Clarke, who continued writing the show even though some of the main characters died off in real life. I am an avid fan of these shows and have seen most of the episodes, so I can reliably state that there are no characters under fifty in any of them and certainly no smart-mouthed eight-year-olds or fashion models posing as grandmothers.

The one glaring omission from these characters is that they never show any of the discomforts that seniors are privy to, such as aching backs, hips, or knees. They will leap out of bed in the morning or in the middle of the night with no hint of any aches or pains. They quaff a pint of ale with seemingly no thought of what it may do to their age-onset diabetes numbers. You never see them eating a handful of pills each morning either. This is so not realistic!

These omissions and the dearth of bibliotheraputic seniors on American TV have prompted me to develop a TV series of my own. It's a female detective show delivered with a dry comedic twist so it should be a hit with the intelligentsia. The 83-year-old heroine, Inita Walker, has had a hip replacement and lives in a senior complex near downtown Kenosha with two Siamese cats, Arthro and Scopy. For a hint of sexual tension I've made her principal protagonist and confidante a twenty-seven-year-old, totally bald, male night nurse named Theo, who has a nursing degree from a prestigious mail-order university. His day job is haunting garage sales and selling the junk on eBay. Some of his cronies at the Dayton Hotel suspect he may be in the witness protection program.

She is really not so much a detective as a consultant to the Kenosha Traffic Enforcement Unit, sort of like a low-key Adrian Monk. She failed the DMV driver vision test, so she was forced to give up driving, but she had no problem getting a license to carry her .357 Magnum handgun. Her principal mode of transport is an adult tricycle which has a police radar detector mounted on one handlebar and a GPS unit on the other. Also, in case of a high-speed pursuit of a parking perp, she also owns an electric scooter that has been modified to attain a speed of twelve MPH in just under twenty seconds.

I hope to get a few support actors from Lakeside Players on the show and an occasional cameo by aspiring thirty-somethings like Bob Dole or Hugh Hefner. I have several story lines festering in my mind that only need a bit of fleshing out. One episode that will be particularly exciting is when she is called out in the middle of the night during a blinding snowstorm to deal with a scofflaw in White Caps who has parked on the wrong side of the street. What makes this such a nail biter is that Theo has forgotten to install the snow tires on her scooter.

I feel I've got a pretty good handle on developing this series. All I need now is an agent, a publicist, and a ghostwriter to help with some minor snags. I wonder what Roy Clarke is doing these days. He turned seventy-six last January. Perfect!

Some novel ideas for the Boat Building

By Thomas J. Noer

A glance at any bestseller list shows that no one reads fiction any more! The only books we buy are about dieting, self-help, or memoirs of substance abuse. As for myself, I'm working on a book called The Drug Abuse Diet that should get me on Oprah! There are still a few novelists who sell and I have asked each to set their next book in the new Kenosha landmark, the vast and ugly Boat Storage Facility.

Here are some excerpts:

Danielle Steel (writer of sexy romances).
Samantha DuBois slowly shed her sheer silk robe and stood nude as the lights of the smelt dippers on Lake Michigan illuminated her ivory skin and long auburn hair. What more romantic spot for a rendezvous with the mysterious Raoul than the Boat Storage Facility? Suddenly, she heard a noise and was shocked to find Jonathan standing before her! How had the brave but boring Jonathan discovered her?

"Samantha. I've come to warn you that Raoul is not the man you think. He is not a UN diplomat but a secret perch poacher and this is where he keeps his illegal catch! You can't marry him. I know I am only a humble multimillionaire, but I love you and fate has brought us together!"

"Whatever," she sighed, "I'm starving. Do you know how to cook perch?"

Dan Brown (author of The Da Vinci Code).
Robert Langdon was still bleeding from the knife wound the dwarf had given him in Istanbul that morning, but now he was near the end of his search. The key had to be in this massive structure near Lake Michigan. Only yesterday, while being beaten by that seven-foot albino in Athens, did he make the connection. Why had this

city suddenly erected such an ugly structure? There could only be one answer ... within it was the deep secret hidden for two thousand years. The pygmy who had shot him with the poison arrow was right! Kenosha was where the mystery would be solved. As he crept past the boats, he noticed they were arranged in an ancient Celtic cross. Yes! In the exact center of this building would be the codebook! Suddenly, he was snagged in the chest by a giant Coho hook. It could only be The Fisherman ... the last guardian of the treasure. Frantically, he grabbed a nearby perch and squirted it to blind his enemy! The search would continue!

Steven King (master of the horror novel).

He was really terrified now. The building was ALIVE and GROWING! Already it had moved into Lake Michigan and captured three jet skiers and even now was headed west towards Frank's Diner! If only he could get into its demented mind and understand the source of its evil. If it was alive it could talk. In a hushed voice he asked, "What is it you want?"

An eerie sound emerged from beneath the yachts, "I want it all, all of the lakefront from here to Winthrop Harbor and Racine. Soon my Civil War Museum brother will join me and we will devour everything in sight. Nothing can stop us. Nothing!"

Tom Clancy (techno thriller writer supreme).

After completing his PhD from Harvard, winning the Nobel Peace Prize, and appearing on American Idol, Jack Ryan had left the CIA for a quiet life in Wisconsin. But now there was one last obligation to save his country ... destroy the terrorist cell holed-up in this boat building. Using a CX47 scope mounted on an 8PR33 stock, he placed a 99LK Smarterthanhell missile on the DK330 launcher. Using the GPS chip implanted in his nose, he calculated the range and fired! A massive roar followed as the so-called Boat Storage Facility erupted into flames. The terrorists fled like rats, but were no match for Ryan's new Alewife Assault rifle. Each splat of the noxious fish downed an enemy agent and America was saved!

Garrison Keeler (Minnesota's famous humorist).

It was a quiet day in my hometown. The Norwegian bachelor farmers had come to the Chatterbox Café to hear the latest on that new Boat Storage Facility. Funny how big buildings had become.

When I was a child we had no buildings. We sipped homemade ginger ale and sang hymns. But things had changed. Just last night, Pastor Lundquist had noted, "Boy, that is one big building out der by the lake. Sure wish we could use it for the confirmation camp. Say, any of that tater tot casserole left?"

Tom Noer (obscure columnist)

I have a novel idea! Why don't we just put the proposed giant WalMart in the Boat Storage Facility? No parking problems since the trolley runs right by.

High Definition TV:
Low daffinition comedy

by Ed Groelle

FCC Chairman Newton Minow once said, "When television is good, nothing, not the theater, not the magazines, or newspapers ... nothing is better. But when television is bad, nothing is worse. I invite you to sit down in front of your television set when your station goes on the air and stay there without a book, magazine, or newspaper to distract you and keep your eyes glued to that set until the station signs off. I can assure you that you will observe a vast wasteland." He said that in 1961, almost fifty years ago. Today, he probably would describe it as an abattoir garbage dumpster.

Recently, my trusty Sony TV died of old age so I needed to purchase a TV. There are strong rumors that universal HD is right around the corner, so I decided to buy a forty-two-inch High Definition thin screen. Some $1,400 later, I have five remotes playing hide and seek in my living room, all with mostly mysterious buttons I have found no use for. In my unconquerable soul, I sort of hoped the TV would come with some new programming. That was not the case, so I decided to take Newton's suggestion and analyze six hours of TV broadcasting to find the cause of my dissatisfaction.

The six hours break down like this: Total advertising time: 2 hours, 8 minutes or 28 percent of the broadcast time. The ad content consisted of: Movies and TV shows: 94, (I assume these are used to fill out the program's allotted time slot.) retail stores: 35, Hospitals, doctors, medicine: 31, Restaurants: 28, Sundries (shampoo, toothpaste, etc.): 14, Food related: 13, Cell phone, cable: 11, Autos: 8, Financing and credit cards: 7, Insurance: 4, Miscellaneous: 10, Total: 255 ads. I did not count those annoying, distracting banners that stream across the bottom one quarter of your screen every minute during the program. Have you noticed they never run those banners during a commercial? Mind you, all these ads were in beautiful high definition. What a thrill!

I'd be willing to bet that if this survey was taken ten or twenty years ago the ad time would be significantly less than today. It's quite probable some experts have researched just how much the audience will tolerate in ad watching before switching channels. In my opinion they reached that point some time ago. I would never watch a TV movie anymore without first taping it so ads can be skipped.

The ads might be tolerated if the program content wouldn't have sunk to such a low level. Is it really necessary to constantly depict two men having a conversation while standing at urinals? In fairness, there is some good stuff to watch like the *History Channel*, *PBS*, and, of course, *Dog the Bounty Hunter*. But, for me anyway, the comedy on TV has deteriorated to the level of sixth-grade toilet jokes. The *Comedy Channel* really is a misnomer. Is there really anything funny on that channel? If there is, I certainly have never stumbled on to it. My cat is funnier when he throws up.

Watch any of the "new" sitcoms being shown now. In the first two minutes they will instruct you in several politically correct situations, several sexual situations will be hinted at accompanied by snicker-inducing type jokes, and, of course, the children are always, always smarter than any of the adults, especially the white adult male who will be cast as the buffoon. It is a comedic formula repeated ad nauseam.

Am I being entertained or chastised? The jokes are not funny, but fortunately, they always turn up the laugh track at the "funny" parts so I know just where to laugh. Is it any mystery that our library's use is increasing instead of decreasing as gleefully predicted?

Television is the first true democratic culture ... the first culture available to everybody, and in theory anyway, entirely governed by what the people want. The most terrifying thing is what people do want. Where it concerns comedy, I know what I want ...

I want Ralph and Alice Cramdon back

I want Rob and Laura Petri back.

I want Bob and Emily Hartley back.

I want Ray and Debra Barone back.

I want my money back.

Let's all give cashiers a break

by Jim Wynne

There has been a movement afoot in the retail industry to improve customer service. It seems that customers are increasingly annoyed by allegedly incompetent and/or complacent workers at the point of sale. One large supermarket chain has *ordered* its cashiers to smile at customers and call them by name. When someone I don't know smiles at me, I always wonder if my fly is open or if I have toilet paper hanging from the back of my pants. I never take it as a sign that the person is genuinely glad to see me. The geniuses that run large retail organizations, most of whom have never had to deal with the public on a daily basis, develop these sophomoric ideas that serve only to demean and demoralize their own employees while ignoring real opportunities to improve things for good customers.

Consider for a moment what your average supermarket checker has to put up with. Many customers are hopeless jackasses. They're rude, sometimes dirty and smelly, demanding, unreasonable, self-centered, and stupid. They think it's perfectly okay to treat store employees like swine. They carry on unnecessary conversations on their cell phones while the cashier is waiting for payment, while five people behind them are waiting, and the four-year-old in the basket seat is screaming at the top of his lungs. They try to get away with more than they have coming, holding up lines while they whine about 'limit-2' restrictions or the shelf tag being incorrect ... a shelf tag which in most cases the customer has misread despite the fact that it was designed to be perfectly clear to the average six-year-old.

They lick their fingers, touch open wounds, and/or pick their noses while handling their money. They are taken by surprise by the fact that merchandise must be paid for, then take their time in determining the method of payment, or finding the checkbook at the bottom of an American Tourister-sized purse filled with cosmetics, candy wrappers, and two yards of topsoil. They'll purposely avoid putting the money into the smiling cashier's outstretched hand, opting instead to put it down on the moving conveyor belt so the cashier has to chase it. If the customer decides to pay by credit or debit card, the even-a-moron-could-figure-it-out electronic card-reading device must be explained in excruciating detail, and even then the customer tries to swipe the card upside-down or backwards, and complains bitterly about how complicated it is. Frequently this complaining is heard from persons who were given the same patient explanation the day before.

Customers take baskets into the *10 items or less* line loaded with enough groceries to winter the Russian army and complain that they are in a hurry and can't wait in the other line where they belong. They bring $100 worth of items to the checkout when they know they have only $9.75 with them. They complain bitterly to the adolescent clerk who refuses to sell liquor because a city ordinance prohibits its sale during certain hours of the day. Sometimes they are drunk or high and babble incoherently and make lewd comments, especially if they are smiled at by an attractive young cashier. Many of them don't speak English and are vexed by the fact that the cashier isn't fluent in Urdu or Portuguese. They study a twelve-foot-long register tape in infinite bloody detail and ask fifty stupid questions about it.

Customer, "What is this? I didn't get any pomegranates!"

Cashier, "It says Polident, ma'am." before reluctantly moving out of the way so someone else can check out.

When a truly unreasonable customer goes beyond every known limit of decent human behavior and the manager must get involved, he or she invariably panders to the idiot, which makes the cashier look and feel like an indentured servant who is expected to take the forty lashes, smile sweetly, and forget about it.

Just remember all this the next time you're buying groceries and the cashier seems disinclined to act really glad to see you. After five hours or so of being abused, there aren't many people who can maintain a pleasant disposition. If you are a normally polite and considerate person, be aware that store management doesn't really care at all about you, because they are too busy appeasing the morons and making them feel welcome, which just perpetuates the whole problem.

If the big retail companies really did care about their good customers and their own employees, they would make it a matter of policy to tell the incorrigible bad ones to hit the road and go shop the competition. Amazingly, the management pinheads haven't realized that customer service is a two-way street and does not consist in kissing the behinds of people who need to have them kicked right out of the store.

College majors for careers in multibillion dollar industries

by Thomas J. Noer

Columbia College in Chicago recently announced they were offering a major in *Video Games*. School officials explained, "Video games are a multi-billion dollar industry and students would have no problem finding jobs."

Now, to some people, this is yet another sign of the end of civilization, but it has convinced me that colleges really do need to offer other majors in multi-billion dollar industries. Students can study Physics, Economics or even History at any college. What we need are schools that understand the marketplace in the 21st century. So, we take you to the Advising Center of Noer University where Sammy Student enters for a conference with the school's Career Counselor.

"Sammy! Good to finally see you. You know you are two hours late?"

"Yeah, well, I'm not into mornings."

"I understand. Now, the reason for our meeting is that I got a call from your parents and they pointed out that this is your seventh year at Noer University. You have yet to declare a major so I thought we would go through some options for a major and career. O.K.?"

"Whatever."

"Now Sammy, as you know at Noer U. we specialize in majors that train students for careers in multi-billion dollar industries so lets look at some possibilities. Do you like to play poker?"

"Yeah, I guess."

"Well, Sammy, poker is a multi-billion dollar industry. It is all over TV and the Internet and video poker games are everywhere. You might consider poker as a major."

"Like, what do I have to do?"

"Well, classes are offered by Fast Freddy Franco at 2 AM in the backroom of Freddy's Lounge. He will teach you all you need to know about the game. There are some additional fees."

"Like how much?"

"Well, it's a $500 buy-in, $100 ante, and minimum $200 raise."

"Whoa dude! I play poker for potato chips. I can't afford that."

"No problem. Let's move on. Do you own a cell phone?"

"Duh! Like who doesn't?"

"Exactly! Cell phones are a multi-billion dollar industry and you might want to major in CP."

"Do I have to like design or repair them?"

"Of course not! What our counseling teaches is how to work with companies to use them to annoy people. The introductory course is *Airport 101* where you practice sitting in a crowded waiting area and speaking as loudly as you can: "HI! I'M IN THE AIRPORT. THE PLANE LEAVES IN ABOUT 40 MINUTES SO I WILL BE IN ABOUT 9:45. CALL YOU LATER." Five minutes later you repeat this until everyone moves away. An upper division class has you with one of those head sets and you walk down the street talking and people think you are either psychotic or speaking to them. Drives everyone nuts! What do you think?"

"Well, I'm not really into walking."

"No problem. Let's move on. How about crime?"

"Crime?"

"Sure Sammy, crime is a multi-billion dollar industry and there are always jobs for good criminals. We start you out with *Intro to Mugging* and then you move to *Embezzlement Theory*. During your last semester you will intern with a politician and learn how to make REAL money."

"Yeah, but don't lots of criminals like, go to jail?"

"Sam, all careers have some risk and N.U. has strong alumni clubs in nearly every state and federal penitentiary."

"Too risky, dude."

"Well, Sammy, we have just started a new major in Steroids taught by professors Bonds and Sosa."

"So, like, what do I do?"

"Well, your job is to take periodic urine and blood tests for famous athletes so they can keep playing. You know, steroids are a multi-billion dollar industry!"

"I'm not much of a jock."

"Sammy, we are running out of choices. Let's see ... *Porno Film Dialogue Coach, Tattoo Removal Consultant, Mall Walking Guide* ... all of these are very popular majors but I don't think they are right for you. It seems to me you lack any ambition, have no social skills, and are basically illiterate, so I think your only option is to major in *Column Writing.*"

"Is that a multi-billion dollar industry?"

"Well, if you are Maggie Gallagher or Armstrong Williams you can get big bucks in secret payoffs from the White House to write in support of their programs, but most column writers get paid in table scraps."

"Table scraps?"

"Yes, editors collect their half-eaten sandwiches, apple cores, and day old doughnuts and then put them in a paper bag on the back steps of the newsroom. When you turn in a column you get the bag."

"Doesn't sound too great. Are you sure that's what I should do."

"Trust me Sammy. I'm an expert. BTW, did you know that *Career Counseling* is a multi-billion dollar industry?"

I look at winter as an occupation, not as a season

by Laurie McKeon

I am writing this column from FLORIDA! Yes, FLORIDA! While I am not trying to rub it in or make you all jealous (okay, maybe just a little), Florida is pretty darn great. It has an ocean, it has sunshine, and it, most importantly, has no snow.

I want to confess something right now just get it out in the open so there is absolutely no confusion on this issue. I hate winter! Let me clarify. It's not actually the winter I hate. I am sure winter in Hawaii or California or in my new favorite place, Florida, would be just fine. It's the cold, snow, sleet, chapped skin, clenched muscles, dirty cars, ugly boots, and chronic static in my hair that come with winter that I really hate. Allow me to continue. I hate washing snow pants, shoveling the driveway, wearing an enormous coat, and sleeping in sweat pants and a turtle neck, (my husband hates that one, too), shivering nonstop, and feeling like I will never, ever be warm again. All I want to do is get into a hot car and feel the warmth of the sun on my face. Is that too much to ask? Well, from November to March in Kenosha, Wisconsin, I guess it is.

I don't know why I hate winter so much. I should have gotten used to it by now. It comes every year and I've spent my whole life in climates that produce freakish amounts of foul winter weather. I grew up outside Chicago, (where bad snow plowing can lose elections) went to college in South Bend, IN, (home of the lake effect snow), spent ten years in Ohio, (ice-storm capital of the world) and actually lived in Duluth, MN for two winters and one summer (the longest two winters of my life) and now, Kenosha. I've never been a fan of the cold and the older I get, the more I hate it.

I must admit that I was humming along nicely this winter. December was mild, rather pleasant, with no big, lasting snow, no annoying shoveling, or deicing the front steps. January started out just fine and that lulled me into thinking that I could actually survive this winter unscathed, intact, and somewhat sane. With all of the publicity of global warming and those holes in the ozone layer I was just so sure that this was going to be a mild winter ... the winter of no discontent. Then the deep freeze hit and all bets were off. I tried to gut it out by wearing three layers of clothes and drinking pot after pot of hot tea but I just couldn't take it for one more day. I needed sunshine and I needed it fast.

To my husband's credit, for the past several years, he has bitten the bullet and paid for us to go some place warm for even a few days to remind me that there is still sunshine in the world and that, soon enough, I can stop wearing two pairs of socks. (a little trick I learned while living in Duluth. It does help keep you warm.) In his calculating mind he totally realizes that a short week in Arizona is cheaper than an inpatient stay in a psychiatric facility and that having a grateful wife during the coldest months of the year is money well spent. As for me, just knowing that reservations have been made for a place in the sun is enough to get me through. Last year we took our whole family to an amazing villa in Jamaica. We booked it in October and every time the thermometer dipped below twenty I just looked at the photos of our villa-to-be and I could persevere.

However, a warm weather vacation was not in the plans for the McKeon family this year. We nobly decided to spend our spring break helping our oldest find the college of our financial advisors choice. Since she has decided that she wants to go to school at least two states away from home, we will forgo our traditional beach holiday for a whirlwind tour of several overpriced east coast universities. We are taking the entire family. It seemed like a good idea in the fall. Now, I'm not so sure.

I guess I overestimated my nobleness because about three weeks ago I just cracked. I honestly couldn't go another freezing minute and my survival instinct kicked in. I shamelessly called our best friends from Ohio who just happen to own a condo on the ocean in Palm Beach. We found cheap flights out of O'Hare and hired a babysitter for the kids. My husband and I then high tailed it to the land of the sun. So, as I head down to the pool once again for cocktail hour in the sun, just remember that I am thinking of you all and wishing you were here.

A letter to Jack from his Grandpa

by Thomas J. Noer

Dear Jack,

A lot of people have been waiting a long time for you to arrive and we were delighted you decided to join us on August 12. You have already met your mom and dad, your beautiful big sister Sophie, your great-grandmother Bernadine, and us, Grandma Linda and Grandpa Tom. In the next few weeks you will be introduced to many others; uncles, aunts, cousins, friends, and your Pittsburgh grandparents, Don and Bebe. We all know you are brilliant, but as you are only two weeks old, I don't think you are quite ready to read yet. But I still wanted to write you a letter about grandparents that you can save and maybe look at in a few years.

Grandparents get to do a lot of really neat things with their grandkids. We get to take care of you when your parents are busy or out of town (even change diapers!) We get to sit with you in sandboxes and dig with sticks. We help you draw purple trees growing out of pink and orange grass that we tape on our refrigerator for everyone to see. We get to read you funny books and make up scary stories. We get to sing all sorts of silly songs together. It is a wondrous thing to be a grandparent!

Grandparents also love to take you places like malls, grocery stores, restaurants, and friends' homes so everyone can see you. Sometimes we like to dress you up and wander around the neighborhood pushing your stroller just showing you off. Silly grandparents!

Grandparents get to watch you enjoy 'special' days. We see your excitement when you look at the bright lights on a Christmas tree, hang up your stocking for Santa, and we help you make the perfect Halloween costume (and maybe even eat some of the candy you get!) We like to help you look for all those Easter eggs and try to figure out where that bunny put them. On your birthday we get to watch you smear cake all over your face, try to blow out candles, and sing, "How old are you? You belong in a zoo!"

Grandparents are great at buying anything you are selling for school, sports, or any other group or club ... candy, greeting cards, raffle tickets ... we are your best customers. We also love to go to anything you are a part of ... soccer games, piano recitals, Sunday school programs. Just let us know the time and place and we'll be there. We also are amazingly easy to beat at *Shoots and Ladders, Hi-Ho Cherry-O,* and *Uno.*

Grandparents also do some very strange things. We take hundreds of pictures of you to show to friends and even to strangers we run into in parking lots. Sometimes we buy really ugly clothes that we think are cute and your parents make you wear them when we visit, even if you don't like them. Many times we talk too much about what your mom or dad were like when they were little and we might tell you the same story over and over again. We like to tickle and make funny noises and pretend we are animals. We also sometimes give too many hugs and kisses, even in front of your friends! Yuck!

There are even a few times when grandparents can be mean. Just like you, every now and then we get tired, impatient, and cranky, so once in awhile we yell when you won't pick up your toys, eat your food, or put on your shoes. We don't always listen carefully and understand what you are saying. When we are busy we may not want to play or talk or even cuddle and that is not very nice. Grandparents are always sorry when these things happen and usually we give big hugs and cold ice cream to make up for it.

We are looking forward to many years of being your grandma and grandpa, but Jack, sometime (10 years, 20 years, 30 years) we won't be here anymore. We hope it is a long time but even after we are gone we will still be with you. When you are sad we will shed a tear and when you are happy we will smile. When you do something great we will cheer and whenever you want to talk to us we will be listening. Just whisper our name and we will be there to hear you. Even when you are a daddy or even a grandpa yourself, we will still be watching and listening. Just whisper very quietly. We will be there waiting to hear from you.

Always and forever ... Love,

Grandpa

I was lucky

by Ed Groelle

I just finished reading a couple of books about war. The first was Paul Fussell's, *Boys Crusade*, a brutal narration about the day-to-day life of an infantry officer in France during the Second World War. The second was, *I Am a Soldier Too*, the story of Jessica Lynch and her ordeal in the Iraq invasion. Both books fascinated me and I didn't realize why until I started comparing my experiences in the Army with those two. My conclusion to that comparison was that I was lucky.

In some ways our experiences were similar in that we all enlisted in the Army for roughly the same reasons. Fussell got involved in college because he thought that the ROTC uniform looked good on him and wanted to join his friends. Jessica enlisted to get away from an economically depressed area. I enlisted to get some additional electronics education and to outsmart the draft. We did this and we all attained our goals but with vastly different outcomes. I seriously doubt that any of us ever thought about the possibility of actually being personally involved in a war. In fact, both Paul and Jessica mentioned several times in their book about how surprised they were to find themselves in a real war.

Paul ended up, through the army's cattle-gating selection methods, as an infantry officer leading an infantry platoon in France. Jessica, who was confident she would never see battle, served as a truck driver during the early days of the Iraq invasion. I got the training and then was stationed in central France for two years, neatly time-wedged between the winding down of the Korean War and the Suez crisis. I was lucky.

Paul was wounded several times and after V-E Day was waiting to join the force that was being assembled to invade Japan. The atomic bomb probably saved his life. He still carries reminders of his war experiences in the form of wound scars and cynicism. Jessica sustained multiple serious injuries and still today suffers and struggles to regain her normal life. I have no visible wounds or scars. I was lucky.

Paul, after discharge, went on to become a university English professor, but his war experience has made him a chronic cynic. Jessica plans to get married and become a kindergarten teacher but will need to overcome serious physical disabilities. I was not adversely affected by three years in the Regular Army and, although it used up some of what may have been the best years of my life, still consider it to have been a beneficial experience. I was lucky.

Paul and Jessica's war was a hot war complete with the accompanying terror, loneliness, and desperation. Mine was the cold war filled with constant readiness, make-work projects, and boredom. Paul saw France lying in the mud with shrapnel and lead flying all about him. Jessica got to see Iraq from the cab of a truck with her friends dying on either side of her. I got to explore France riding a Lambretta scooter. I think I owe a great deal to the Paul's and Jessica's of our country. Someone had to do it and they did it. I was lucky, they were not. There, but for the Grace of God …

If you asked a thousand veterans you will get a thousand different opinions of their time of military service ranging from hate to love but all the non-professional draftees and enlistees would probably understand Jessica's feelings when she received her medals at a ceremony. She sat in a wheelchair, looked down at the medals on her lap, turned to her mother, and said, "I want to go home." That about says it all.

Here's to the new year and another chance to get it right

by Laurie McKeon

It's all over, finito, done. The champagne is flat, the wrapping paper's recycled, the needles are hovered, and the fat lady has sung. That would be me. The Holiday season is officially over, at least at my house. Without the holidays I must admit that I am at loose ends.

Ever since we put the Halloween costumes away it's been a non-stop press toward the Yuletide. For the last two months my life has been fully consumed by frenzied seasonal preparations ... sixty full days of constant shopping, cooking, eating, wrapping, list making, and cavorting (and we did cavort). Every year the trifecta of Thanksgiving, Christmas, and New Year's sucks me into its shiny, spinning, vortex on November 1st only to spit me out on January 2nd, five pounds heavier and five hundred dollars lighter, slightly dazed, very confused, and not sure what to do with myself. I think I am in holiday withdrawal.

I hate this time of year. The weather is iffy, the world looks dingy, the kids are pale, and there's not a decent holiday in sight. Let's face it. All the good holidays are over until Easter. Sure, there's Valentines Day (which my husband calls, 'amateur night') and St. Patrick's Day, but whom are we kidding? A one night shot of lukewarm romance or green beer? Kind of puny. Mail is still delivered, the banks are open, and the kids have school. That's no holiday. I don't care what Hallmark says. So, I've got three full months until Easter and its wild sidekick, Spring Break. How am I ever going to pass the time waiting for my next holiday fix?

I suppose I could make some resolutions ... you know, eat better, spend less, exercise more, floss regularly, (all made, all broken-too many times to count) eradicate world hunger, find Bin Laden ... the usual. But honestly, after weeks and weeks of eating to excess, spending beyond my means, ignoring the treadmill, and mocking the floss, I just don't think I can be so resolute so quickly. Besides, I like to postpone any personal improvement plans until the Lenten Season when the fear of burning in the eternal flames of hell greatly bolsters my own flimsy will power.

So, resolutions are out, I do recognize the need to wean myself from the past two months of festive excess and self-inflicted anarchy as well as to keep my sanity and get past these cold, dark winter days. Since I am not willing to go cold turkey, I am proposing some very gentle guidelines or suggestions, if you will, on how to fill this holiday void and bring some structure back to my days.

~ **Go to bed early** - Now is the time to make up for all the sleep I did not get over the holidays (up till 4:15 AM on Christmas Eve, wrapping crap I forgot I even bought). I'm tempted to just go to bed and not get up until April or at least until Valentine's Day when I'll take my Whitman Sampler back to bed with me. A self-imposed 10 PM bedtime should make me a better person, or at least less cranky.

~ **Clean something** - Most people put off their cleaning until spring. Big mistake! Not me! I know myself and so know that come March I'll never get to that messy closet. Once the sun starts shining on a regular basis I'm not staying inside to sort old uniform pants. Nothing makes me feel more virtuous than color coordinated closets and an alphabetized spice rack.

~ **Read some decent books** - It's time to put away the *In Style* magazine and the Neiman Marcus catalogue and crack out something with a spine. While I am huddled in my bed I may as well try to gain some knowledge. Barack Obama's new book and a biography of England's Mitford sisters beckon from my nightstand.

~ **Eat some soup** - I could have said make some soup but that seems like a lot of work. I'm just going to eat some soup prepared by others. It's hot, it's steamy, seems slightly medicinal, and will make up for the Whitman Sampler I plan to eat in February.

~ **Write my Thank You notes** - Man, it almost makes me want to stop getting gifts. I said 'almost.' Again, I fear I will not be able to fully enjoy my long winter's sleep until I get this holiday monkey off my back. In the immortal words of Nike, "Just do it!"

God willing, these five little proposals will help me adjust to post holiday reality, see me through the darkest days of winter and bring some *feng shui* to my off-kilter life. If nothing else, I should at least be able to make it until Ground Hog Day.

Brave columnist confronts evil bureaucrats:
Secret memos exposed

by Thomas J. Noer

Dear Readers:

The following memos have been recently leaked to the public and appear in print despite possible legal ramifications. Under no circumstances should you inquire as to the source of this information and you should immediately burn this page when finished. (If you live in the city of Kenosha where burning is banned, shred this column and take the remains to the recycling center.)

From: Tom Noer, Occasional Columnist

To: Steve Lund, Editor Editorial Page

My Dearest Steve: As I ponder my next column it occurs to me that I have been writing these for several years but have received no increase in my meager compensation. Now, we all know how brilliant and humorous my work has been, so how about a little more cash for the effort?

Your pal, Tom

From: Steve Lund

To: Tom Noer

Dear Tom: Got your memo regarding pay increase. Unfortunately we have a very tight budget given the cost of colorizing our comics, paying for Howard Brown's tennis balls, and buying those new Mercedes for the editorial staff, so I'm afraid I can't offer more. Sorry!

Steve

From: Tom Noer

To: Steve Lund

Steve: I was sorry to hear your response, but have a possible solution. I notice you printed re-runs of Bill Guida's columns and assume he still got paid. How about the same for me? Seems only fair.

Tom

From: S. Lund

To T. Noer

Bill's columns are of interest to a large audience and actually have some content. I cannot say the same for your pieces. Bottom line ... no re-runs.

From: Noer

To: Lund:

I am shocked to hear such comments and have no choice but to take my request to higher powers and am forwarding my previous memos to Craig Swanson and Howard Brown.

From: Craig Swanson, Editor

To Tom Noer:

I have received your correspondence with Steve Lund. I must admit I have never actually *read* any of your columns and was unaware that you wrote for our paper. I have since looked at some of your work and am surprised that we pay you anything at all. Regards to whoever you are.

C. Swanson.

From: Howard Brown, Publisher,

To: Tom Noer:

Dearest Tom. God bless you! Do you play tennis? How is your lovely wife?

Howard.

From: T. Noer

To: "Scrooge" Lund

As you insist on your miserly ways, I must inform you that I have received some rather interesting information (and photos) about your personal life and feel compelled to reveal them unless you come through. If you want to play hardball, be prepared!

Noer

From: Lund

To: "The Whiner"

My lawyer will be in touch and you better get ready to reveal your sources. You should be reminded that a New York Times reporter is currently sitting in jail for not giving up HER sources. Hope you like it in Waupun!

From: Noer

To: Lund

Hey, threat boy, bring it on! I am certain the News will stand by me and the pursuit of journalistic purity. (cc: Howard Brown, Craig Swanson, the ACLU, and Karl Rove) P.S. Nice moustache! Do you know the 1970's are over?

From: Secretary, Mr. Howard Brown

To Tom Noer

I have forwarded your memo regarding jail time to Mr. Brown who, unfortunately, is on a six-month trip to study press freedom in Antarctica. He will be in touch when he returns, but asked if you would like to buy an ad in the classified section.

From: C. Swanson

To: T. Noer:

Some fine writing has been done in prison.

From: Heidi Otto, Payment Tsarina, Kenosha News

To: Tom Noer

Mr. Lund has asked me to remind you that often you have used improper, "funny" numbers on your invoices and has instructed me to withhold payment for any future columns. Have a nice day!

Heidi

From: Fred Ricker, Chief Account and Money Launderer, Kenosha News

To: Tom Noer

Steve Lund requested an audit of your account for the past few years and I have discovered that you have actually been OVERPAYED. I must ask you to reimburse us with interest for the excess. You should know I have contacted the IRS and they seem very interested. Also, a Mr. Rove called from Washington and is looking into possible violations of the Patriot Act based on your continued anti-Green Bay Packer statements.

Fred.

From: Lund

To: Noer

You have a column due on Sunday and we have heard nothing from you. What sort of rot are you going to inflict on readers this month?

From: T. Noer

To S. Lund

Oh! I wouldn't worry. I have something in mind that should be of great interest to the public and to you in particular.

Love,

Tommy.

I wrote this poem of Art, one of my wife's relatives who works as a biologist for the Wisconsin Department of Natural Resources.
He manages a fish hatchery raising muskellunge fish (Muskies). It pokes fun at State bureaucracy and Art's meticulous record keeping.

Art

by Ed Groelle

There was a young man named Art
Who failed in his try to impart
Knowledge to his fish bureau
That one plus one equals zero
Because it just didn't plot on their chart.

He kept writing memos to the State
Fed them a line, they took the bait.
He convinced the fish bureau
That one plus one equals zero
Now all their fish refuse to mate.

Art said, "Well, that's just fine.
I'll prove on a chart of spherical design
That, if fish there are none
Then, zero plus zero equals one
And just how efficient I'm."

He had his spherical chart all drawn
When he noticed something was wrong
He turned his chart inside out
Thereby proving without a doubt
That one plus one does equal zero

Art's fame is now certainly won
Tho his math is still questioned by some.
You see, to me he is no hero
One plus one isn't zero
He forgot to carry the one.

The last two words of our national anthem … 'Play ball!'

by Kenda Buxton

Be it enacted by the Senate and House of Representatives of the United States of America in congress assembled, that the composition known as "The Star-Spangled Banner" is designated as the national anthem of the United States of America. (March 3, 1931)

Most Americans can't hit the high notes. Only 46% can name the war our country was engaged in when it was written. When asked to recite the words, two in three (61%) Americans can't do so. Just 5% know the tune we sing it to comes from an English drinking song. Though 72% admitted that they're generally holding a beer while singing it and 47% thought they could sing it better if drunk. One in three (38%) Americans don't know its official name, 82% think it has just one verse, while fewer than 35% of American teens can name its author. When quizzed about how many stars and stripes our flag held when it was penned, 20% of Americans didn't know our flag *had* stars and stripes, 33% claimed it wasn't fair to ask them Jeopardy audition questions, and the remainder said that while they have no idea how many stars and stripes the flag contained 194 years ago, they do know that every McDonald's restaurant has two golden arches. You can't get much more patriotic than that.

Although as a group we don't know nearly as much about our national anthem as we should, we sure do get enraged when someone messes with it. After all, righteous indignation over something we know nothing about is the American way.

What has many Americans enraged lately is the Spanish-language version of the national anthem entitled, "*Nuestro Himno*", which translates as "Our Anthem." The idea for this rendition comes from British music executive, Adam Kidron. Evidently, he's still holding a grudge over that little Boston Tea Party incident of some years ago. Mr. Kidron said, that while he sympathized with recent immigrant demonstrations, the number of Mexican flags present troubled him. He hopes the Spanish-language version, which includes changes to the anthem's original lyrics, will display Latino patriotism along with more displays of American flags at these gatherings. Since word of the song has gotten out, Mr. Kidron said he's never received so much hate mail in his life. All of it written in English, I presume.

Americans from President George W. Bush, to singer José Feliciano, to Charles Key, the original author's great-great grandson, have voiced their displeasure over *"Nuestro Himno"*, saying the song is unpatriotic and should only be sung in English. "I think it's a despicable thing that someone is coming into our society from another country and changing our national anthem", Key said.

Well, of course, it's despicable! As evidenced by the 61% of Americans who don't know the words, most of us can't even sing our national anthem in English. No wonder we're so threatened by the thought of having to sing it in Spanish. President Bush, no lightweight when it comes to his own challenges with the English language, declared, "I think the national anthem ought to be sung in English," to which the masses cried, "Here, Here!" in resounding agreement. Unless they meant, "Hear, hear!" that is, which implies the president's microphone wasn't working. See, this is why we want everyone to learn English. So they can be as grammatically confused as the rest of us.

Although many of us don't know that it was written during the War of 1812, that its official name is *The Star-Spangled Banner*, that it contains four verses, was authored by Francis Scott Key, and that at the time it was penned, the flag had fifteen stars and fifteen stripes. Americans, including many Hispanic Americans, are adamant about what they do know … they want their national anthem sung in English. It's not about trying to erase anyone's culture or heritage. Instead, it's about those rare occasions when we come together as one nation to sing a song about the endurance of our flag and country in a time of war.

So, regardless of what language you speak, the next time you're asked to stand and sing our national anthem, don't worry if you don't know all of the words. Given that more than half of all Americans don't, you'll be in good company.

Christmas wears me down. I must be claus-trophobic

by Laurie McKeon

HO, HO, HO. Merry Christmas, Happy Holidays, and every other perfectly appropriate, non-offensive, seasonal greeting. Only eight shopping days left until Christmas and I'm nowhere near ready. Please believe me when I say that I'm not usually a Scrooge, but for some reason, this year I'm waving the white flag. I'm just plain giving up. I don't want to shop, cook, wrap, carol, bake, or holly jolly. I am the ultimate Bad Santa and can't seem to get over it. While the rest of the world is feeling peace on earth and good will to man, I'm just feeling tired, stressed, cranky, overweight, and broke.

Frankly, although I know this is "the most wonderful time of the year", a time for peace, love, joy, and brotherhood, I find that I really can't stand much of anyone. So, rather than counting my blessings this year (oh, don't worry, I know how lucky I am. I just don't need another viewing of *It's a Wonderful Life* to remind me), I am creating my own naughty list filled with all of the people who should be getting coal in their stockings this holiday season. Here they are:

~ **Anyone who's finished their shopping** - especially those jerks who have been done since Halloween.

~ **Anyone who's finished their wrapping, cards, baking, decorating, holiday cooking, and cleaning.** Just shut up already. We know you are superior. There, I've said it out loud and it's even in the newspaper. Now, get on with your perfect lives.

~ **Anyone who sends me a gift whom I didn't already buy for** - Man, you're killing me. Now I have to find something for you in my random gift closet. I hope you like the unicorn webkin. It's all I have left.

~ **Anyone who expects me to wrap their gift** - If what you want can't fit into a gift bag, you're not getting it from me.

~ **Anyone who expects a 'Thank You' note** - Listen up! Anyone who gave me a gift, is thinking of giving me a gift, has ever given me a gift, or has ever thought of giving me a gift, please consider this column to be your 'Thank You' note. I'm not kidding!

~ **Most of my family** - They are all coming for Christmas dinner and expect me to cook and feed them. Right now this seems like an incredibly unreasonable demand. My sister Wendy had the good sense to plan a trip to Europe with her family and will not be at my table. So far, I still kind of like her.

~ **All of my in-laws** - Please, please, please, for the love of God, can't we just do a gift exchange or buy each other a book? Who are we kidding? Your fifty dollars in cash to me and my $50 gift card to you just cancel each other out. How about we eliminate the middleman, keep our own money, or make a donation to charity?

~ **My husband** - He should either have the guts to tell his family to do a gift exchange, (no daughter/sister-in-law can voice these heretical opinions), be forced to do their shopping, or stop complaining about how much this Christmas is costing us.

~ **All the people who lose weight over the holidays** - Because they are sooo busy that they just forget to eat. Sorry, it's not just me and everybody hates you guys.

~ **The person who got the last decent parking space at the mall** - I don't know who you are, but you're on my list.

~ **The whining kid ahead of me in the checkout line** - Hey! FYI, Santa is watching and you, my friend, are a very long way from getting the *Spiderman Web World* toy that you were crying about back in aisle five.

~ **The forty people ahead of me in line at the post office** - Especially the dude with the eighteen packages going over seas and keeps changing his mind about buying postal insurance. Does the phrase, "Going Postal" mean anything to you? It should!

~ **Anyone who looks younger than me in their Christmas card photo** - I know that this is totally irrational because generally most every card I receive has a killer photo, but I still hold a deep-seated resentment.

~ **Anyone who sends an obnoxious Christmas brag letter** - telling me that their kid just won the Nobel Prize. Why doesn't anyone ever write to say that their kid is in rehab, prison, or, better yet, just a totally average kid? I seriously cannot believe that every single child of every single person who sends us a Christmas letter is playing first chair violin with the New York Philharmonic, center field for the Yankees, or both.

~ **My editor at The Kenosha News** - for expecting me to write some precious, festive column about the happy holidays. Hey, Steve Lund, guess what? It's not happening. You're stuck with this. And it doesn't come with a gift receipt either. HO, HO, HO

Eat your pablum (and your peanuts,) Jimmy Carter

by Thomas J. Noer

Nothing makes you feel old like talking with young people. This was brought home by two recent conversations with the under-thirty set. A while ago I mentioned to my kids that a book I had read was pablum, meaning soft, easy, and with little nourishment. Blank stares followed and I suddenly realized neither of them had heard of the word *pablum* as meaning baby food.

More recently, I ran across one of my students in the hall eating peanuts and I cleverly said, "You look like Jimmy Carter!" Silence ensued and I soon understood that she had no recollections of Jimmy Carter. He was like Millard Fillmore, a vague name from the distant past. The first president she remembered was Bill Clinton.

Pondering these moments, I realized that the generation gap widens daily and many of the references of my baby boomer colleagues are lost on those who have no idea what we are talking about. Below are some cultural landmarks that should jar memories for those who check their Social Security statements regularly. If you are under age fifty, you may need a translator. (But, no one under fifty reads the editorial page anyway!)

Once upon a time students and office workers used ditto fluid, carbon paper, and erasable bond typing paper. Doctors actually came to your house, police walked a beat, the mail came twice a day, and mean teachers carried wooden paddles.

Not too long ago, women wore girdles and white gloves and bra straps were hidden. Men wore hats (not baseball caps), tie clasps, and handkerchiefs in their suit pocket. Cool guys in high school had church keys around their neck and Ivy League pants with buckles in the back. Nerdy guys hung slide rules on their belts and ran boring filmstrips in biology class. Sweatshirts were only for gym class and you NEVER wore green on Thursdays.

I can remember when a mouse was something a cat chased, hip-hop was what rabbits did, and a hard drive was on the golf course. Gas stations sold only gas, had attendants who wore ties, checked your oil, and gave away cheap dishes. Except for *VW Bugs*, people drove AMERICAN cars (DeSotos, Studebakers, Ramblers) without air conditioning, power windows, or FM radio.

Back in the dark ages, my mother cooked with a pressure cooker, washed clothes using a mangle, and defrosted the freezer with pans of hot water. She also collected and pasted *Green Stamps*, talked on a black, rotary phone, listened to radio soap operas, and paid with cash since no one had credit cards.

When I went to the movies in my distant youth, there were banners hanging outside with a penguin that said, 'It's Cool Inside!', ushers showed you to your seat, there were cartoons, serials, double features, and the whole audience sang by following the bouncing ball.

Way back when, baseball had only sixteen teams, hitters did not wear batting helmets, and World Series games were during the day. Football players did not have facemasks and went both ways. Basketball had no shot clock, sprinters ran on cinders, and tennis was played with wooden rackets.

When dinosaurs still roamed the earth, we turned on the TV (by hand!) and watched (in black and white!) Arthur Godfrey, Bishop Sheen, and Jack Paar. There were only four channels (and one was educational that nobody ever watched) and no re-runs. My dad read *True* and *Argosy* magazines, my mother *Colliers* and *Look*. My brother Sport and I squeezed a plastic bag of margarine to make it turn yellow.

In distant times, the most popular wedding gifts were TV trays (likely purchased with Green Stamps), fondue pots, and ugly hand-made macramé flowerpot holders. There was no decaf, no sugar-free, no fat-free, and no microwave popcorn, but there were freezer pans, milk boxes, 3.2 beer, and *Fuller Brush* men. We didn't have Kmart, Wal-Mart, or Target, but there was Sears-Roebuck and Montgomery Wards (with GIANT catalogues), and in the fall, trips to *Robert Hall*.

And, of course, we started fires by rubbing sticks together, killed buffalo for meat, walked five miles to school (uphill both ways), and lived in mud huts. If we were lucky, our parents served us a nice, big, bowl of pablum!

The English assignment my dog never got a chance to eat

by Ed Groelle

Some might consider this as an eighth grade English assignment ... 'People I Admire.' The point is that I was never assigned this in school and have always felt slighted so ... I'm doing it now with your indulgence. All the selected are dead and had an incredible driving ambition in their particular area of life. None had clay feet or were phony in any aspect of their lives.

Sacagawea

Little is known of this intrepid, Native American woman other than that she was on the Lewis and Clark expedition and was *critical* to its success. Contrary to popular lore, she didn't guide the team so much as act as an intermediary to the Indians met along the way, and in several instances kept the party from being massacred. She was married to one of the men and six months pregnant when starting the trek. The silver dollar minted to honor her was a failure but she was certainly not. Without her presence the US map might look very different today. No one knows what eventually became of her or where she is buried. If we did, she might have a monument on the D.C. mall instead of the silver dollar.

Eric Hoffer

A completely self-educated philosopher, he never attended any school since he was blind for most of his childhood. When he regained his sight he was never known to be without a book. He educated himself to the point of becoming a very popular lecturer at UCLA. He doesn't seem to be as highly regarded as he should be since he is a bugbear to liberals, but most would agree with his commonsensical philosophies. I have a grudging admiration for him not only for his philosophies but also because he is the only person I know of who totally ran his own life, no matter what the consequences. The closest any of us could come to experience his kind of personal freedom for a few days might be to travel the Pacific highway end-to-end, alone, on a motorcycle.

Marie Curie

Polish-French physicist held in high esteem and admiration by scientists throughout the world who began her preliminary education by secretly attending 'floating universities' in Poland when it was illegal to teach women the sciences. Later, Marie studied physics and mathematics at the Sorbonne and quickly received her master degrees in both subjects in spite of a limited knowledge of French. She was the first woman to receive a doctorate in France, first woman to win a Nobel Prize, and the first person to win a second Nobel Prize. She is mainly remembered for her experimental work with radium, which at that time was considered a benign, useless, substance. She ultimately died from effects of radiation. Still today, if you want to examine her notes, it is necessary to wear a radiation suit.

Joanne D'Arc

This is my choice for 15th century *Person of the Year*. How does a meek, pious, seventeen-year-old girl manage to rally the French army? I'd like the opportunity to look into her eyes to see what was there. An internal divine power must have empowered her. She inspired the army to defeat the English only later to be handed over to the English who treated her like an animal, castigated, and accused her of all sorts of religious crimes. She was eventually compelled to attend an outdoor barbecue in Rouen as the guest of honor. What a tragic injustice!

Richard Halliburton

This guy is one of the world's most admirable nuts, an erstwhile Steve Irwin, but with the added distinction of having written several books of his exploits that I practically memorized by age fourteen. His thirst for adventure was insatiable. He flew around the world, visited Timbuktu, climbed the Matterhorn and Mt Fuji solo, sat on the Sphinx's head, swam the Hellepont, Sea of Galilee, and Panama Canal (paying a toll of thirty-six cents,) and did enough crazy stunts to fill several books. He once said, "I'll be especially happy if I am spared a stupid, common, death in bed." Well ... he died happy at age thirty-nine trying to pilot a Chinese junk across the Pacific.

Kingsford Smith

Here's another admirable nut deemed by many to be the greatest aviator of all time. Shortly after Lindbergh crossed the Atlantic, Kingsford crossed the Pacific in a 1920 fabric covered Fokker plane in which the seats were not even bolted down. A far more ambitious enterprise because the scale was much bigger and flying conditions much tougher. Many considered his attempt to be insane. After 1927 Lindberg seldom flew again and rested on his laurels but Smith went on to establish more flying records than anyone else on earth. Australians regard him as a hero and an excellent role model. He disappeared over the Bay of Bengal in 1935 at age thirty-eight.

So there it is ... my missing eighth grade assignment. My dog is long gone but I feel much more complete now.

Feel free to grade it.

The arduous curse of the Cub fan ... undying loyalty and optimism

by Kenda Buxton

As curses go, the infamous *Billy Goat Curse* that looms over the Chicago Cubs is mild compared to some others. There are Irish curses:

~ May your cow be flayed.
~ Death and smothering on you.
~ May you be mangled.

There are literary curses, used to deter thieves prior to the invention of the printing press when books were handwritten:

~ Steal not this book, my worthy friend,
for fear the gallows will be your end.
Up the ladder, and down the rope,
there you'll hang until you choke.
Then I'll come along and say,
"Where's that book you stole away?"

Then there's the 'Mummy Curse', found in King Tut's tomb:

~ Death will slay with its wings whoever disturbs the peace of the pharaoh.

And curses in the Bible:

~ *Will a man rob God? Yet ye have robbed me. But ye say, "Wherein have we robbed ye?" In tithes and offerings. Ye are cursed with a curse - this whole nation.* (Malachi 3:8-9)

I certainly wouldn't want my cow flayed, if I owned a cow, that is. Since I own pigs, I assume they could be flayed too. Therefore, I'm being careful not to rile anyone who might curse me with, "May your pigs be flayed!" Although, given the hog market these days, a mass pig flaying would be more of a blessing than a curse.

'Death and smothering' is self-explanatory, and I prefer not to die, or be smothered until I do, any time soon. Nor do I want to be mangled, suffer a painful death because I disturbed a pharaoh's tomb, or tick off God by short changing the offering plate.

While all of the above curses could cause a person worry, it's the *Billy Goat Curse* that supposedly plagues the Cubs. According to legend, in 1945, Sam Sianis tried to enter Wrigley Field with a goat. Since Sam had purchased a ticket for the goat, it's understandable that a *lot* of cursing was prevalent when the goat was refused admittance. It was then that Sam declared, "Cubs, they not gonna win no more!" Either Sam was far more prophetic than even he realized, or it's not wise to anger a man with a goat.

I spent my childhood following the Cubs, blissfully unaware of the *Billy Goat Curse*. Whether the Cubs won or lost, it didn't matter. I loved baseball, playing it, and watching it. I mimicked Jose Cardenal's crouched stance in the batter's box. When I swung at a pitch, I looked more like a contortionist in bad need of a chiropractor than I looked like a baseball player, but I didn't care, because I aspired to be the first girl in the Major Leagues. No matter how often I was laughed at upon replying, "Play right field for the Cubs," whenever I was asked what I wanted to do when I grew up, no one could take that dream away from me.

During my teen years, my interest in the Cubs waned, and my dreams of being a Major Leaguer were replaced by reality. Even if a woman broke into the Majors, she wouldn't be me, because I wasn't good enough. I was a decent player on a neighborhood vacant lot but that was the only baseball diamond I'd ever circle.

For seven games this fall, my enthusiasm for the Cubs was rekindled. In my mind though, it was José in right field and not Sammy Sosa, and I was ten years old again, watching the Cubs play on a black and white Zenith console.

The one thing that hasn't changed since I circled the bases is the faith that lives in the heart of every Cubs fan and the firm declaration that, "There's always next year." When I was a kid, 'next year' always seemed so far away and so full of possibilities. Maybe those are the exact reasons why Cubs fans flock to their team with renewed hope each spring.

As for the *Billy Goat Curse*, the Cubs should consider themselves lucky. Sam could have imparted that old Irish curse of, "May yourself go stone blind so that you will not know your wife from a haystack!" Although I'm sure there're times when a man would rather *not* know his wife from a haystack, being stone-blind sure makes it tough to play right field.

A few words of practical advice for the class of 2003

by Thomas J. Noer

We are fast approaching commencement season and I calculate that I have sat through over fifty commencement addresses in my life. I have lost track of the number of times I've heard, 'You are the future,' 'Commencement means beginning,' and 'I will be brief!' As a veteran of graduation speeches, I feel able to offer my advice to the class of 2003 on how to survive in the real world that awaits.

Talking is important. You have made it through school communicating with shrugs and grunts, punctuated with an occasional 'like' and 'you know,' but in the real world you likely will have to speak in complete sentences. Life is 'essay' not 'multiple choice.' People will ask: 'Why do you want this job?' Not, 'You want this job, a) because it pays well, b) because it is easy, or c) all of the above.' Remember, it is unwise to refer to your boss as 'dude' or to answer all questions with 'whatever' or 'for sure!'

Learn how to cook a meal, iron a shirt or blouse, and repair a car. We know you are all going to become millionaires and hire servants, but that might take a year or two. Meantime, you need to eat, look good, and get around. Maybe you can recite Plato, but can you fry an egg or change your oil? Out in the real world some practical skills are often more crucial than knowing what caused the Seven Years War.

Work is hard and long. You will be shocked to find you will need to go to your job at least five days a week and stay there for eight or more hours a day. This is hard. This is why it is called, 'WORK!' There are no 'skip days' or 'study halls' or 'make-up tests.' I also hate to have to tell you this, but there are no ten-week summer vacations, no two weeks at Christmas, no spring break, and no teachers' conventions. Bummer!

Your parents are still alive after you graduate. Many students forget this and assume that once you are out of the home, your parents go into a state of suspended animation until you have kids and they then will awake to provide free babysitting. Your parents may actually want to hear from you now and then and even offer some advice. You have learned to ignore them, but they can be quite helpful at times. You may want to jot down their phone number or even their address to send a letter … a form of written communication few of you have used.

You will lose touch with most of your friends. You may have sworn everlasting love with your buddies, but in a few years you will have lost contact with most of them and will actually have to make NEW FRIENDS who did not go to school with you. Now, you do not need to abandon all your school pals, but be warned that sitting around in your letter jacket or sorority sweatshirt talking about that crazy English class or wild prom party gets old quickly.

Beware of the evil word 'interest.' As soon as you graduate you will find people eager to offer you credit cards and loans and sell you things with *No Money Down*. Be warned that all of these include a strange thing called *interest* that will appear in a statement every month. This may be unfair and confusing but be aware or learn the phrase, 'Chapter 7.'

Find something to do besides work. I warned you that work is long, but you still will have sixteen hours a day of free time. Even if you sleep eight of these, about one-third of your life is still unaccounted for. You can play video games, drink beer, or calculate your credit card debt, but perhaps you should have some other options. If you live to be 75, you have over twenty-five years of free time to fill. What are you going to do with it?

It's not too late to turn back. Sure homework sucks, some teachers are nerds, and you have no money, but you may never have life as good as you have now. Most of you have free room and board, someone to pay your bills, and you can wear whatever you want. I stayed in school until I finally ran out of degrees and had to get a job. I then became a college professor, the closest thing to being a student I could find. You may also want to consider avoiding the real world for as long as possible.

So, class of 2003, as I leave you, always remember, 'You are the future' and 'Commencement means beginning.' I hope I have been brief.

Adventures of a 10-day snowbird

by Ed Groelle

I know that listening to other peoples' vacations can be excruciatingly boring, but I was told that if I didn't come up with an article they would be forced to reprint one of Jimmy Carter's campaign speeches. Consider yourselves lucky.

It all started while putting on my mukluks during the last snowstorm when we were treated to another fifteen inches of snow. There *had* to be better weather somewhere, so I used my credit card and influence with Expedia to book a flight to Phoenix on Midwest Airlines with an Enterprise car rental.

We arrived at General Mitchell Airport three hours ahead of the flight, but due to lines and computer glitches, just managed to get to the boarding gate as they were about to close the doors. FYI, the comfortable, wide seats on Midwest are gone and we weren't offered any warm chocolate chip cookies.

Enterprise Rent-a-Car has been for years my only choice due to their outstanding personal service. In Phoenix, the girl took us to the lot and showed us fifteen cars from which we could choose. You will never get options like that from any other car rental company. I picked a new Ford Taurus. I had heard that Fords are exceptionally well designed in 2008 and that turned out to be true ... an excellent car, beautiful handling, and luxurious comfort.

I always travel with my own GPS unit and it, as usual, was a godsend. It saved us a lot of time from being lost. GPS works on the same principle used by the bug that commits suicide onto your windshield right in your line of sight, usually just after washing the windshield.

We drove 2300 miles in a big circle starting with a portion of the old Route 66. Unfortunately, it was through the Sonoma Desert, so was flat as a pancake and not of much interest.

The Grand Canyon is overrated and for all its grandeur, can quickly get boring. The Indians gouge tourists as much as possible, even to asking $67 to walk through the Antelope Canyon and

$150 to stand on the Skywalk. Turned down both. The best way to see the Canyon is to drive the road east along the south rim towards the Glen Canyon Dam. This dam is just as impressive as Hoover Dam but lacking the thrill of being able to stand or drive on the top.

Then we took the Coronado Trail Scenic Drive. It was the best mountain drive I've ever driven and that includes the Alps. It was five hours of pure driving pleasure on a perfect highway with 145 miles of curves and swoops, and get this ... no cars going in my direction and only three or four from the other way. It was like those TV car ads in which there are never any other cars on the road.

Cochise's Stronghold is reached by a dirt road to the base of some mountains made of rocks similar to our Wisconsin rocks but as big as houses. It is a very quiet, serene location with unlimited visibility. The only sound is of the wind rustling through the cacti, all equipped with razor sharp spines and leaves. Cochise is presumed to be buried somewhere there, but we were not allowed to dig for him.

I expected Tombstone to be a tourist trap but it is, in reality, a pleasant town with Boot Hill, Ok Corral, etc. The residents were very welcoming to tourists. I got the impression that they party every night after the tourists leave. I wouldn't mind living there.

Only a few miles east of Phoenix is the Apache Trail Historic Road. The last half is washboard dirt and driving it is as thrilling as any ride at Great America. If you ever get to Phoenix don't miss this drive.

We spent the last two days in Scottsdale. It is a definite advantage to have money there. I get a kick out of morphing into my billionaire persona and then going to Nieman Marcus to haggle price with the clerks.

There isn't space to mention all the places we visited. Overall, it was a good trip and I liked Arizona. I wouldn't want to live there permanently, but a few months a year? Bring it on!

Never overestimate the decency of the human race

by Laurie McKeon

Do you remember your mom or grandma telling you that, "family business stays in the family" or "the neighbors don't need to see our dirty laundry?" Well, that thudding sound you hear right now is my grandmother rolling over in her grave. Hey, stop laughing! Your grandma is rolling over too.

I just saw a commercial for some new TV show in which people get hooked up to a lie detector while a host asks them ridiculously personal questions that I assume they are required to answer in front of a live television audience and in an insatiably voyeuristic nation. Here's one query I heard in the promo for the show, "Have your ever had sex for money?" Nice! I'll bet her mother is so proud. I'm assuming these contestants volunteered to be on this degrading show and I realize that they will get some sort of monetary compensation for their public humiliation, but my real question is, "When in the course of human history did people stop being embarrassed of their indelicacies and become willing, eager, and shameless exhibitionists? When exactly was the day that people no longer wished to keep their private lives to themselves and started acting out their peccadilloes in front of a television audience?" Think about it! Within two generations or so, we've gone from people (basically my parents and their friends) who could barely whisper the word 'sex' to people clamoring to bring their babies to *The Maury Povich Show* for a DNA test that will very publicly answer the burning question of, "Who's your daddy?"

There is a strange and disturbing phenomenon going on in our culture. It seems that our puritan, private, and closed-mouthed ancestors who kept family secrets and indiscretions quiet for decades are officially extinct. Sad to say, they've been replaced by tattooed, chair-throwing, heavy-drinking, hot tub soaking, and foul-mouthed, reality TV and talk show participants who live out their every word, tear, sneer, conquest, and bad decision on national television. Obviously, with modern mass communication, television, emailing, texting, and camera phones, it is virtually impossible to keep much of anything a secret, but whom are we kidding? Is there anyone left in the world, other than my sister and I, who even wants to keep things under wraps? We have turned into a people hell-bent on projecting our deepest, darkest, and most intimate moments across the airwaves for the entire world to see. Even more frightening, not only do these knuckleheads lack the good sense to be embarrassed by their actions, they couldn't be more pleased with themselves. Nothing is private, nothing is sacred, and just about everybody from Paris Hilton's mom to Hulk Hogan's kid is lobbying for their own reality series.

While I am amazed that people would actually want to go on television and reveal their inner struggles, issues, and ugliness, I am equally amazed at just how many people enjoy watching these train wrecks, (or else why would the networks keep them on the air?) I honestly don't care at all that people are shacking up, hooking up, lighting up, or indulging in any other self destructive, detrimental, or embarrassing behavior, but does it all have to be so public? I must be missing something, but I fail to see the attraction in airing and hearing peoples' personal dramas and major mistakes. I truly have absolutely no desire to see someone marry a millionaire. I don't want to see people forming alliances on a desert island, and I sure as heck don't want a shot at love with Tila Tequila, Flavor Flav, or even that Firestone tire heir who runs his family's winery. What sort of attention-seeking weirdo chooses to date in front of a camera crew and a viewing audience salivating for heartbreaking mortification?

I fully understand that every human foible and failing from infidelity to substance abuse has been around since biblical times, but when did informing your significant other that he is not the father of your child, confessing to your partner that you've been sleeping with his brother, searching for marital contentment, attempting to land a high profile job, or celebrating your sixteenth birthday become prime time entertainment? Is Jerry Springer to blame or have we just turned into a ludicrous, over-the-top nation that will sell out all good taste and decency just to be seen on television?

I do fear that all of this hyper, over-the-top reality impacts us more than we realize. I'd like to believe that in the course of humanity we, as a collective people, are moving toward some greater good or ideal and that every generation becomes a little kinder, smarter, and more civilized than the one before. But, as any one who has ever seen an episode of *The Hills*, *I Love New York*, *The Real World*, or *The Bachelor* knows that's just not true. Thank God Grandma is not alive to see it.

Everyone is entitled to be stupid, but some abuse the privilege

by Kenda Buxton

Hurricane Katrina had barely blown out of New Orleans before speculators claimed this storm was a sign that the end of the world will be here quicker than President Bush can take another five-week vacation. Considering what it costs to put gas in our cars these days, many of us will welcome the second coming of Christ, provided we don't have to drive to Heaven.

Ever since the world began, speculators have speculated as to when it will end. Which means every time there's a fire, flood, earthquake, drought, hurricane, plague, war, or Michael Jackson hosts a sleepover, someone warns us to clean house ... both literally and spiritually speaking, because there might not be another opportunity to scrub the soap scum off our bathroom tiles or make things right with the Lord.

Throughout the centuries, we can only assume others have tried to clean house in some manner as learned men and women have given us these predictions:

90 AD – Saint Clement the First predicted the world would end at any moment. 1,915 years later, it's safe to say Clement wasn't particularly talented where this end-of-the-world prediction stuff is concerned.

365 AD – Like Clement the First, Hilary of Poitiers announced that the world would soon end. And also like Clement, I hope Hilary wasn't attempting to make a living off the accuracy of his predications.

375 AD – A student of Hilary's, Saint Martin of Tours, predicted the world would end before 400 AD. While apparently not the brightest man when it came to learning from the failings of his teacher, Saint Martin did excel at making inaccurate predications.

January 1, 1000 – European Christians predicted the world would end on January 1st, 1000. In an attempt to spread the word of God, Christian armies waged war on Pagan countries, hoping to convert the Pagans before the final hour. Meanwhile, many Christians gave their belongings to churches in anticipation of the end. When Christ didn't appear, the churches didn't deem it necessary to return those belongings, though they did deem it necessary to kill anyone who complained about his lack of tables and chairs.

1843 – William Miller predicted Jesus would return on March 21st, 1843. When Jesus didn't show up, William predicted Christ's return for October 22nd, 1844. As a result of Miller's predictions, many Christians sold their possessions, meaning that once again, a lot of people were left with nothing to sit on.

1925 – My great-great-grandfather and Civil War veteran, James Cather, predicted *little men* would invade the United States … their appearance signaling the end of the world. When we went to war with Japan, my family thought they finally had confirmation that Grandpa Cather's predictions really *weren't* brought on by that Confederate shell fragment lodged in his skull. Being good Baptists, we prepared for the coming of Christ. Being smart Baptists, however, we kept our furniture.

1988 – NASA scientist, Edgar Whisenaut, published the book, *88 Reasons Why the Rapture Will Occur in 1988.* Shortly thereafter, Edgar published a book entitled, *88 Reasons Why We're All Still Sitting Here.*

Future Years – A group calling themselves, "The Family" predicts the world will end in 2006. They're stockpiling food, with plans to hide in caves in India. Not exactly where I'd choose to ride out the end of the world, but to each doomsday predictor his own.

Annie Stanton predicts that a 14.4-mile long asteroid will hit the Earth in 2006 and that Jesus will arrive right behind it.

2006 is evidently the year to sell your possessions because numerous people predict the end of the world will come on June 6, 2006 … the number '666' representing the beast mentioned in Revelations.

Despite these predictions, I wouldn't turn my tables and chairs over to anyone just yet, if I were you. According to Matthew 24:35-36, Jesus said that no one will know the exact date and time of His second coming. And as one line of an old Statler Brothers song goes, "You may not find him coming in a chariot of the Lord. Jesus could be riding in a '49 Ford." (Or perhaps on an asteroid.)

Regardless of when the world ends, if Jesus *is* riding in an old Ford, I hope he has plenty of money with him to fill up the tank.

Headline: Local man
offered perfect job

by Ed Groelle

Since we are now daily knee deep in political polls this might be a good time to comment on the amusing subjects of polls and statistics. For a long time I've been collecting dubious statistics and polls which seem to me to be not only questionable but downright foolish.

George Gallup, an undisputed authority on polls, once said, "I could prove God statistically." There was someone who understood the inherent fallacies underlying statistics. In judging the validity of any poll or statistic it is important to know who is doing the reporting, who do the results benefit, and who is paying for the poll. This information is seldom stated so most polls and statistics should be rejected as being just a lot of fluff. Polls can be slanted with loaded and leading questions and by conducting the poll in the area where your outcome will reflect your opinion. For example, if someone wanted to get an approving response to abortion, wouldn't it be advantageous to take the poll in a liberal university town like Madison, Wisconsin instead of a small town in Kansas?

Smoking is one of the leading causes of statistics. One of my favorites was gleaned from an article in the Racine Journal quoting a woman who worked for one of those anti-smoking organizations. She stated that if our Governor Doyle approved the tax increase on cigarettes, 22.4% of smokers would quit. Did you get that? Not approximately 20% or 25% but exactly 22.4%. How could anyone know that? Could it be she was trying to justify or impress someone as to her job importance? She doesn't dare report that 100% of smokers will quit because she would then be out of a cushy job.

There was a Senator in the 1980's who pegged the value of statistics. I'm sorry I can 't remember his name. He was ninety-one years old and had been smoking cigarettes since he was eleven. He believed that if he was hit by a bus and killed, his death would be counted as a smoking related death. He was, sadly, probably correct.

Here are two of my all-time favorite statistics that should insult every reader's intelligence: American companies will lose $780 million in lost productivity due to Super Bowl. Gosh, stupid me, I thought it would only be about $500 million. Another: 90% of the ocean's large fish species are now extinct. Wouldn't it be significant to know what span of time he is talking about? Is it one year or 10,000 years? There is no hint of that in the article. At any rate, he should be given a big raise for ascertaining information like that.

Statistics are like bikinis. What they reveal is suggestive, but what they conceal is vital.

When it involves statistics on the intimate side of life, I am reminded of what Bill Shakespeare once wrote, "Ah, the eyes of youth wherein the love light lies ... and lies, and lies and lies." I don't care how protected and anonymous the surveys are, I simply can't imagine anyone telling the truth when it is about personal relationships. Boys will brag, girls will protect their reputation, and adults, especially seniors, will check off their dreams and/or regrets. My favorite statistic in this area is that condoms have a 1 in 1,000 failure rate. Think about this one for a moment. Did the gatherers of this information have a few gazillion spy flies on the walls of bedrooms or spy cameras in every motel room and parked car in America? Give me a break!

I wonder how I could get a job taking and extrapolating surveys or dreaming up statistics. It has been said that you need to know someone to get into jobs like that. In 1953, I shook the hand of Jack Dempsey. In 1957, I once stood within ten feet of Marshall Tito in Postojna, Yugoslavia and our eyes met for one fleeting moment. I wonder if those two incidents can qualify me for having "known somebody." I'm certain I could do a good job of it. Just give me the opportunity. After all, any fool must now and then be right, if only by chance.

The Short Book Club: A brief list of quick reads

by Thomas J. Noer

Both of the major Chicago daily newspapers have recently begun printing condensed versions of their papers aimed at young readers. These editions feature lots of photos and graphics and have no story longer than 300 words, because the publishers assume people under thirty will not pay attention to any longer article. This Reader's Digest approach to the news is the latest example of a trend that assumes readers will not finish anything longer than a paragraph. Even television has shortened ads to ten and fifteen seconds, as they fear nobody will watch a commercial that is any longer.

America's short attention span syndrome (SASS) is especially troublesome for those who write and publish books. If people won't read more than 300 words and can't watch TV for more than fifteen seconds, why would they ever buy a four-hundred-page book? The obvious solution is to publish short books that can be read in less than a minute. Below are ten really brief volumes that even the most distracted reader can finish in less than sixty seconds and get back to their video game:

Kenosha After Dark! - A Guide to Downtown Entertainment. A comprehensive listing of the major evening recreational opportunities in downtown Kenosha. It includes how to get into a Bingo game at the Dayton, the best places to watch motorists try to turn left off Sheridan Road, and an architectural tour of abandoned buildings.

The Democratic Party's Strategy for Winning Elections - Practical advice on how to turn victory into defeat through organized incompetence. The book discusses the planning of Paul Wellstone's memorial service to help lose in Minnesota, how to sound just like a Republican and where to find really inept candidates. Introduction by Representative Dick Gephardt and Senator Tom Daschle.

How to Solve Major Crimes - The crack Boulder, Colorado police describe their on-going five-year investigation of the Jon Benet Ramsey Case and Washington, D.C. detectives show how they are only a few years away from finding who killed Gary Condit's intern, Chandra Levy. In the introduction, O.J. Simpson explains how he is still looking for 'the real killers' on Florida golf courses.

The Kenosha Guide to Road Construction - The traffic gurus of Kenosha explain how to get roadwork done quickly with a minimum of inconvenience for motorists and businesses. Chapters on the Sheridan Road project and the work on 75th Street and 39th Avenue are especially brilliant. Don't miss the photos showing how to arrange orange traffic cones in patterns that distract drivers.

The Brewer's and Cub's Book of Winning Baseball - The geniuses of these two franchises share their secrets for building a pennant winner. Be sure to read the section by Chicago officials on '*Our 75 Year Plan for Success!*' and Milwaukee's '*Your Taxes Paid for Miller Park so Who Cares About Winning Games?*'

Movies Where Nothing Blows Up - A summary of all the films in the last decade that stressed plot and character rather than special effects. Less than a page, this book includes no video game or action figure marketing tie-ins. (A sequel to the successful: *Great Ideas in American TV: The Intellectual Content of Fear Factor, Jackass, and The Howard Stern Show.*)

The Complete Wisconsin Fashion Book - Yes, you can wear a Packer sweatshirt to your prom! Yes, long underwear is OK in July! Of course, a John Deere hat goes with everything! This tiny volume documents the best of the state's sartorial statements. Be sure to read the section on *Sweatpants Make Everyone Look Good.*

Memorable Editorials of the Kenosha News - Looking for hard-hitting commentary on the major issues of the day? You won't find it here as this extremely tiny book looks at all of the controversial editorial statements in the past twenty years. Don't miss the sections on *Hash: How to Cover a Complex Issue in One*

Sentence! and, *Darts and Laurels: Filling-Up Space When You Have No Ideas!*

The Complete Love Lyrics of Eminem - Explore the soft side of the Detroit rapper with a list of all his sweet and tender words about women, gays, and loving your neighbor. If you order now you will receive, free of charge, a second, even shorter book, *The Social Significance of the Music of Britney Spears.*

Tom Noer's Greatest Columns - Chuckle at the wit and wisdom of the best of his sarcastic ramblings! This collection is published on a postcard with an introduction by, 'A Kenoshan.'

I guarantee you can read all ten of these works in less time than it takes you to make a left turn off Sheridan Road, watch all of the non-Packer stories on Sunday night Milwaukee TV, or read all 800 words of this column.

How is Halloween celebrated in a nudist colony?

by Kenda Buxton

The phrase 'weapons of mass destruction' didn't exist, a new car cost $3,600.00, and we were watching *The Mod Squad* and The *Flip Wilson Show* on TV. The former included the grooviest gang of fuzz ever to wear a badge and the latter included Flip cross-dressing as a woman named Geraldine, back when people still thought men dressing as women were funny.

It was 1970, the year they took Halloween away. It was like a year without Santa Claus, only a million times worse to an eight-year-old who'd spent weeks rummaging through costume boxes at Wilson's Dime Store, trying to decide if she should go Trick or Treating as Batman, Mr. Spock, or Marcia Brady. It was one of my 'defining moments,' as Dr. Phil calls the significant events that determine whether you'll be a well-adjusted adult who doesn't hear 'weirdo' or 'nut job' muttered as you leave a room, or are destined to spend your life running from house to house wearing a Marcia Brady mask, ringing door bells, and yelling, "Trick or Treat!" on President's Day, Ground Hog's Day, Labor Day, and any other day that might provide a good excuse to collect candy.

At one time, Halloween was a simple little celebration in Celtic Ireland. The Celts believed that on October 31st, the spirits of those who'd died during the year returned in search of bodies to possess. Since the Celts weren't too thrilled at the thought of being possessed by some dead guy, they'd dress up in scary costumes (no self-respecting Celt ever went Trick or Treating as Marcia Brady) and race through the neighborhood being rowdy and destructive in order to frighten the spirits away. What the Celts didn't know was that, while they wouldn't be credited for inventing Halloween, they would be credited for holding the first tailgating party.

The good thing about a Celtic Halloween was that you never had to stand in line to get your candy X-rayed. The bad thing

309

about a Celtic Halloween was that if you gave out hard candy or an orange, your neighbors might decide you were possessed and burn you at the stake. Not that I blame them. Nothing ruins a night of Trick or Treating more than Brach's peppermints or something nutritious like fruit.

In the 1840's, Irish Immigrants brought Halloween customs to America. It took a mere 100 years for a night of a few tricks and treats, to become our second-largest grossing retail holiday, which just goes to show what good old-fashioned capitalism can do for a Celt and his evil spirits. Or at least until some well-meaning, but grossly misguided parents in Kenosha County decided it was dangerous for unsupervised children wearing masks with eyeholes sized for chipmunks and costumes sized for giants, to be dashing across streets after dark, knocking on strangers' doors and asking for candy. I don't get it, but you know how it is … there's always one do-gooder in the crowd who has to ruin everyone else's fun.

Suddenly, Halloween festivities were at school, the last place a kid wanted to be at night. No longer did we have shopping bags and pillowcases overflowing with candy. Instead, we were given a puny bag of donated candy, which meant for every Milky Way we found, we found twenty peppermints and an orange. So much for the Batman costume I'd finally settled on. The PTA gave prizes for the best costumes. My cheap Batman suit didn't stand a chance against a kid whose mother could make a Christmas tree costume from nothing but tin foil and green felt. The result was that even with prizes, games, and a bag of candy we didn't have to walk five miles on a blustery October night to collect, Halloween just wasn't fun anymore after the grownups took charge.

And so, the disappointment of that Halloween became my defining moment, which is why people whisper, 'weirdo' and 'nut job' behind my back. But at least no one's burnt me at the stake yet, because I know better than to hand out peppermints and oranges on a night when every kid deserves all the chocolate he can eat without worrying about whether or not he's wearing a prize-winning costume.

Life ... There are no rewards for just showing up

by Kenda Buxton

The third Friday of each new school year is known as 'School Attendance Day' in the Kenosha Unified School District. In light of this, kids all around Kenosha will fall over and die when I reveal that, back when I was in school, every day was 'School Attendance Day.' Many of you remember the dark ages I'm referring to. The only way your classroom could have air conditioning was if your teacher worked at a hardware store during summer vacation and scraped together enough of her own money to buy a fan at half price. If she liked you, she might have even pointed it in your direction once or twice during the day. Lunch menu 'choices' meant a fried fish square, applesauce, and green beans every Friday. And we could refer to the break between mid-December and the first of January as 'Christmas vacation' without being sued or accused of being politically incorrect.

Yes, kids, as pitiful and deprived as it made the childhoods of millions of baby boomers, there were no special activities, socials, ice cream, or McDonald coupons passed out just because we'd shown up at school ... a place we were expected to show up each day whether we wanted to be there or not. I know, it sounds cruel, doesn't it? Imagine the nerve of our parents and the school officials, expecting us to be in school five days a week without rewarding us for it. You'd think they were trying to prepare us for adulthood or something. That's right, adulthood ... the place every kid dreams of reaching where no one will tell you what to do, when to do it, or how to do it, and where you'll be rewarded for every mundane accomplishment from washing the car to doing a load of laundry. Here's where I burst your bubble, youth of America. The only reward you'll get from washing the car and doing a load of laundry is a clean car and clean clothes! Not nearly as exciting as McDonald's coupons, but them's the breaks when it comes to being an adult. Even if you figure that 90% of everything you do after you're eighteen will go unrewarded, you'll still be off by at least 5%.

That's right! 95% of everything you do after you're eighteen won't earn you a darn thing but a paycheck that the government will take half of for various benefits they'll promise you, like Social Security and Medicare, that will either be bankrupt when you reach retirement age, or will be so inadequate that you'll have to keep working just to have health insurance long after you're using a walker and a hearing aid. What more of a reward could a person ask for than that? In between age eighteen and retirement, you'll attend six dozen wedding and baby showers, numerous birthday parties, anniversary parties, and housewarming parties. You'll be expected to bring a gift to all of these events, meaning that throughout your lifetime, you'll spend thousands of dollars on rewards you're giving someone else, only to get nothing in return. And when you do get something in return, it'll be the wrong size, the wrong color, or dishtowels. Yeah, dishtowels. Now there's a reward, huh?

Speaking of rewards, on the rare occasion in your adult life when your employer does reward you with something more than just your paycheck, it may be similar to what you're used to being rewarded with on School Attendance Day. The problem with that is, you'll no longer think of ice cream, pizza, doughnuts, and McDonald's coupons as rewards. Instead, you'll think of how the ice cream will raise your cholesterol level, how much weight you'll gain if you eat a doughnut, and whether or not the peppers and onions on the pizza will give you indigestion for the rest of the day.

So to quote some guy named Kreeshna, "Let the motive be in the deed and not in the event. Be not one whose motive for action is the hope of reward."

Good words to live by, although admittedly, I have no idea who the man is. I must have been absent the day Kreesha's philosophies were taught, since back when I went to school, there was no reward for just showing up.

No one likes little monsters

by Laurie McKeon

My family really enjoys going out to dinner, but lately I'm finding it unbearable. Not because my teenage boys eat like longshoreman and not because feeding a family of eight at any place without a drive-thru can cost more than my first car, it's just that every time we go out to eat, it's bratty kid night ... but not at my table.

By and large, our kids have been fine out in public. They've eaten in some pretty fancy places (especially when a grandparent is picking up the tab), they've flown across the country, they've attended plays and concerts, and we've taken them to Mass since they were born. (no cry room) Even when a waitress once dumped hot syrup on one of the boys (hey, free breakfast), no one peeped. I'm not saying that our kids are perfect by any means and they certainly are not any more naturally well-behaved than any other children, but we always made it crystal clear that we had zero tolerance for poor behavior. We've always been hyper-concerned that our little circus should not bother other diners, fliers, shoppers, worshippers, or whatever. Manners, courtesy, politeness, and consideration for those around you are a BIG deal in our house. I still say to my brood (ages 7-17), "Maybe families with two kids can act like that, but families with six kids? No way! They'll call Children's Services."

I have to admit I'm tired of having my meal, flight, movie, or event spoiled by some kid who is just out of control. Way too many parents have no idea how ill-mannered their children are. I'm not kidding! Last week, we were seated at a mid-scale family restaurant with chaos all around us. On my right were three children who just kept doing laps around their table, periodically stopping to throw themselves at their mother, and whining for food. The table behind us had two kids, maybe four and five years old, who did sprints up and down the banquet bench, pounded on the glass divider between our two tables, and pressed their ketchup stained faces against the glass. It was kind of funny at first (for about a minute) and then it just became annoying. I kept motioning for junior and his little brother to sit down and turn around. I even gave them 'the eye,' a never fail discipline trick in our house, but they never flinched.

Sad to say, these children were not orphans. They were there with several full-blown adults who presumably, were their parents. However, none of these adults made any real attempt to rein in these monsters. Instead, they did what so many parents do today. They give that look that conveys, "Oh, I know this behavior is kind of irritating, but I don't really want to stop my conversation to actually discipline this child and frankly, isn't my kid just so cute?"

Well, I'm here to tell you, because some one needs to, "No, your kid is not cute. Of course, YOU think he's cute. You're his parent." That's just nature's way of ensuring that you don't kill him when he's a teenager, but no, no one else thinks he's cute. They may say so or may even act amused but what they are really thinking is, "Please go home, please go home, please go home." A poorly behaved child does nothing to endear himself to anyone. And, here's a news flash; as the parent, it's your job to teach your kid to behave. Sorry, that's part of the parenting program. It's in the handbook ... look it up.

And here's an even bigger news flash; your kids can actually behave. Trust me, they can do it. It is not too much to expect a four-year-old to sit in a chair in a restaurant long enough to eat a meal. It is absolutely reasonable to make your five-year-old sit through Mass without a coloring book, a cold beverage, and a bag of cheerios. Your kids can make it through a movie, a concert, an airline flight, and a doctor's appointment without throwing a fit, without making a fuss, and without spoiling the experience for you, them, and all the unsuspecting people you will come in contact with. You just have to make them and keep making them and keep making them. Don't make excuses ... she's tired, she's hungry, she's upset, she's coming down with something ... I've heard them all. Don't make exceptions ... just this once, as long as you drink your milk, because you have a friend over, etc. You are the adult so you get to make the rules. Don't be afraid to say, "NO!" and don't be afraid to actually follow through. Your kids will be happier, you will be happier, and if you are sitting anywhere near me in a restaurant, I will be way happier. Here is the deal, and I'm telling it to you straight … if you can't control your seven-year-old, God help you when she's seventeen.

How many Euros for that T-shirt? An Italian travel quiz

by Thomas J. Noer

Buongiorno, faithful readers! I have just returned from two weeks in Sicily, Naples, and the Almafi Coast of Italy. In the faint hope of making the trip tax deductible, I offer a brief quiz to help you determine if you are a rude, ugly, American tourist or a cultured traveler in the old world. Scoring is at the end.

1. You enter an Italian restaurant and notice that all the customers, waiters, and most of the dogs are chain-smoking unfiltered cigarettes:

    A. Ignore it, eat quickly, and don't inhale.

    B. Ask for the non-smoking section and listen to the laughter.

    C. Bum a butt from the busboy and light up.

2. The waiter brings you a lengthy menu, in Italian:

    A. Carefully take out your Italian-American dictionary and translate.

    B. Point at dishes with the longest names thinking you might get more food that way.

    C. Order a pizza and a coke.

3. You have a sudden need for the toilet but find a stern woman demanding some coins to enter. You have only a 20-Euro bill:

    A. Turn around and walk to a store to get change.

    B. Bolt past her and hope she does not hit you with her mop.

    C. Go in the street like everyone else.

4. You are at a railroad station and see a sign that your train departs at 1850.

    A. Use your handy European time card to figure out when to board.

B. Hop on the first available train and hope it goes somewhere interesting.

C. Return to the hotel as your train left over 150 years ago.

5. You are driving on the *autostrada* and everyone behind you is flashing their lights and making obscene gestures:

A. Calmly stay in your lane and maintain your speed.

B. Push the pedal to the metal, flick your lights, and give them the bird.

C. Abandon the car on the side of the road and walk to the nearest wine bar.

6. You meet a Sicilian and want to talk with her about her country:

A. Discuss Sicily's rich history and culture.

B. Ask if she has seen the movie, *Patton*.

C. Sing the theme from *The Godfather* and make noises like a machine gun.

7. You need to exchange some dollars for Euros:

A. Shop around at several banks for the best exchange rate.

B. Approach the nice stranger lurking in the alley with a wad of cash.

C. Ask shopkeepers if they take 'real money.'

8. You have visited 34 cathedrals, 27 castles, and 18 museums in five days. When you arrive in a new city:

A. Try to see all of the forty-four attractions listed in the guidebook.

B. Select one or two sights for the day.

C. Buy a copy of *USA Today* and read it in the park.

9. You want a taste of real Italian culture:

A. Purchase tickets for the local opera company.

B. Visit a neighborhood disco and dance to ABBA songs.

C. Find a sports bar and ask if they can put the Cubs game on.

10. You want to practice your Italian:

A. Ask a grocer the price of a half a kilo of fresh lemons.

B. Ask a cabdriver in Naples for directions to Rome.

C. Ask the kid on the motorcycle to watch your luggage for an hour.

11. You need a hotel room for the night. Be certain to ask the clerk:

A. If the room has a view and if breakfast is included.

B. If they take credit cards and can carry up your bags.

C. If the bathroom is located in the same city.

12. An Italian asks you whom you most admire from their country. You answer:

A. Michangelo, Dante, and Leonardo DiVinci.

B. Columbus, Pavarotti, and the Pope.

C. Sophia Loren, Frank Sinatra, and Tony Soprano.

13. You find all of your underwear and socks are dirty:

A. Find a local Laundromat and see how long the drier runs on five Euros.

B. Take out a second mortgage and buy new, Milan-designed undies.

C. Go home!

14. It is your last day and you have not bought anything for your kids:

A. Locate an antique store and purchase some fine Italian ceramics.

B. Run into the airport souvenir store and buy some cheap T-shirts.

C. Give them your leftover Euros.

Scoring: If you have ten or more 'A' answers you are a sophisticated traveler who should take your next European trip with Rick Steves. If you have ten or more 'B' answers at least you won't be an embarrassment to your country. If you have ten or more 'C' answers, you might consider the Wisconsin Dells for your next vacation. *Arrivederci!*

You think retirement is a snap? Guess again!

by Ed Groelle

Why do I usually prefer the 'before' photo rather than the 'after' in diet ads? That was my first thought on awaking a 6 AM. Wondered if anyone else feels the same way and then abandoned the thought. First order of business is to clomp to the basement and fire up the old two-cup coffee maker. When did I last clean it? Too late now. Maybe tomorrow. While I'm down there may as well check the emails; three Viagra, two 'can't miss' stock investments, requests for aid in getting some money out of Africa and, of course, the ever popular Classmates offer. Make a mental note to contact Bill Gates and thank him for the miracle of e-mail.

Get the paper with coffee in hand and then make breakfast. What'll it be this morning? I decide on my favorite, Waffle Crisp soaked in blue milk with a banana sliced on top. Skim the front page. Same-O, Same-O. School scores, too high, too low? Someone who appears to be blaming me, personally, for lingering discrimination, a journalist reporting the latest and worst news he can find about Iraq trying to win a Pulitzer a la Jack Anderson. Then to the obits. Look at the names for some recognition and diligently take note of the ages. It's a good day! All the deceased are older than me. Then to my favorite, the Editorial page. I still miss the rapier wit of Tom Noer. My spirit brightens when I see an article by Tom Sewall, the only man I could get politically active for. The rest of the articles are the same as always, Bush-bashing and sour grapes.

Then to the comic section. Hopefully, the Kenosha News hasn't, once again, deleted my favorites. I try to imagine what would happen if they bashed women the way they do white males in *Real Life Adventures*. Skim the other pages for interesting headlines and that's it. I like the days when the inane ranting of Sound Offs are printed. I finish the paper by cutting out the crossword puzzle for later in the day. I've done every one for the last ten years.

Next order of business is to get ready for a Volunteer Driver Escort trip. Today I have my favorite, Terri. She is blind and I accompany her as she counsels people who are losing their sight. I usually shop, read, or do the crossword puzzle while she works. Terri is always up and raises my spirits. The time never drags. Sometimes we stop for lunch. I feel like having KFC's chicken wrap today.

Back from the trip it is time for mail call. My wife put a wastebasket next to the front door. A stroke of genius. Most of the mail goes into this receptacle unopened, except for the bills, although the offer of buying a car with no money appears inviting. Nah, both my cars only have 80,000 miles each. Good for a long while yet.

Can't forget my daily walk. Usually from my house to Lake Michigan. Admire the lake for ten minutes and then back ... a distance of three miles. If I'm really in the mood, I'll walk further to Common Grounds and have a cup of Earl Grey's tea. I start walking with a lot of aches and pains and then finish feeling fit. Love it.

The rest of the day is for maintenance projects; mowing the lawn, admiring the tenacity of Creeping Charlie, and just keeping everything going. I might have someone's PC to fix or I could work on my long-term project of converting all my VHS tapes to DVD. At 6:30 it's a half hour of the *Everybody Loves Raymond* reruns, the only TV that I can stomach anymore. My wife is an excellent cook so dinner is always a pleasure. After dinner, I read to keep up my goal of reading at least one book a week. This week it is Taylor Caldwell's, *Answer As a Man*. Her last and a good one!

Suddenly, it's midnight and time to hit the Select-Air mattress. One my best investments. Click!

Joining a posse is one helluva lot more fun than working

by Kenda Buxton

Ever since I read about Sheriff Beth's proposed budget cuts, I've been practicing everything I know about being a cop:

~ "Stop or I'll shoot!"

~ "Freeze, turkey!"

~ "Book 'em, Danno!"

~ "Go ahead, make my day!"

Years of watching *Adam-12, Starsky and Hutch, Hawaii Five-O,* and *Dirty Harry* movies have prepared me to take the law into my own hands. If we citizens of Kenosha County band together, we can replace the twenty-four deputies whose positions might be eliminated when the sheriff is forced to trim his budget by 1.7 million dollars. Instead of subsidizing the county golf courses, maybe that money should be redirected to the sheriff's office. Oh, but wait, if we do that, there goes my plan for all citizen-deputies to arm themselves with golf clubs. Never mind, scratch the idea about not subsidizing the golf courses. The golf clubs will be too valuable when we all take turns patrolling on the graveyard shift. Graveyard shift. See, I've already got the lingo down. This deputy stuff isn't gonna be so hard after all.

Getting deputized will be the easy part. I've seen this done on Bonanza thousands of times. All we have to do is raise our right hands and when Sheriff Beth asks us if we promise to uphold the law, we say, "I do." or "I will." or "Ya' betcha ya' der, Sheriff. Ya' kin count on me." This last guy had usually stumbled out of the Silver Dollar Saloon about the time Sheriff Coffee was looking for volunteers and was too drunk to know what he was volunteering for. While nonetheless eager to serve his community, sadly, he was usually the first one shot when the bad guys showed up to rob the bank.

After we've completed the deputizing ceremony, we'll jump in our "Black and Whites" (or whatever color car you own) and go on patrol, looking for bad guys doing bad things. Remember, we're on a tight budget, so forget about using one of those fancy new white patrol cars or even one of the old maroon ones. We're on our own for transportation with this job.

The bad guys we're looking for will fall into one of the following categories: con men, cat burglars, call girls, bed bugs, dirt bags, mutts, gang bangers, geek monsters, and gutter junkies. According to the book *Cop Speak*, these people are up to no good and we should "take 'em down" and then send them "up the river" (or maybe that's "down the river") to the "Big House," the "Pokey," the "Slammer," the "Joint," and throw away the key. We can forget about a fair trial and all that other nonsense that's just a waste of our tax dollars, because we're deputy-vigilantes and can do whatever we want.

The drawback to catching these bad guys is that the budget cut won't allow for weapons (See, I told you those golf clubs would come in handy), or for any fancy surveillance equipment, which is why I'm thinking Paul Revere had a pretty good (and cheap) idea when he had those lanterns hung in the church tower. So remember, "one if by land, and two if by sea." Upon getting the signal that trouble is a brewin', we'll sprint through Kenosha County screaming, "The British are coming! The British are coming!" We might be a little confused over exactly who we're to beat senseless with our golf clubs, but if nothing else, it's a historic call to arms that deserves a noble revival.

Yes, folks, it's lonely at the top, which is why we citizen-deputies must support our local sheriff at a time like this when the budget might not allow for deputies who are actually *trained* to catch the perps. So, arm yourselves with your golf clubs, jump in your black and whites, and challenge some dirt bag to, "Go ahead, make my day." I'm not sure what we're supposed to do after that, but hey, we're not getting paid for this job, so what do they expect from a bunch of volunteers? When all else fails, we'll just ride through the county shouting, "The British are coming! The British are coming!" and hope like heck someone who knows what he's doing shows up to help.

Updating children's classics for the 21st Century

by Thomas J. Noer

As a grandfather, during the past two years I have become reacquainted with childrens' books, and have become convinced they need to be updated. Not many of us today live in castles, herd sheep, or grow beanstalks, and even 20th century stories need to be adjusted for our time. I offer below some contemporary rewrites of famous children's books to make them more relevant to today.

Pat the Money - A modern version of the classic 'first book' aimed at today's yuppie couples who want to teach their kids what is really important. Children can touch and feel Mommy's mink stole, the keys to Daddy's BMW, and play with a Platinum American Express card, Palm Pilot, and cell phone. Gucci, Gucci, Goo!

Free Little Pigs - A group of perky young PETA vegetarians, aided by Jack Spratt, who eats no fat, and Peter, Peter, the Pumpkin Eater save the three little pigs from an evil, meat-eating wolf and liberate four and twenty blackbirds about to be baked into a pie. At the end, they all join together for a delicious turnip, okra, and pine nut casserole and a night of politically correct clog dancing.

Little Red's Ridin' in the Hood - Famous gangsta rapper Little Red and his personal posse, The Woodsmen, are riding around the hood in his new sled when they hear that his archrival, Big Bad Wolf, has broken into Red's grandma's crib. While The Woodsmen get medieval with the cross-dressing wolf, Red and grandma break out the bag of goodies.

Anne of Three Cables - Bored to tears by hours of bad Canadian TV, perky Anne orders three different cable packages for Green Gables. Grumpy Marilla gets hooked on *The Food Network* while silent Matthew never misses *The Home and Garden Network*. After watching Entertainment TV, Anne splits from Avonlea for L.A. where she finds work as a waitress in a trendy Internet cafe. A talent agent wanders in and casts Ann to star in a Canadian version of *The Bachlorette.*

The Shrinks and Treehorn - Kenoshan Florence Heide's young hero still thinks he is getting smaller and his distracted parents continue to ignore him. Fortunately, an alert school counselor notices that he can no longer reach the drinking fountain and brings in a team of psychiatrists to examine him. They conclude Treehorn's problems are the result of reading all those cereal boxes and suggest he eat only generic cornflakes with no label. The Shrinks then sign a made-for-TV deal based on the case.

Brown Bear, Brown Bear, Why Can't You See? - Perky junior ophthalmologist Dr. Goldilocks performs emergency laser eye surgery on a large bear with severe cataracts. When he regains his sight, the bear accuses her of sitting in his chair, sleeping in his bed, and eating his organic porridge. Fortunately, three formerly blind mice she has recently fitted with tinted contact lenses, arrive and save Goldilocks.

Raggedy Ann and Andy Finally Find Work - After years of wearing shabby clothing and panhandling on the street, a social worker gets the two waifs into a homeless shelter, a job training program, and some decent clothes. Tutors find they have a gift for music and wind up touring the country with their *Tribute to Sonny and Cher* and *A Night with the Osmonds.*

Green Kegs and Spam - The *Cat in the Hat, the Grinch,* and *Sam I Am* throw a wild St. Patrick's Day party in Whoville with green beer and canned meat. After a few hours, they find they can no longer recite *Hop on Pop* clearly and call Horton the Elephant to drive them home as they are totally Seussed.

Peter's Rabid - A hopped up rabbit (get it?) high on chamomile tea and brown bread plots revenge against Mr. McGregor for the strange disappearance of his father. His sisters, *Flopsy, Mopsy, and Cottontail,* stage an intervention and get Peter into an anger management program run by *Jeremiah Puddleduck* and *Squirrel Nutkin.* You will also want to read the sequel, *Peter's on Prozac.*

Dr. Do-too-little - A lazy physician is fired by mean HMO Director, Willy Wonka, for spending all day talking to animals rather than seeing enough patients. Fortunately, he finds work on a Pacific island as the medical adviser to *King Babar and Queen Celeste* where he adopts a monkey known as *Curious George,* a large red dog called Clifford, and a pig named Olivia. He eventually marries his pale nurse, Snow White, and they have seven extremely small children.

Goodnight Soon - Unable to sleep until his monthly column is finished, a Kenosha writer lives for days on nothing but mush. When he finally completes 800 words, a mysterious little old lady in a rocking chair whispers, "Hush!" and he falls asleep.

There are five elements: earth, air, fire, water and Big Macs

by Laurie McKeon

On Monday, August 14th, the McKeon family received a shocking blow. Not to be overly dramatic, but life as we know it has taken a seismic shift. We are all still a little shaken, but we're rallying.

On this particular morning, I realized that we had absolutely no food in the house ... no milk, no bread, not a frozen waffle or an egg to be had, but I wasn't overly concerned. I must confess that in the summer, food purchasing, storage, and preparation at Casa McKeon is a little haphazard. I hate wasting warm, sunny days navigating the aisles of Woodman's for my usual two-cart, $400 visit. Add on the time it takes to unload and put away all that food and you're looking at a three-hour ordeal, minimum. So, during June, July, and August, you won't see me in any super market checkout line until we are truly Mother Hubbard desperate.

We had no food but I wasn't worried because, well, we'd been down this path before and obviously, I did have a plan. We had to be at St. Joe's by 9 AM to pick up school packets for the big kids and then on to the north side for 10 AM tennis lessons for the littles. Simple! I would just drive through McDonalds on our way to St. Joe's, grab some McBreakfast, let the kids eat in the car (no syrup, no ketchup ... car rules), run into school for the packets and then on to tennis. After tennis, I'd bite the bullet and go to buy groceries.

As we headed north on Sheridan Road, our gateway to the city of Kenosha and the route we travel innumerable times a day, anticipating those golden arches, we were shocked, no stunned, to discover that McDonalds, our McDonalds, was closed for the next four months. No way! For the love of God and all things holy, why didn't any body think to confer with me on this? A little advanced warning would have been nice or some sort of community forum possibly, or a psychologist on site to break the news gently. Didn't anybody do an impact study before taking such drastic measures?

When my kids were smaller I was one of those overly smug, slightly irritating, parents who doled out Happy Meals only as a very special treat. Dinner was usually a home-cooked, food-pyramid-friendly, culinary experience. While I still strive for that Betty Crocker perfection, as the kids have gotten older with schedules rivaling the landing at Normandy, the McDonald's drive-thru on Sheridan Road has become our auxiliary kitchen. Now that it's closed, some of the McKeon progeny are a little nervous

I know fast food isn't the healthiest, (although the Asian chicken salad isn't half bad) but on those days, and there are a lot of them, when we've got a tennis match after school, Junior High football from 4:30-6:30, varsity soccer at the same time and at different places, two kids with CYC football practice from 5-7 PM (GO VIKINGS), and a band concert at 7:00 PM, a home-cooked meal is physically impossible. Just making the requisite pick-ups and drop-offs takes the fine precision of an Indy pit crew. I know! I know! Today's kids are ridiculously over scheduled, but we do stick to a very strict one-sport-per-season rule and no travel teams. However, even that, multiplied by six kids creates a logistical challenge. Frankly, I'm keeping my kids in organized sports as long as possible in the hopes that they will be too tired from practice to hold up a liquor store.

In all honesty, it's not the food we're addicted to, it's the fast. We're always pressed for time and the Sheridan Road McDonalds, strategically located in the middle of my route, is just so convenient. Maybe I've gotten a little complacent, lulled by the siren song of fast, easy, food. Since that is no longer an option, we're soldiering on. I know it's a stretch but I'm actually considering leaving my loop and driving all the way to the Pershing Boulevard McDonalds. Who knows? We may even try Burger King or KFC, and God forbid, if I get truly desperate I may even pull out the crock-pot ... but I doubt it.

Need free, quick, bad advice? Just write to Dr. Tom

by Thomas J. Noer

Until a few years ago, confused Americans seeking anonymous advice about their most private issues had only two choices; Write to *Ann Landers* or write to *Dear Abby*. Now we are overwhelmed with columnists and talk show hosts eager to offer us quick solutions to life's difficult problems. Ann has been replaced by Amy Dickinson and Abby by her daughter, but there is also *Dr. Joyce Brothers, Dr. Laura Schlesinger* and, of course, *Dr. Phil*. It seems that if all you need to tell people how to live their life is a Dr. title then, I qualify. So, here are my helpful hints to those in desperate need.

Dear Dr. Tom,

My husband's recent behavior has me very worried. For nearly a month he has not moved! He just sits in front of the TV muttering, "Fourth and 26!" It was fourth and 26! What can I do?
Perplexed in Wisconsin.

Dear Perplexed,

Your husband is suffering from what psychologists call PPPP (Post Packer Playoff Paralysis). If he has a large piece of cheese on his head remove it and then gently whisper, "It was just a game! Brett had a sore thumb! Sherman should never have punted." He should regain partial consciousness by fall.

Dear Dr. Tom,

Hope you can give me some quick marriage tips. A while back I ran into my old high school sweetheart. (Let's call her Brittany.) I proposed, she accepted, and we were married in a quaint chapel in Las Vegas at 3:00 AM. But, the next day she was gone! Sure, we were both a little drunk, but what went wrong?
Jilted Jason.

Dear Jilted,

Dr. Tom has found that marrying intoxicated, pop idols at dawn rarely results in a lifetime commitment. I suggest some marriage counseling with Liz Taylor, Larry King, and Lisa Minnelli to ensure your next romance is more permanent.

Dear Dr. Tom,

I am the editor of a mid-sized newspaper in Southeast Wisconsin and my boss wants me to fill space without paying for reporters, wire service copy, or expensive columnists? Can you help me out?
Steve in Kenosha

Dear Steve,

What you do is offer readers the chance to be Guest Columnists on Fridays. You pick a few and then they write FOR FREE. You get to fill your paper without spending a cent. After a year or so you just get rid of them and find new ones. You can use the money you save to color your comic section or PAY YOUR SUNDAY COLUMNISTS MORE!

Dear Dr. Tom,

I hope y'all can help me. I grew up with a guy in Texas named George but he has left the state and I just can't get that good old boy out of my head. I write about him near every day, but he never notices me. I am just so angry!
Mad Molly.

Dear Molly,

It seems that you have sort of a love/hate relationship with this guy and you need to get over it. There are plenty of other men to obsess about. You might be interested in this new governor of California.

Dear Dr. Tom,

My wife and I are caught in some strange time warp. Each night the same TV show runs over and over and over. It's like the movie, *Ground Hog Day*. What's going on?
Ground Hog Day Couple.

Dear Hogs,

I fear you have fallen into the TNT *Law and Order* black hole where there is nothing but endless reruns and re-reruns of McCoy, Lenny, and sexy assistant D.A.'s making plea bargains with sleazy lawyers. You MUST switch channels immediately or you might be forced to sit through *The Goodbye Girl*.

Dear Dr. Tom,

For the past three years I have held a pretty powerful position in Washington, D.C. but need to do something new to make sure I keep it. Can you suggest some wild new idea to help me stay employed? Money is no object!
George W.

Dear George,

Well, you could reform the health care system, create some new jobs, or clean up the education mess. But these are all really tough and would take a lot of work. I think you need something really stupid and crazy, like say ... going to MARS! Just kidding! Let me think about it and get back to you with a real idea!

Dear Dr. Tom,

The people where I work are getting pretty fed up with your sarcastic comments and constant criticism. How do we make sure nobody reads your sick columns?
Howard.

Dear Howie,

If you really want to make it impossible to read my column, why not bury the Sunday editorials in the business section. Even the hardest working reader will never find it there.

After September 11th ... now there is no safe place to hide

by Kenda Buxton

For those of us born after World War II, "a date which will live in infamy," is an event we've only read about in history books. As the children and grandchildren of what Tom Brokaw coined the "Greatest Generation" ... men and women who gave of themselves during the Second World War, the majority of us grew up with middle-class comforts, and a sense of security that so many preceding us had never known. From the inception of this country our citizens have fought to gain and to preserve the freedoms we have today. Progress hasn't always come without a fight and often for each step forward, we've taken two backwards. Almost one hundred years passed between the end of the Civil War and the beginning of the Civil Rights Movement. We have as much to be ashamed of since the birth of our nation as we have to be proud of. We are Americans, united as one people, yet still flawed enough to have the Ku Klux Klan and often divided over the exact things our country was founded on, like political and religious freedom.

On September 11th, 2001, Americans experienced another date that will live in infamy. Unlike sixty years ago, this time we viewed the act of evil as it unfolded. It could have been a Spielberg thriller, only it wasn't. The best actor couldn't have projected the terror on the faces of those fleeing the collapsing towers. And no actor pretending to mourn could make us feel the sorrow of firefighters crying for comrades lost beneath the rubble, as though that sorrow was our own.

It was a time when we came together as a nation. It was a time when we held candlelight vigils, gathered to pray, and gave blood. It was a time when we raised our fists and vowed revenge. It was a time, like so many times before, when we were united, yet divided. Mosques were vandalized. Our countrymen of the Islamic faith were harassed. We were suspicious of those who worship or dress differently than we do. We couldn't agree if we should make war or peace. And if we did go to battle, who were we fighting and would the end justify the means? One year has passed, and still so many questions are left unanswered and so many scars remain.

Regardless of who we are, which presidential party we support, where we worship, or if we worship at all, there will always be facts about September 11ᵗʰ we won't forget:

The New York City firefighters and police officers who lost their lives while doing the jobs that earned them a living.

The people who boarded planes to attend business conferences, take a vacation, visit friends, or return home.

The military personnel in the Pentagon, considered to be one of the safest and securest buildings in the country. It only took one act of terrorism to make us realize that there is no safe place if someone has the element of surprise and planning on his side.

The passengers of United Airlines Flight 93, who exemplified all that it is to be an American, as they undoubtedly ignored racial, religious, and cultural differences, while banding together to fight back. For those few moments left between life and death, I'm sure the hijackers learned what Americans are made of.

And finally, the estimated 3,275 people who lost their lives that day, and the children, mothers, fathers, siblings, and friends left behind to mourn them and to wonder why.

We are a nation of people who come from all around the globe. We practice more religions than any other nation in the world and we are free to publicly speak against our president. Yet, despite our age of 226 years, we still have problems that aren't resolved. But it's our differences that make us strong and although dividing us at times, it's those same differences that also unite us. Soon, we'll come together to remember this dark day that will also live in infamy, September 11, 2001, when so much went so tragically wrong, while at the same time so many heroes from all walks of life made us proud to be Americans.

Sage advice from the dearly departed

by Laurie McKeon

Believe it or not, my two-year term as a Sunday morning columnist for the Kenosha News has come to an end. For a while I had delusions of going out on a high note with some sort of hard hitting, controversial, Pulitzer-worthy column. I quickly realized that such ambition might actually require research, effort, and ability that I do not currently possess. So, for my final column, I am sticking with what I know and I'm leaving you with my top ten pearls of wisdom ... little tricks of the trade for raising a pack of kids with out going certifiably insane. Please understand that I am giving this advice not as an expert, but as a veteran, one who has been there, done that, made more than my fair share of mistakes, and is willing to impart the fruits of my hard earned lessons. Consider it my little gift to those who have invested the time to read my rambling columns.

Be the grown up - First and foremost, do not ever forger that you are the grown up. You are the one with the adult judgment, the bank account, the credit card, and the driver's license. You pretty much call all the shots. Don't be afraid to use your God-given advantages to rule with impunity.

Just say, "No!" - I once read somewhere that a parent is supposed to say 'No' twenty times more than 'Yes', or I might have just made that up, but it really does work. Kids incessantly ask for everything ... a candy bar, a puppy, a new car, a nose ring, a handgun ... your job, as the parent, is to say, 'No' pretty much all the time. In the short run it may seem easier to just give in, but I've learned the hard way that even one half-hearted, wholly qualified 'Yes' will open the floodgates for a lifetime of whining. The earlier your kids learn to take 'No' for an answer, the better off you will be.

Get Organized - This seems pretty obvious, but I really mean it. Life with children is filled with countless variables. Take total control of those you can. Many, many, ugly situations will be avoided if sneakers, library books, team jerseys, doctor's appointment, school schedules, and such are guarded, monitored, and regulated like state secrets.

Certain traits are hard wired - There are many things that you as a parent can and must control; bedtime, bath time, meal time, behavior, manners, school attendance, etc. However, there are some things that you will never change, so just deal with it. There is nothing sadder than a parent trying to force a bookish kid to be an athlete or an artist into an engineer.

Grooming counts - I swear to God, people will cut you big slack if your kids are clean and well dressed. I know that it is terribly superficial, but it is true. You may assume the world will see right through that ketchup stained Spiderman T-shirt into your child's sensitive soul, but trust me, every waitress, teacher, physician, and clerk will treat him (and you) a whole lot better if you clean him up. At least you'll get points for trying.

Bed time is the best time - Children need sleep and, more importantly, so do grownups. There is no greater gift you can give your child (or yourself) than the ability to put herself to sleep. Do not underestimate the number of very bad decisions that have been made while suffering from sleep deprivation.

Remember the goal - It is very easy to forget that the whole point of raising children is to turn them into self-sufficient, fully functional, reasonably happy adults. There is no scientific proof that French flash cards, a personal trainer, or a Nintendo Wii will insure a secure adult regardless of what other parents or your kid may tell you.

All kids lie - While you may think you gave birth to a little Georgie Washington, you didn't. Your kid (and mine, too) will lie to save his skin to avoid his homework, get a second dessert, or to throw his sister under the bus just for the heck of it. It's your job as the parent to try to discern the truth or just do what I do … punish regardless.

Ignore them - Unlike our parents, we tend to hover over our kids, orchestrating their every sport, friend, activity, and class. While I do not advocate total neglect, a little distance is not bad.

You really do not need to referee every battle, chart every slight, or negotiate every relationship. If someone is bleeding or needs money, you'll be the first to know.

Enjoy it all, because it goes way too fast - It's been a lot of fun writing for the Kenosha News. I want to thank Steve Lund and all of the nice people who actual read the words I wrote, even the guy who stopped me in the grocery store to tell me that he hated every one of my columns. Hey! At least some one is reading them.

Constructive criticisms coming from a confirmed curmudgeon

by Ed Groelle

I am a born-again Kenoshan and having lived here and paid taxes for over 45 years I feel justified in pointing out some conditions around town that are deserving of comments.

Starting on the western edge there is that monstrosity of a monument located on a traffic island between woodman's and I-94. The Kenosha News can rave about it all it wants but, as work of art, it just doesn't cut it. Or maybe it does since it looks like a giant cheese slicer. It is heavy, clumsy, and can actually induce nausea if looked at long enough.

Speaking of Woodmans, what discerning mind decided to put a faux brick floor in the produce section? I doubt that any of those responsible have actually shopped there. I have a blind friend who cannot shop there because the cartwheel noise disorients her.

Moving east we come to the parking lot at the new St. Catherine's Hospital. Possibly a noble effort to break with traditional parking lots but whenever I drive there I am reminded of the song, MTA, by the Kingston Trio of poor Charlie who couldn't get off the Boston subway. On the awful traffic plan hall of fame it ranks just below the I94/Hwy 50 interchange and the parking lot of the Pleasant Prairie Post Office. Wouldn't a plain, open lot be more practical, especially to senior citizens?

I love the Rec Plex and go there almost every day. The "NO Spitting on the Track" sign posted on the walking track always intrigues me. Some slob at one time must have been observed doing just that. Personally, I had never considered spitting until I read that sign. It's sort of like telling a child, "Don't put beans up your nose."

The new Southwest Library is a beautiful asset to our town but ... who in the world selected those gawd-awful seats in the coffee bar? They are totally nonfunctional for human use. The seat-to-back connection radius is so large there is no room for the tailbone. Shifting forward to make room causes you to slowly slide off the chair to the floor. Didn't anyone test-drive those before purchasing?

More East and a little North we find Pike Creek flowing through Washington Park or, as the locals call it, the River of No Return Bottles. Nothing much can be done about this but, just maybe, the authorities in the county and city could get together and divert the Fox River through there. Illinois doesn't need it anyway since all they ever do is to build ticky-tacky condos along its banks.

The harbor area has a couple of aesthetic slip-ups. I don't know why it should, but the giant memorial to the east of City Hall with the globe always upsets me because the globe is not round. It is oval with the horizontal diameter narrower than the vertical, sort of like an upright egg. To be technically correct the poles should be slightly flattened. Again, didn't anyone notice that before signing off on it?

The North façade of the Harborside condos deserve a mention. If you stand on the north bank of the harbor, look south, wait for a trolley to appear and then squint a little, you can see a perfect replica of the south side of Chicago in the 50's. All that is missing is some peeling paint and those continuous-loop clotheslines running between the porches hung with long johns to complete the picture. They will probably appear in time. Compare this to the beautiful facades at St. Catherine's Commons. Mr. Tarantino, the developer, has taste and that makes all the difference.

I've criticized some areas in this city and I think it only fair to award some praise for balance. Big applause to Andrea's, Tenuta's

Delicatessen, Larsen's Pharmacy, Crystal's Clothing, Model Market, Bjorn's Clothing, and a host of other family-run businesses for defying the big conglomerates and retaining some of the heart and soul of a disappearing segment of Kenosha. Good going guys and hang in there. We all love you.

I want to give an especially big hand to 80-year-old Al Gallo who said in an interview, "Phone? I don't need no steenking phone. It would only ring anyway." Good for you, Al! You are an icon to a great many Kenoshans. Are there any more at home like you?

I regret to announce that this is my last article. I have many more educational and amusing stories to tell but Steve Lund is down-sizing me. Writing these articles has caused me to reflect on a fairly interesting life. I want to thank Steve and all my loyal fans for the past four years. It's been a hoot.

About the Author

Ed Groelle is a graduate of DeVry Technical Institute in Chicago. He is retired, lives in Kenosha, Wisconsin, and spends his time bicycling, writing, and volunteering, mostly with the blind and visually impaired. Groelle has been married forty-five years to Charlene and has two beautiful daughters, Laura and Melissa.